PENGUI

# Cecilia

# Cecilia

An ex-nun's
extraordinary journey

## CECILIA INGLIS

PENGUIN BOOKS

Penguin Books

Published by the Penguin Group
Penguin Books Australia Ltd
250 Camberwell Road, Camberwell, Victoria 3124, Australia
Penguin Books Ltd
80 Strand, London WC2R 0RL, England
Penguin Putnam Inc.
375 Hudson Street, New York, New York 10014, USA
Penguin Books, a division of Pearson Canada
10 Alcorn Avenue, Toronto, Ontario, Canada M4V 3B2
Penguin Books (NZ) Ltd
Cnr Rosedale and Airborne Roads, Albany, Auckland, New Zealand
Penguin Books (South Africa) (Pty) Ltd
24 Sturdee Avenue, Rosebank, Johannesburg 2196, South Africa
Penguin Books India (P) Ltd
11, Community Centre, Panchsheel Park, New Delhi 110 017, India

First published by Penguin Books Australia Ltd 2003

3 5 7 9 10 8 6 4

Cover and text design by Susannah Low, Penguin Design Studio
Typeset in 10.5/15 pt Sabon by Post Pre-press Group, Brisbane, Queensland
Printed and bound in Australia by McPherson's Printing Group, Maryborough, Victoria

National Library of Australia
Cataloguing-in-Publication data:

Inglis, Cecilia, 1935– .
Cecilia: an ex-nun's extraordinary journey.

ISBN 0 14 300129 9.

1. Inglis, Cecilia, 1935– . 2. Sisters of Mercy – Australia – Biography.
3. Ex-nuns – Australia – Biography. I. Title.

271.9202

www.penguin.com.au

*For all my families*

– the Cahills, my sisters in Religion and the Inglises

# *Contents*

Prologue        1

## PART ONE • Growing Up Catholic

1    Being Catholic      7
2    Where It All Began      17
3    Going to Ag's Place      24
4    One Sunday Afternoon      37
5    The Road to Singleton      47

## PART TWO • Religious Life

6    Entering the Convent      63
7    My Eighteenth Birthday      71
8    Mr Nickerson      87
9    Leaving Home      91
10   Initiation into Teaching      97
11   Living in a Branch House      106
12   Teaching at Hamilton      115
13   Dad's Death      137

14     University and Other New Things    144

15     My Mother Dies    155

16     Falling Apart    171

17     Home to the Convent and Changing Times    178

18     *The Fruity Melodrama*    193

19     Time for a Change    200

20     Countdown    215

## PART THREE • A New Path

21     Into the Deep End    223

22     The Final Leaving    235

23     Adventures with the Law    245

24     Stacey and 'Midnight Matchmaker'    254

25     Dracula Romeo and Inner-city Life    263

26     Moving to Chippendale    277

27     Mary Comes to Town    284

28     Never So Bad Again    293

29     More Men    298

30     'Midnight Matchmaker' Again    310

31     Men and Sex    321

32     Married at Last    329

33     On Becoming a Gran    334

34     My Sixty-sixth Birthday    338

35     Reflections on the Journey    346

Epilogue    354

Acknowledgements    359

*There's a season for everything,*
*a time for everything under heaven:*

> *A time to be born,*
> *A time to die;*
> *A time to plant,*
> *A time to uproot what is planted.*
> *A time for killing,*
> *A time for healing;*
> *A time for knocking down,*
> *A time for building.*
> *A time for tears,*
> *A time for laughter;*
> *A time for mourning,*
> *A time for dancing.*
> *A time for throwing stones away,*
> *A time for gathering them up;*
> *A time for embracing.*
> *A time for searching,*
> *A time for losing;*
> *A time for keeping,*
> *A time for throwing away.*
> *A time for tearing,*
> *A time for mending;*
> *A time for keeping silent,*
> *A time for speaking.*
> *A time for loving,*
> *A time for hating;*
> *A time for war,*
> *A time for peace.*

*ECCLESIASTES   Ch. 3: 1–8*

# I am Cecilia

I am a woman,
A 66-year-old woman.
I am a wife, a stepmother, and – thank God –
a grandmother.
I am an Australian.
I have been a child in an Irish-Catholic home;
A nun for thirty years;
A teacher;
A school counsellor;
And a psychologist–hypnotherapist.
Now I am a retiree who is aspiring to be a writer
so that I can tell you my story.
It is a story of being planted, and growing;
A story of being uprooted and replanted –
several times.
It is a story of striving to find my roots again,
and eventually growing into the kind of
spreading tree which lives in the sun;
The kind of tree in whose branches creatures
find shelter and rest.
It is a story of family and good friends,
Of laughter and tears,
Of momentous decisions, and great distress,
A story of searching and finding, and losing again.

Most of all, it is a story of survival.
Through all the things that have happened
   in my life,
I have become the person I am now –
   happy, content with the way things are
And able to let go of the things that have been,
   that I wish had not been so.
Walk along with me on my road to Emmaus,
And listen as I tell you my tale.

# *Prologue*

'Dong! Dong! Dong!'

The big bell in the convent tower rings out.

'The Angel of the Lord declared unto Mary,' I say to myself, 'and she conceived of the Holy Ghost.'

'Hail Mary full of grace, the Lord is with thee. Blessed art thou among women and blessed is the fruit of thy womb, Jesus.'

'Holy Mary, Mother of God,' I answer again, 'pray for us sinners now and at the hour of our death. Amen.'

'Dong! . . .' the bell continues its call. I continue to respond. The habit of a lifetime.

It is the 6 o'clock Angelus, in the evening of 11 November 1981, one of the longest days in my life. I am sitting at my desk in the superior's office of the Convent of Mercy, Singleton, getting ready to leave forever.

It is just a few weeks short of thirty years since I first drove up the sweeping gravel path to the front door with my mother and father. I was seventeen. Now I am almost forty-seven. I was young and idealistic. Today I am older and tired. Maybe disillusioned. I'm certainly sad.

It is nearly time. I tidy the few things left on my desk for my successor to follow up. There's a knock on the open door and Sister Mary comes in.

'Need anything done? Any help?'

The nuns know I'm packing to move from Singleton, but not that I'm packing to leave the Order for good.

'No, thank you. I'm right,' I say.

'Any time,' she says. 'Just ask.' And she goes out again.

Right! I think. Then – how can I know if I'm right?

The community will be going to dinner at 6.30. That's when I plan to leave. I won't say goodbye. That would be too painful for me and probably also for them. Best that the provincial superior tells them later that I have left. I will write to them in a few days. Try to explain.

A few friends in the community know I'm going, but most don't. Some will understand, but be sad. Others will feel shock, even a sense of betrayal.

I don't need to leap over the wall. The convent station wagon waits, near the side door. I parked it there earlier. My cases and a couple of boxes are in a nearby room – the pitifully small accumulation of a lifetime.

It is 6.30. I hear footsteps as the sisters head for the refectory, and voices floating on the air. I wait a few minutes in case there are stragglers, then begin loading cases and apple boxes into the wagon. I'm wearing my habit – a plain blue dress with the Mercy Cross on the collar. No veil – they went out long ago. But in my overnight bag I have pants and a shirt: secular dress.

# PROLOGUE

I've finished loading the car. I take one more look around my office where so many fine women have sat at the roll-top desk before my turn. Most of them are at rest beneath a white cross among the trees in the little convent cemetery. I close the door.

I let myself out the convent side door and shut it wearily behind me. Into the station wagon, which I will deliver to one of the Newcastle convents in a day or so.

I head down the red gravel drive, and out through those same imposing gates I entered almost thirty years ago.

The sun is setting as I turn towards the highway.

# Part One

Growing Up Catholic

# 1

## Being Catholic

That evening as I drove down the highway, I probably wondered how it had come to this. Thirty years of dedicated religious life over. What had inspired my sixteen-year-old self with such a strong desire to be a nun, in spite of the life just beginning to open out before me?

Why had I left?

And where would my life go next?

The reasons I became a nun lie wholly in my early life. All the things that made me who I was – my family, my schooling, the Church – led to my decision, but most of all it was my own personal religion.

My earliest experience of religion was the praying of the family rosary at home. We'd all kneel together and be absorbed in the peace and repetition of the prayer flowing over us. The times I remember best are winter evenings with the coke fire sputtering red in the grate, and the room warm and cosy while we prayed. Being close to each other – praying together – was important to the family. Everyone who was home had to come to the family rosary, which was always after the news on the wireless at 7 p.m., before Dad could settle to his paper or his book.

We took it in turns to lead the prayer: 'Hail Mary full of grace, the Lord is with thee. Blessed art thou among women and blessed is the fruit of thy womb, Jesus . . .'

Then the answer: 'Holy Mary, Mother of God, pray for us sinners now and at the hour of our death. Amen.'

Then it was repeated, over and over again, with each decade – the 'Our Father' prayer and ten 'Hail Marys' – introduced with a part of Christ's life to be meditated upon. For example, 'the third joyful mystery – the birth of Our Lord in the stable at Bethlehem'. The words might be hurried and slurred, but the rhythm would go on.

For me, a lively seven-year-old, the rosary was a very tedious experience. My little rebellion was to create a diversion by kneeling at the table opposite Maurice – my nearest brother, who would have been eleven. I would put my head devoutly in my hands on the table, then raise it slowly, part my fingers and pull faces at Maurice when I could catch his eye. Eventually, if I was lucky, he'd sputter, giggle and laugh. Then we'd both giggle, and the devotion would be destroyed. There'd be a terrible frown and 'Tch! Tch!' clucking noises from Dad. Mum would pull my arm and reef me over to the settee beside her where she sat in her evening spot.

Soon my restless soul would surrender to the waves of calming repetition. Peace would descend on the room and the fire would add a glow to the devotional semidarkness.

The warmth and family togetherness would seep deep within me.

When the prayer finished, Dad would get up from his knees and sit on his chair with the paper spread out on the table in front of him. The others would go about their own affairs and Mum would pick up her sewing basket again to finish darning a sock, or sewing a torn shirt. But I'd stay on my knees, with the calmness still upon me. Sometimes I'd move over close to Mum to put my head in her lap. She'd put aside the sock and her basket, and begin to stroke my head. We'd both be quiet, no word spoken.

After a while the spell would be broken. She'd pick up her sock on the wooden darning mushroom and resume the back-and-forth movement of her needle. I'd move aside and go on to whatever a seven-year-old does till bedtime. Or perhaps by then it *was* bedtime.

This was religion. Spirituality.

Dad – big strong Dad – worked so hard in both the heat and freezing cold making buildings grow out of heaps of bricks. Dad, kneeling there by his chair, devout and given over to the prayer . . . Mum, radiating calm from her corner, and the family together.

All of these rituals were tied up with being Catholic – part of the one true holy Catholic and Apostolic Church, outside of which there was no redemption . . . whatever all that meant. Being Catholic was a way of life, like breathing in and breathing out. Being Catholic was the very fabric and colour of my whole existence – the whole of my life.

There was Mass on Sundays at 7 a.m., summer and

winter, and I was always up and dressed in time to walk up the hill with Mum and Dad. Sometimes this was in the winter darkness with coats and hats on against the cold. I generally sat with Mum while Dad had his own place, in a transept where a lot of the men seemed to sit. My brother Maurice was an altar boy, so he was up with the priest.

Once a month it would be Sodality Sunday. Sodalities were devotional groups set up to encourage people to go to communion at least once a month. A spirit of severe unworthiness seemed to have been part of religion in the nineteenth century, and these sodalities were designed to help relax this fear. People were encouraged to attend as part of a group. Mum would wear her special ribbon and sit with the ladies of the Sacred Heart Sodality; Dad would wear his sash and sit in the main body of the church behind his banner of the Guilds. When I was old enough I would dress in my blue cloak and white veil and sit proudly with the Children of Mary. I'm sure it was all part of the Irish tradition of the Church which was so strong in Australia when I was young.

School at Rosary Primary School, Waratah, began and ended with prayers. We had the Angelus at midday, and prayers before and after lunch. There were religion lessons every day, and we learnt and recited our prayers: the Our Father, the Hail Mary and longer prayers like the Hail Holy Queen. We learnt off by heart the whole of the little *Green Catechism*, which summarised most matters of faith and morals.

'AMDG' was written at the top of the blackboard, and by the end of primary school, I put it at the top of every page of my work. It was a summary of the Jesuit motto 'Ad Majoram

Dei Gloriam' – to the Greater Glory of God. I thought it meant 'All my deeds for God' and I was happy with that.

On Saturdays we had a trip up to the church for confession. I made that trip far more often than I made the trip to the Saturday afternoon pictures. Then there was Mass on Sundays. Sometimes on Sunday evenings we also went to Benediction with its candles and incense, and joined in the singing of the old Latin hymns, like the 'Tantum Ergo'.

Add to this routine saying the family rosary together every night, morning offering as soon as you woke for the day, morning prayers beside your bed and night prayers on your knees before you got into bed. If you couldn't be bothered kneeling beside the bed – perhaps it was a cold winter's night – you said them in bed, unless you were too busy reading a book smuggled in under the covers by the light of a similarly smuggled torch.

By the time I got to high school we were also having a retreat for three days once a year. A priest would come and give talks about living a good life, saying your prayers, or about the scriptures or saints. There'd be silence everywhere, confessions with the visiting priest (which made a nice change from the parish priest), and there'd be holy books to read. I liked retreats. There was a part of me that enjoyed the quietness, the spiritual atmosphere and the time to sit and just 'be'.

It was at the retreats that the idea of 'vocation' first became real for me. A person was called by God to give their life to His service. Vocations were serious stuff. They were real and had to be followed, even if you would rather have been doing something else. Religious vocations, it was quite clear, were a privilege, not optional.

The nuns, parish priests, mission priests and the priests who gave us retreats at school all told horror stories of what happened when people stood in the way of someone's genuine vocation. Parents who opposed their child's vocation somehow fell on hard times, or lost their child to crime, a bad marriage, or to untimely death.

As for the person who had a vocation and refused to follow it – the consequences were just as bad. The boys fell into bad company, got tangled up in crime and ended up dead, in jail or attempting suicide to cover their shame. The girls were likely to marry dreadful rotters who were unfaithful, abusive, bashed them and eventually abandoned them with a brood of unruly children to support and raise.

As I grew older I often went to morning Mass during the week, because success would come by 'working as if all depended upon work, and praying as if all depended upon prayer'. The nuns had told us so. I hated getting out of bed early, but there was something I did like about the bike-ride up to the church in the chilly dawn, and being part of that small early morning congregation seemed very special.

Every year at the end of October there was a procession at the Newcastle Showground in honour of Christ the King. I'd walk with the Children of Mary in my blue cloak and white veil, swinging rosary beads and praying 'Holy Mary, Mother of God . . .' with the thousands of other Catholics who came along in those days. There was green grass under my feet, sun on my back and I fervently sang 'Faith of Our Fathers, living still . . .' and 'Ave! Ave! Ave Ma-ri-i-ia!', as they do at Lourdes.

Then we had Benediction from the altar set up high in the

middle of the ground, and the bishop spoke. It was a good afternoon. Usually all of my family would go along. Maurice would be on the altar with the altar boys, Mum with her Sodality, and Dad wearing his Guild's sash with the men. It was quite something to be there with all those devout people – a really 'feel good' event.

When I was in early high school someone gave me a statue of Mary. She stood a bit over a foot tall, and Dad made me a little shrine for it in the corner of my room above my bed. He rounded the edge of the shelf at the front, and had a raised dais at the back where the statue stood. I found a small blue kerosene lamp with an opaque top somewhere, and bought a glass vase just big enough for a few flowers. When I wanted to say my prayers, ask a favour, or even if I just felt like it, I'd light the wick and the tiny glow would warm the statue and the corner. This was what religion was about: in your bedroom kneeling beside the bed, praying and thinking about whatever concerns you had right then, while Mary watched over you.

There was a picture I had seen somewhere that I liked so I got a small copy of it and kept it in my prayer book. I called it the 'Madonna of the Storm'. The Mary pictured was young and held her baby so protectively. The cloak gathered around her was blue and her hood was a golden russet brown against gathering purple storm clouds. The child slept, peaceful, in her arms. That was religion, too – being carried securely against the storm and being at peace.

Many years later I heard someone say that God was the still point at the centre of a turning world – the calm in the eye of the storm – and that picture said the same thing to the fifteen-year-old me.

I liked the human Jesus I found in the Gospels – kind, compassionate, hungry, tired out. He even had a sense of humour. I liked the things He said about loving your neighbour, and the story of the Good Samaritan. How His Father in Heaven knew when a tiny bird lost a feather from its wing and cared for it, thus how much more must He care for all of us.

A copy of a painting that hung on the wall of our classroom in fifth year at high school was called 'Jesus Weeping Over Jerusalem'. It was an oblong of evening colours and tones, and in the background were the flat roofs of an ancient Middle Eastern city as I imagined it may have been. Jesus was in the foreground on a hillside and looked out over the city. It made me feel so sad.

I would sit and look at it and absorb the colours and emotions. 'Jerusalem, Jerusalem – how often would I have gathered your children under my wings as a hen gathers her chicks – and thou wouldst not . . .'

I felt the sadness of the rejection suffered by Jesus. Peace, security, love – all offered and rejected. All that Jesus wanted to give – to gather; to bring all peoples into the harmony of his Father's house. 'And thou wouldst not . . .' This was the religion and the Jesus I was drawn to.

Once I had made up my mind I had a vocation to be a nun, I took it for granted that entering the convent was the 'right' thing to do. I had to follow this vocation, in spite of all the other things I might want to do. I just had to give them up for God.

*It is 1934 and the house is a brick Federation-style home
in Aberglasslyn Road, Rutherford, just out of Maitland,
New South Wales.*

*It's late at night and my two elder sisters are in bed
when there's the sound of a footfall in the hall.*

*The younger one sits up and shakes my older sister.*

*'There's a noise!' she whispers, clutching her arm.*

*'Hush,' says the older. 'It's only Dad going in to see
Mum. Go back to sleep.'*

*Dad sleeps on a stretcher bed on the side verandah
'because he likes fresh air', which is only partly true.*

*The side verandah is not a fail-safe method of
contraception, and I arrive in February 1935, four years
after my nearest brother, Maurice, when Mum is forty-three
and money is scarce. I am the seventh in the family.*

# 2

## Where It All Began

Maitland was the home of both the Cahill and Edwards families, so it was there I was born in 1935, when the pall of the Depression hung over the land, and the trauma of World War II had not yet begun.

My father's people had come from Ireland in the latter half of the nineteenth century, and my mother's family had emigrated from Liverpool to Queensland. My mother's father was born there, while his father worked on the spreading railways. My father, Joe Cahill, was the second youngest of eight children, and my mother, Alice Edwards, one of five.

One Sunday evening outside the local church after Benediction, Joe Cahill asked Alice Edwards if he could walk her home. He was twenty-nine and she was twenty-five when they were married in the cathedral at West Maitland in 1919.

That's where it all began.

I was only four in 1939 when Dad decided we should move from Maitland to Newcastle, as he thought he could get a better job there, which he did. He worked for a local builder, and must have got a bigger wage as he and Mum were better off, except when it rained. Bricklayers couldn't work in the rain, and no work meant no pay during that time.

Dad had designed our house and arranged to have it built when we moved from Maitland. It had three bedrooms, a lounge room that we only used on special occasions, an eat-in kitchen and a 'breakfast room' where we mostly lived. The dining room table and sideboard stood in the middle of the breakfast room, which seemed to also be called the dining room half the time, though we hardly ever had either breakfast or dinner there, except on special occasions like Christmas. I think the dining room table must have acquired its name from a dining room in Maitland, but I was too young when we left to remember this, so I just took the name for granted.

There was a back verandah with one big old chair where you could sit and read. The old couch – or 'settee' – along the wall in the breakfast room with its back to the verandah was where Mum sat every night after tea to do her mending while Dad read the paper at the table.

It was not a very big house for parents with a family of seven, but the older members of the family had already begun to move out. My two eldest brothers came and went from their army camps, and my sister Bet was at boarding school most of the time.

By 1944, World War II was well under way, and I was in fourth class at Rosary School, Waratah. Each day I walked up the hill to the school near the church, and walked home lugging my Globite schoolbag.

In winter when we had a coke fire in the corner fireplace, I'd sometimes make toast on a long wire toasting fork and eat it with hot butter melting through. On the mantelpiece above the fireplace there were photos of my eldest brothers, Joe and Jim, in their army uniforms. Joe seemed to have been grown-up for as long as I could remember, and he probably had been, as he was fifteen years older than I was. He was a butcher before the War, slept on a bed on the back verandah when he was home, and owned the big Sunbeam motorbike out in the shed. It was only ridden when he came home on leave. During the War he was an engineer with the army in Darwin.

Jim had wanted to be a teacher, but the army caught up with him first, at age eighteen. The recruiting officer told him he could be a teacher after the War, with complete disregard for the changes war might bring. He could easily have added, 'If you come back'.

Jim owned the record player and the records, and the books on the bookshelf he had built in the back room – the boys' bedroom. I was allowed to play his records as long as I turned the handle slowly to wind it up, and was careful not to scratch the records with the needle. It was here I heard my first classical orchestral music, and tenors like Joseph Schmidt and John McCormack.

There were also some records of very stirring patriotic songs about the heroes of the Irish Easter rising of 1916 – like the one about the hanging of Kevin Barry, a mere lad of nineteen summers. I was interested to hear recently that he and several others were re-interred with hero honours in

Dublin in 2001. When I listened to these songs I began to understand my father's dislike of the English. Though he had never been to Ireland, he was very Irish at heart and shared their resentment of the harsh treatment of the Catholic Irish by the ruling English power. On his wedding day in 1919 he had even worn the colours of Eamon de Valera, the Irish hero who led the movement for independence from England, and who eventually became the first president of independent Ireland.

Jim gave me books for Christmas and birthdays when he was home, and I dipped into his bookshelf as I grew older. He worked in the post office in the army camps, and moved mainly around New South Wales.

Though Tony was only fifteen months younger than Jim, he didn't have to join the army during the War. He worked at the Newcastle Steelworks, so he was exempt from call-up to the army. He had auburn curly hair and was quite a lad. One Sunday afternoon he decided to try to ride Joe's big Sunbeam motorbike, but it got away from him and crashed into a telegraph pole up the street. Tony was all right, but the bike was not.

That night I climbed under the dining room table so that no one could see me and wrote a letter to Joe in Darwin. I couldn't spell very well, so I agonised over some words before deciding to ask.

When my head appeared with the innocent request, 'How do you spell motorbike?', Mum reacted. 'Give me that!' She read out my letter: 'Dear joe tony broke your . . .' Then she tore it up, so Joe never heard about the crash. Not from me anyway.

The elder of my two sisters was Mary, and I shared an old

double bed with her till she married and moved out. She was twelve years older than I was, and also seemed all grown-up to me. She had trained at technical college and became a dressmaker, with a business at home. I was very proud of the sign-written notice on the front of the house that read: 'M. Cahill – Dressmaker'.

Mary sometimes took me to town to go shopping or to the pictures, and this was quite a treat. During the War she decided she'd work at the Ritz Milkbar in town for a while for more company, as dressmaking was a lonely business. It was there she met her airforce fiancé, Bill.

I must have been a nuisance, because they paid me three-pence to walk ahead of them on the way home from Mass on Sundays so I wouldn't talk, and sixpence to stay out of the lounge room when they were talking in there. They kept the door shut and I couldn't imagine what they might talk about, so I was fascinated and took every opportunity to spy. When Bill was posted to Darwin, he and my brother Joe met there.

My second sister Bet was eight years older than me, and was always away at boarding school because she got a state government bursary that she had won in an exam at the end of primary school. When she came home she slept on a little single bed in our room, and I loved it because she mothered me and read me stories.

Our dog Nip – a foxie – completed the family. He defi-nitely lived outside, except that sometimes Joe would bring him into the kitchen when Mum wasn't there. He was never happy there, though, always looking around expecting Mum to appear, and ready to make a bolt for it.

Just up the street there was a family – the Joneses – who had three kids with whom I played, and who were in and out of our place a lot. The friendship wasn't wholeheartedly encouraged because they were 'publics' and didn't go to our school or church. Anne was a bit older than I was, and Paul was a bit younger. Daisy was younger than Paul. Sometimes I went to their place to play, but more often they came to our place – all of them.

I was always inventing impromptu plays for us to perform, and we'd dress up and take the parts assigned. The best game we played was 'hospitals' under the peach and nectarine trees in the backyard near the fowlyard fence. We took it in turn to be doctors, nurses and patients. The patient was 'in bed' – fully clothed – on the old train-line sleepers around the trees, and diagnoses involved lots of exploring of bodies, and feeling of tummies and other interesting places.

The friendship that *was* actively encouraged was with Mary Flanaghan, who was in my class at school and lived in a street near the school and church. Her family was Catholic, and I was allowed to go to their place to play. The Flanaghans had lots of kids and were poorer than we were. I could see that by the way their jumpers were stretched and had holes in the elbows, and from the boys' pants, which had holes in the knees.

The kids got homemade presents for Christmas and birthdays. They had rag dolls with buttons for eyes, and funny stitched faces with wool hair. The doll's cot was all lopsided, made of roughly sawn pieces of wood nailed together. Santa Claus never brought me expensive presents, but he definitely brought a better range of gifts to my house.

The boys were a bit smelly and none too bright. One of the boys always had a big yellow boogey hanging out of his nose, and no one ever insisted he get a handkerchief and blow it.

Playing with the Joneses was much more fun than the Flanaghans, given their accessibility and willingness to go along with the games I was always inventing. I suppose if I thought about it, I might have wondered if Mum would have approved of these games of hospitals, and I might just have wondered if it was somehow a sin. But then the Joneses were publics, and they didn't have sins, so it must have been all right.

# 3

## Going to Ag's Place

Going to Ag's during the holidays was one of the great pleasures of my life when I was in high school. My Globite bag – a larger one by now – would be emptied of school things and packed full of clothes and books to read, and I'd walk down to the station at Waratah for the train to Maitland.

The first time I went to Ag's for a holiday Maurice took me, but when I was a bit older Mum agreed I could go by myself. I'd feel very grown-up sitting on the train, thinking about the time to come.

Ag was Dad's unmarried sister, my aunt, who lived in the old house where Dad and the rest of his brothers and sisters grew up. She was such a great person I used to wonder why she never married, but Mary, who always seemed to know lots of family information, told me she was engaged once but her two older sisters told her she shouldn't get married. Aunty Mag was married and had children in Newcastle, and Aunty Mary was a nun, Mother Michael, who taught music in Lochinvar with the Sisters of Saint Joseph. Anyway, these two sat Ag down and told her it was her responsibility to stay at home and look after her parents. So she did. She sent her young man packing, looked after her parents till they died, and then settled down to living with Mick, her tailor brother, who never married either. He died before I was born, and Ag just became everyone's favourite aunty.

I was the last in a long line of nieces and nephews who had holidays at Ag's. I had cousins who were much older than I was because Dad was at the bottom of his family of eight. Dad and Ag were close because she was just above him in age and as good as any boy when it came to getting into mischief, Dad used to say.

I would get off the train at West Maitland, and catch the local bus which rattled around the countryside till it got to the stop near the old Rutherford Hotel on the Pacific Highway. Then I walked. I walked across the highway and round the corner, past the house where I was born. I'd stare with interest at the pillars and lattice, but I could barely remember living there. Ag's house was about a mile down the dusty Aberglasslyn Road, past the other houses. Beyond her house there were only paddocks and trees.

I'd go in through the sagging gate in the tired, unpainted fence, along the cracked cement path, up the three steps onto the wooden bull-nosed verandah with its nameplate 'Cashel' proudly mounted beside the old front door, and I was there. Nothing was ever locked at Ag's, and the front door would be wide open when I got there, as she'd be expecting me.

The house is still there, but no longer in the family. Last year I drove past it on a nostalgia trip to Maitland, and it has been done up and cared for. It was originally a timber four-roomed cottage, with skillion verandah and kitchen added on at the back. An extra big room with a concrete floor was also added later behind the kitchen. When I had holidays there that room had become an internal laundry and bathroom with its copper, bath and toilet replacing the copper in the yard, the round tin bathtub now hanging on the wall. The 'little house', well up the yard, was used as a garden shed.

The large room with the concrete floor was originally an extra bedroom for several of the five boys as they all grew up, and it answered my questions as to how a family of eight had all lived in a four-roomed house. There was also a little closed-in room on the back verandah that was a bedroom for one of the boys, but Ag had shelves in it and used it as a pantry. I guess there was also a parents' bedroom, one for the three girls, and a third bedroom for some of the boys. This room was known in the days I visited as Mick's room. None of the rooms were very big.

I would knock on the open front door and call out, 'Ag! I'm here!' and she'd come bustling up the little hall, arms outstretched to greet me. We'd go down the hall, through the 'parlour' room with its unused fireplace, piano and old-fashioned furniture, and down the step onto the back verandah. Along the verandah there was another step down into the kitchen, which was large and likely to be warm with delicious smells of cooking food coming from a large saucepan on the stove.

Still talking, Ag would produce cups and saucers, a milk jug and sugar basin, a plate of freshly made little cakes with currants, and a teapot of tea. We'd sit and eat with our elbows on the oilcloth table cover, and she'd want to know all the news.

Ag must have been about sixty years old. She was comfortably round, without being small like my mother, and had short, straight grey hair, parted on the side and held with a bobby pin. Her eyes would light up in her face as we talked, and she'd be interested in everything I had to say. Then it would be time for tea, the evening meal, and the contents of that aromatic large saucepan would be revealed.

After tea, we'd go for a walk in the evening air, as the light was fading. We walked a lot. Sometimes we'd go out along the road to the Waterworks (I never did find out what the Waterworks was used for, if anything). There were big round eels in the water, and you could see their slippery bodies slithering about if you sat quietly. We walked through the paddocks among the tall grey gum trees trailing ribbons of bark as they sloughed their old skin, and the magpies carolled us along the way.

We'd go out to the paddock where my grandfather, who had been a butcher, kept the animals he bought at the sale yards. He had his slaughter shed there too, as well as the trees where he hung the beasts to bleed. In those days there was no abattoir, and he did everything himself, from buying the cattle and sheep till the meat went to the butcher's shop. Ag would point out where they had had their first house, where now only the ruins of an old brick chimney stood.

We'd also visit the old Campbells Hill cemetery, and she'd show me the family graves. We'd tidy them up, and put the flowers she'd brought on them.

Another day we'd go over the hill to the next valley, to

collect mushrooms after rain, or blackberries for the pie she'd make when we got home. Or we'd walk the mile or so to Gorings, the corner store on the highway. Next day Ag would make scones and biscuits in her old green stove which needed to be fed a constant diet of shillings. I never knew why she kept the jam jar of shillings on the mantelpiece. When the stove was full, she'd empty out the shilling slot and start again. I have since thought that because the stove was old, it must have still worked on a system prior to when the meter was installed. We'd eat hot scones dripping with butter and grape jam while we read our books under the old grapevine out the back.

Ag grew a few tomatoes, had some chooks and a cat which terrified me by hiding behind the kitchen door to spring out and grab my heel as I came in. It didn't really hurt, but our cat was never allowed to come inside, and I didn't understand it was just playing with me.

These holidays were full of discoveries. Ag's stories were fascinating, and she introduced me to the Cahill and Brennan side of the family. Granny Cahill was born Elizabeth Brennan. Ag said she was a small woman with an incredible Irish accent, and was kind to all. I've heard my big brothers – Jim and Tony – tell stories about Granny and her kindness. They were terrors, with only fifteen months between them, and there was one story about how they got into mischief at Granny's when they hadn't yet started school. They painted her newly whitewashed inside copper with red paint they found, then decided she just might not like it. They thought they'd better go home before she found out. As they ran off, Granny saw some red paint on one of them and was all concern.

'Oh! Come here child! Ye've cut yo'sel!'

But with 'Mum'll fix it!' they fled out the back gate and along the lane to home, where they washed off the paint and said nothing more about it.

Ag was very proud to say Granny Cahill was the business head in the family, as she had the house built in 1896 at a cost of £163.7.0 (one hundred and sixty-three pounds and seven shillings). The architect's fees were £9.6.1 (nine pounds, six shillings and a penny) added onto this. She had saved up and paid it all off in small instalments, in spite of having to feed and clothe her brood of eight. Ag had the accounts to prove it.

Ag talked about Seamus, Granny's alcoholic brother, who was quite a character, and whom Granny always looked after when his demons beset him and he needed to dry out. I discovered that there was more to being Irish than a sense of humour and a love of poetry. Ag told me about 'the curse of the Irish' – the demon drink that was known to beset our family.

The best stories were about 'Red Ned', her father and my grandfather, who was a wild and rebellious red-headed Irishman. His family feared he'd end up in jail or transported somewhere, so they saved the money to send him to Australia to join his brother in 1866.

There is a letter he wrote to his mother as an eighteen-year-old waiting on the ship in quarantine off Sydney after the trip out. He tells how he 'dressed' several sheep for the captain's table on the journey, and won money at cards to add to his pay from the captain.

The stories flowed. The one about shooting up the pub

was the most lurid. When his son, Uncle Dan – the gentleman of the clan, generally regarded as a bit of a snob – was doing his teaching training he had to get to the Marist Brothers' school down in West Maitland. My grandfather got him a pony to ride to and fro. Coming home one day, he was roughed up by a few young yokels as he came round the pub corner. I guess they had had a few drinks and decided to take the mickey out of the snob on the horse in his suit and tie.

When he got home looking all messed up, Red Ned was very angry. He put the old horse in the cart and was off like a shot to the hotel with his gun, with murderous intent. Fortunately, someone spotted him coming, and the publican put the young louts out the back door, out of harm's way. Red Ned was so angry when he couldn't find them, he made do with shooting up the bar instead, and poor Granny took a long time to pay off the damage, bit by tiny bit.

On Saint Patrick's Day, Grandfather would put on his green scarf and set out for a day of carousing with his cronies. In the evening there was a big concert at the Maitland Town Hall, and the family would dread Grandfather's appearance there. He'd be likely to be heard bellowing from the back of the hall, 'Give us something Irish!' when he didn't approve of the program. Often, Ag told me, Granny would have to go and collect him from the police station the next morning, sheepish but unrepentant.

Grandfather was from the little town of Cashel, in Tipperary, hence the nameplate proudly displayed on the verandah wall as you came up the steps. One of his big stories was how, as a young man, he could throw a stone over the Rock of Cashel, and was known as the 'Tipperary Stone Thrower'.

When one of my older cousins, Pat Cahill, went to Ireland, Ag said he saw the dimensions of the Rock of Cashel and came back to tell the family about it. He said it was a small mountain with a ruined cathedral and cemetery on the top. 'Throw a stone over it?' he said. 'Ya couldn't fire a 303 over the bloody thing!' he added in colourful Cahill language. The story was larger than life, like Red Ned, who never let the want of a few facts spoil a good story. When I visited the Rock of Cashel a few years ago myself I could see what our cousin meant, but also felt pride and a sense of wonder to be standing where Red Ned had stood, and to find the family graves near the Celtic cross at one corner of the ruins of the burnt-out old cathedral. There were old gravestones, but they weren't readable. Since then, a nephew of mine – Jim's son Michael, from Wellington – did some research to pinpoint the exact location of the family graves and invited the clan to contribute to having the lichen cleaned from the old gravestones so the text could be read once more. However, he found that the Rock of Cashel has been classified as a national heritage site, and no changes to the monuments are permitted. Perhaps one day I'll get back there to see it all again. I also found a 'Cahill's' butcher shop in the main street of the little town and saw the family trade was still alive and well. The fascination with our roots stretches down the generations of my family.

Grandfather was very proud of his family and given to some pretensions, such as when he had a piano brought in from Sydney for Aunty Mary to play after finding out she was musical. But he was a chauvinistic Irishman at heart. When their first new house was mooted, he saw no reason to put a wooden floor in the kitchen. If a dirt floor was good enough for his mother in Ireland, he didn't see why it wasn't good enough for his wife in Australia.

Ag had letters from cousins in Ireland and America, and photos of them on the mantelpiece in the parlour. She was especially proud of the photo of a handsome young priest there, and she said he was Father Luby from America. Ag and his mother wrote to each other. When I was in the USA in 1988 I visited an aging cousin, Eileen Nott, in Richmond, Virginia, with whom my brother Maurice had made contact somehow. When I mentioned the Father Luby on Ag's mantelpiece in the 1940s, her eyes grew big with amazement and disbelief. He was her brother, though she'd never heard of Ag, but only of 'Australian cousins' her mother wrote to.

I discovered that Ag was everybody's Aunty Ag: to the mums and kids down the street, to the orphans at Monte Pio, and to the nuns who looked after them. She did volunteer work for the orphanage, and ran stalls at their fete. She helped in many ways at the church too, where she took me to clean the brass, sweep the floor and do the flowers.

As we walked down the road to the Rutherford Hotel, and then the mile or so down the highway to the Sacred Heart Church, Ag would tell me how she made this journey years ago with me in the old family pram when I was only two or three days old. She was my godmother and took me to be baptised as soon after birth as possible. If I died without baptism I could never go to Heaven, and would be in Limbo for all eternity – hence the haste with which I was christened. My mother didn't go as she was still recovering from the birth.

Mum used to say she never saw any of her babies baptised. Instead it was Ag who held me while the priest poured the water on my head, and Ag who spoke on my behalf. She promised to renounce Satan and all his works and pomps, and to be faithful to the Church and its teachings, and promised on her own behalf she would look after my spiritual welfare.

Ag may never have married and had a family, but she had a very wide family of nieces and nephews and folk from the parish that loved her.

Ag was special, and was an integral part of my life till she died at about eighty-five, still living in her little house with its steps and split levels in spite of having lost a leg to diabetes a few years before. She went home with a walker and an artificial leg of which she was inordinately proud, and joked that it was a much nicer shape than her real one. She always said she had bandy legs, in spite of never having ridden a horse.

She was buried in the old Campbells Hill cemetery with Mick and Granny and Grandfather Cahill, though there isn't anyone left to tidy the graves and put flowers on them any more.

*My father has me on his knee.*

*'Tell me again,' I say, 'about when I was born.'*

*'It was the middle of the night,' he says. 'Three o'clock in the morning.'*

*I am looking up at him, drinking it in.*

*'There was a terrible storm. There was lots of lightning, and thunder was crashing all around.'*

*He pauses. I wait. I've heard it all before but it's still exciting.*

*'I thought I heard a little knock at the front door.'*

*I nod.*

*'I went and opened the door, but there was no one there.' He shakes his head. 'Then I saw these little wet footprints coming up the steps out of the rain, across the verandah, and towards the door. So I looked down, and there you were. On the doorstep.'*

*'And then?' I say. 'And then?'*

*'Then I picked you up in my arms, and took you inside, and gave you to Mum.'*

# 4

## One Sunday Afternoon

It is late on a Sunday afternoon in October, 1951. I am sixteen and standing outside my mother's bedroom, quaking in my shoes. My heart is thumping in my throat. From inside, I can hear small sounds of movement as Mum is freshening herself up and getting her face on before she makes Sunday tea.

My hand is on the knob of the half-closed door. I only have to say, 'Mum, can I come in?' and give the door a push, and I'll be in there telling her I'm going to enter the convent and become a nun.

In the twelve months since I made the decision to enter the convent I've been very careful not to give away any clues about what I've been contemplating. I didn't want my family to know and expect me to be goody-goody and pious. I could just imagine Mum saying to me, 'Huh – and you say you want to be a nun!' every time I fell from grace, or showed a tendency to be a bit wild.

But now the time has come to drop the bomb, and I'm

very nervous. I know Mum doesn't think I am *the type* to make a good nun, and she'll be opposed to the idea. But I've been to see Father Cronin this afternoon, and talked it all over with him. He's known how I've been feeling for the last year, and today he said, 'It's time to tell your mother and father. They need to know.'

I quailed. 'Don't you think it's too soon?' I said. 'The next intake is not until March.'

'No,' he said. 'Now's the time. Your Leaving Certificate exam is coming up, then Christmas, and after that you'll have to be getting ready.'

'Oh dear,' I said, my heart sinking to my boots. 'My mother's going to get a shock. I don't know what to say.'

'Just tell her. Tell her you've been to see me, and I said to say you're going to Singleton next year.' He moved some papers on his desk. 'Simple.'

'Oh dear,' I said again, palms beginning to sweat at the thought.

'It'll be all right,' he said. 'No need to say any more than that. Just let her know what you're thinking.'

I've been sitting out on the back verandah with everyone in the sun, just waiting for this moment. We've got a visitor for tea tonight. Enid has arrived, who's been part of the family for years, and they've all been talking, talking. But I've hardly heard a word. I've been peppering to get it all over with. When Mum eventually came inside, I followed her, and here we are.

I look down at my hand on the doorknob, quivering. I think perhaps it would be easier if I leave this till tomorrow and imagine myself stepping back quietly. Then – no, it will never be any easier. Better just *do* it.

I give the door a tiny push.

'Mum –' I say, 'can I come in?'

She's sitting at her dressing table, with a pot of Ponds face cream in her hand, looking at me. She's wondering what this is all about.

'Mum –' I say. My voice doesn't come out right, so I start again. 'Mum – I didn't just go for a bike-ride today like I told you.' I take a big breath and blurt it out. 'I went to see Father Cronin and he told me to come home and tell you I'm entering the convent. I'm going to Singleton next year.'

She's just sitting there looking at me. The Ponds is suspended in mid-air and her mouth is slightly open.

'Wh – what? What did you say?'

So I start again. 'I've been to see . . .'

She doesn't wait for me to finish. Her eyes have gone a bit funny, and she's looking hard at me. She says, 'You go to blazes!'

I back away, find my feet, and go for my life.

Looking back from a distance of fifty years I feel for that sixteen-year-old fleeing from her mother's bedroom. She was so young; so idealistic. So sure that what she was doing was right. So vulnerable. So inexperienced. Sixteen – sweet sixteen? – yet planning to enter the convent.

My experience of life was very limited. In primary school I had known boys who had been largely rough and loud and obnoxious. They had christened me 'Tojo' because of the glasses I had to wear. Even I could see why they called me that, because I looked like every cartoon of a Japanese soldier that was in the paper. My glasses were of round wire, covered with black tortoiseshell, and Mum chose them because they had secure spring arms which wouldn't fall off.

Anyway, I hated those glasses and the boys who called me 'Tojo Cahill' till the end of sixth class. I had no liaisons with, or even kind feelings towards, any of them.

There were the entirely innocent Saturday afternoon dance classes in town with my girlfriend, Carmel, where we had crushes on one or the other of the instructors. They were quite spunky young men, who could also dance, and I'm sure were as happy as a couple of roosters in a fowlyard. There were plenty of simpering young women to hold and guide around the floor.

I'd devoured lots of books with romance and sex in them, but that was hardly practical experience. I didn't know how to talk to boys. I didn't really know many boys. My brother Maurice had gone away to the seminary to become a priest when I was fourteen, so there weren't even any of his friends about the house any more.

There was Frank, the Marist Brothers' boy, who was a music student at the convent and practised each afternoon after school in one of the infants' classrooms. It had been very pleasant to stay back for an English honours lesson after school, do a bit of homework, and then sneak over there when the nuns had all gone back to the convent for prayers, and have a mild flirtation. He was good-looking and friendly, and welcomed the interruption to his music practice. We'd compare teachers and lessons, swap lesson notes and laugh a lot. Hardly experience, though.

❖ ❖ ❖

The lady next door – Mrs Harris – was a widow with one son a bit older than me, and had a spare bedroom that she decided to fill with a student called Peter, who was from the country. This new neighbour and I were soon on speaking terms. Peter was the first boy who showed interest in me, and he was close enough for me to spend time responding to such interest. That summer before I entered the convent I spent a few hours on and off talking to him over the fence at the front gate on warm evenings. We'd sit on our opposite sides of the dividing fence, me on our solid bricks, and he perched on Mrs Harris's post-and-rail fence, or lounging on her front lawn.

I even went bike-riding with him once. He was always asking me about the Catholic religion so I decided to take him across to the local Redemptorist Monastery in Mayfield when they had an information night. Even then I suspected Peter's interest in Catholicism wasn't totally genuine, but just a way of getting me interested in him. We went along anyway, as I told myself it was good to spread the faith, but it also seemed the closest thing to a date I was likely to get at that stage. I had a twitter of excitement in my tummy at the thought. I talked to my mother about it and she said, 'All right', though she must have had misgivings.

We set off on our bikes, but had to walk them up the hill to the monastery. Peter changed sides so he was walking beside me. We were talking away about his family in the country when his arm slipped around me. I felt myself stiffen and my breath came in sharply. Instinctively I knew I'd like to snuggle against him. My breath came faster, and then I remembered, I'm going to be a nun! and I pulled away. I kept the bike between us after that, but I felt sorry to have missed the opportunity. It'd be nice to kiss a boy, I thought, before I give all that away forever.

While I was out, Mum told my father where I was and who with, and by the time I got back Dad was in a high state of anxiety. He was so cross with me that he forbade me ever to go out with Peter again, and said I was not to 'waste time' talking to him. I was furious. He's just so unreasonable! I thought. What does he think I was doing?

Seething, I complained bitterly to Maurice, who was home on holidays from the seminary. 'Nothing happened!' I said. 'I was doing a good thing, taking Peter to the monastery to hear about Catholicism.' (I didn't mention the arm-around-me bit though.)

Maurice was very understanding and I felt he was on my side. He explained to me that fathers tend to be very protective of their daughters, and that this was partly because they remembered how randy they were as young men. Fathers just didn't trust any boys. This concept helped and was new to me. I couldn't imagine my father, young man or not, as randy – though I *am* number seven in the family! And what did he think of me, if I wasn't to be trusted on a simple bike-ride?

Anyway, this effectively restricted any further relationship with Peter, though he was still interested in me and I felt flattered by that. Now that I'd told my parents I was going to enter the convent, I guessed that put an end to anything else developing.

Mum was confused by all this, and told me years later she was never sure she should have let me enter the convent. All this 'interest' in dance classes and boys didn't seem to her consistent with someone who said they wanted to be a nun.

Bet, my sister who was already a nun, had never been like that. She had seemed right for the convent – quiet, and not interested in going out, or boys.

'Boys' was a bit excessive, I thought, as Peter was the only boy I'd ever really talked to. We'd never held hands, sat in the back row of the pictures or kissed. I'd never been physically close enough to any boy to kiss, and wouldn't have known how. I suspected Peter would have liked to have a try, and my heart would skip a beat when I thought about it, but that's where it stopped.

The death knell to Peter's interest was sounded when Mrs Harris told him I was going to be a nun. She picked this up from Mum, but he was disbelieving and scoffed at the idea. She produced the final blow when she took him outside to view my calico nighties hanging on our line next door.

Old Sister John had insisted on making them for me according to the convent ten-gallon pattern in totally unbleached calico, and Mum had been trying to soften them with bleaching, washing and hanging out in the weather. Later, during the novitiate, three of us would get into one for a concert item, and the stiffness would prickle me at night for months. There was no mistaking they were strange items of clothing to be hanging on a suburban clothes line.

Peter confronted me, and there was no way I could answer his question, 'But why?'

When I said, 'I just feel I should', it sounded empty and unconvincing. He had no concept of 'vocation' with which I'd been brought up, and saw the whole idea as a waste of a life.

'Don't you want to have a boyfriend? And play around?' he said. ' Don't you want to get married? Have kids?'

I said, 'No, not really. The only other thing I ever really wanted was to be a journalist. If I wasn't going to be a nun, I'd like to go to Sydney University and become a journalist.'

'Then why not do that? First?'

'I applied for an Exhibition [similar to a bursary that paid university fees] when I did the Leaving, and got one. I've asked them to hold it over for twelve months – just in case.' I looked at my shoes. 'But there's no "just in case".' I intended to enter the convent for life.

He said, 'Yes – but after that? After uni? I can't believe you don't want to have a boyfriend and all that.'

'There's no "after that" in my plans either.'

So that was that. I'd enter the convent unkissed, and possessed only of a conviction that I was called to be a nun, so all that side of life was not for me . . . just as study at Sydney University was a pipedream, and not for me either.

Anyway, it was just as well I wasn't going to Sydney University. The nuns warned us and told us stories about girls losing their faith there. This was laid at the door of Professor Anderson and his school of philosophy undermining faith, and the consequent hedonistic lives girls led.

I knew I had a wild streak tucked away inside me, and might possibly have become one of those grains of wheat who fell by the wayside, withered and died, and have given myself over to the sinful lifestyle.

Dad would be very disappointed in me.

So, considering all this, there was conviction in my decision that it was the right thing to do, but also sadness and a sense of loss.

*We are in the kitchen in Rutherford and Dad throws me high up in the air. It seems very high to a three-year-old. I scream with delight, and bow my head over in fear of hitting the ceiling.*

*I say, 'Throw me up and catch me again, Dad!'*

*Into the air I go – above his head, towards the ceiling, and he actually lets go. I feel his hands let go of me as I fly up. I scream with mock terror and delight, and he catches me again as I come down.*

*Then, 'Again! Again!'*

*It's a very rowdy business, with me screaming and Dad laughing, and Mum is frowning. She doesn't quite approve of such noise and frivolity.*

# 5

## The Road to Singleton

It was 25 March 1952, the Feastday of the Annunciation, and there I was sitting on a picnic rug on a green verge over-looking a most picturesque valley below. It was a glorious day – sunny, blue sky and a fresh breeze. We were having a family picnic: me, Mum, Dad and my brother Jim.

Why then did I have this feeling of dread and anxiety?

It was because we were on the way to Singleton for me to enter the convent there. This day had been looming for months now, gradually creeping closer, and my dread had been mixed with anticipation.

I looked down at the car Jim borrowed from someone to drive us up, and could see the large brown case sitting in the open boot. It contained part of my 'trousseau', and I thought about the dead nun's battered tin trunk behind it that I had been given by the convent holding the rest of my things.

What a trousseau it was! Sheets, towels, pillowslips and lots of clothing. We had to go to Sydney to a supplier of nun's apparel to get long black dresses and convent-style underwear and singlets, both cotton summer sleeveless ones and winter woollen numbers with long sleeves and portholes in the front to allow for the bust I didn't have. Six of everything. I shuddered at the thought of such alien garments.

Mum had made the long black half-petticoats, the several dozen blue check handkerchiefs and the long, blue check aprons that covered all. Mary, Mum and I had a lot of hilarity at the fittings and trying bought things on, but the fun was wearing thin now as I had a sinking realisation I was actually going to have to wear all this stuff pretty soon. And not just for dress-ups.

Mum said, 'Another sandwich, anyone?'

I shook my head. The one I was eating was stuck in my throat, and I had another drink of tea from the thermos to wash it down.

Why am I doing this? I turned aside and looked down into the valley. It's not too late . . . yes, it is! Everything is decided. I'm expected. Anyway, I've made this decision. I'm going through with it and there's no turning back.

Dad was toying with his cup and watching me. There was a jolt in my tummy. He knows how I'm feeling. I gave him what I hoped was a reassuring smile, and he smiled back. His eyes were warm and encouraging. Mum was fussing with the food and plates as she packed things up. We had to go soon. We had to be there between 2.30 and 3 p.m.

Suddenly, a big truck came hurtling down the road and round the bend. What if it can't take the turn, I thought, and crashes into me? I won't have to go! Then I put aside the thought, because if the truck hit, it would probably take all of us and go over the edge into the valley, and I didn't want everyone to die.

Looking back across the fifty years since that day, I can still clearly remember the dread I felt sitting there in the sun, putting on a brave face for my dad. Mum was oblivious to it, fussing with practical details. If I felt so bad, why was I going? Why did I feel so bad?

*Why* was I going at all?

There was that sense of 'calling' I had – a vocation to save the world, or at least my corner of it. There was the Jesus of the Gospels that I loved to imagine: sitting among His disciples, at weddings, tired by the well, having compassion on the hungry and tired multitude, talking about the ways His Father in Heaven cared about us. I think I wanted to share this Jesus with other people who didn't know Him.

There were also those feelings of peace and devotion during the family rosary, at morning Mass, and during retreats. I looked forward to living in a place where this devotion was cherished and nourished, and where people cared about each other.

On the other hand, religious life was a drastic choice. It meant leaving behind family and friends, and everything familiar – even the clothes I was used to. It meant wearing all this funny black stuff, being locked away behind walls, and I couldn't even imagine what I'd be doing all day there.

There were some other disturbing thoughts too. If religious life was Heaven on Earth, where people really cared about each other, why were some of the nuns I knew so tough, unjust and even cruel?

My mind ranged over the nuns I'd known who'd impressed me – one way or the other.

I lied about doing my homework when I was in fifth class in primary school. I said I did it when I didn't. Mostly I was a good kid at school – obeyed the rules, was polite and fairly quiet. But I didn't always do all the work I should have done – all that learning stuff: spelling, poetry, and pages of the *Green Catechism* by rote. As for homework, I usually did it, but this day there were some sums I was supposed to do and I hadn't.

Sister Jerome could be a dragon. She was the only teacher who ever gave my brother Maurice the cane. This was a few years earlier, but was still the cause of family outrage because Maurice was such a good, gentle boy, and all he had done was get the giggles in the church with his mate Peter Ryan.

Maurice noticed that Peter's prayerbook he was supposed to be reading was upside down. He nudged Peter, and pointed at the book. They both went into helpless giggles. Some interfering pious do-gooder had reported to Sister Jerome that the boys were seen laughing in church. (This was at morning Mass, which was completely voluntary.) She gave them six of the best, with no questions asked.

You could usually expect to get into more trouble at home if you reported having got into trouble at school, but Mum still got annoyed years later when she thought about Maurice getting the cane.

One day Sister Jerome decided to have a federal inquiry into homework. Sometimes she checked it daily, while at other times she took up the books at the end of the week.

Each day she did the homework sums on the blackboard, and we were supposed to correct ours from the ones on the board. If you were quick, you could copy down her solutions as she went, but just had to be careful to pop in a couple of mistakes to cover your tracks.

'Leave your sum books open on the desk,' she would say. 'Open your Bible history books and read page ninety-four.' Then she would walk around the room, inspecting the books.

But that particular day she wanted an immediate inspection of work. Boys were being marched out to the platform and caned in front of the class.

'Hold out your hand!' Swish – whack! 'Now the other one.' Swish – whack! again, and the boy tucked his hands into the opposite armpits and slunk back to his seat.

Packing death and lucky not to wet my pants, I remembered the sixer she gave Maurice.

When she got to me I said, 'Yes, Sister. I did some of it but I left it at home.'

She stared down at me, her eyes glinting behind the steel frames of her glasses.

'All right,' she said, all frost. 'Go home and get it!'

What was I to do? I knew it wasn't there. I hadn't done it. Somehow I smuggled the textbook I would need to do the sums under my tunic, and tightened the belt so it wouldn't fall out in front of her. I rushed down the hill and arrived home in breathless tears.

Mum was annoyed to see me but went along with my plans – doubtless in view of Sister Jerome's great mistake with Maurice. I dug a brand new exercise book out of a drawer where Mum kept supplies for emergencies. This was an emergency if ever there was one. I started the sums. I had ten minutes, no more. I was so anxious I couldn't think straight. I smudged the first page, made blots, and couldn't do the long division.

I rushed back up the hill and into the classroom.

'Well?' Sister Jerome was icy. I handed her the book. She looked at me standing there, puffed and pale. All the evidence was there before her – the new exercise book, the smudges and blots, the half-completed sums, the trembling child. Sister Jerome was no fool.

'Is this it?'

'Yes, Sister.'

'It's not all here.'

I shifted from one foot to the other.

'I said I only did some of it.' This sounded weak, even to me.

She looked at me again, hard. Then she handed me the book.

'All right,' she said. 'Go and sit down.'

Perhaps there *was* a heart beating under those yards of cream serge after all! Or perhaps Sister Jerome thought one mistake with the Cahills was enough.

Sister Jerome was not soft, kind and gentle like Sister Manes, who taught me in infants class, or Sister Julie who taught me in sixth class. Sister Jerome was hard, but you certainly did your work for her. Well, mostly. She was the first nun I knew who made me wonder why she was like that. However, she was a teacher. Maybe she thought that was how teachers were meant to be. Then again, weren't they supposed to be understanding and encouraging too?

Then there was old Sister John who taught me maths in first year at high school, then in fourth and fifth year for the Leaving Certificate, and who had insisted on making my convent nighties. There were contradictions in her treatment of me, and I was confused and ambivalent about her.

In first year Sister John would sit out at the table where she presided over the classes. She was deaf, and seemed very old, with a craggy face dominated by big grey beetling eyebrows. She was not so old, I discovered later, but we all thought she was ancient.

We'd have a maths problem to solve. When I took off with maths I'd be finished in a flash and out to the table to show her, which was the way it worked. She'd look at my book and shake her craggy brows.

'No,' she'd say, her black eyes piercing me. 'Go and do it again.'

I'd be confused. I'd know it was right. At least, I'd think it was. I'd go back and do it again, then stand in line at the table to show her.

'Yes', and 'Yes', she'd be saying to the ones ahead of me. I'd look over someone's shoulder and they'd have exactly the same result as I had. I'd think, this time she'll say 'Yes'.

It was finally my turn. 'No,' she'd say again.

After this happened a few times I gave up taking my book out first. Instead I'd do the problem, then read it out to the girl sitting beside me. She'd take it out and get a 'Yes'. I'd take it out and get a 'No', so I gave up. I'd do the work, but spent a lot of time reading a book under the desk, or talking to the other kids. If you kept your head down so she couldn't see your lips moving, it was safe because she couldn't hear you. This didn't do me any harm, because I could do the work, but I'm sure it disrupted others.

But Sister John was canny. She'd know something was going on and Cecilia Cahill was the centre of it, so I ended up down the back of the class by myself, with a few spare desks separating me from everyone.

I didn't understand why. No one talked with me about it, so I was hurt as I sat in isolation, and cracked more and louder jokes to show it didn't matter to me.

Later, as a teacher, I would also get impatient with the smartarse who was twice as quick as everyone else, and I discovered the way to deal with her was to have something else lined up for those who finished first.

Sister John worked in a different way which she probably thought was 'cutting me down to size' or 'teaching me a lesson'. The lessons I learnt were that it wasn't good to be bright, to finish first, and that sometimes people picked on me unfairly for reasons I didn't understand. I also learnt to be class clown to cover it all up.

The best I can say after all these years was that she thought I was a strong personality and needed to be pulled into line, to learn to deal with adversity. 'Character building' I think she would have called it. Yet she was pleased I was entering the convent, and really wanted to make those nighties for me. I thought she might even like me, in a perverse way.

Were there many like her in the convent? I had an uneasy suspicion that cutting down tall poppies might be a convent custom, and that I might be seen as one.

◦ ◦ ◦

Good things also happened at school. Some teachers gave me recognition and encouragement. I did well in essay competitions, like the ones the Newcastle Council used to have for Health Week, and I had short stories and articles published in the school magazine. The principal was a gentle, totally fair and understanding teacher called Sister Mary Raymond, who would often give me responsible jobs. She became for me a model of what a teacher and a nun should be. There were also others on the staff whom I admired and liked.

Sister Louis was our maths teacher in second year. She was young and very human. She treated the girls as people, said funny things, laughed out loud when things happened in class, and ran the joke competition for the school magazine. She would sit at the table in the front of the class, tell us she'd finished marking the test we did last week and was ready to give it back. There'd be a shiver of excitement and apprehension among the girls.

Sister Louis would hand bundles of papers to the girls in the front seats, and they'd start running around the room, giving them out by the name on the top. One day when someone dropped my paper in front of me, I couldn't believe my eyes.

Written on the top of the first page in big red writing was 98 per cent, with a large red ring around it.

I looked at it for several seconds in disbelief, but it didn't disappear. A thrill of excitement welled up in me. I looked up to Sister Louis, sitting at her table.

She was watching me, and smiling at my reaction. She nodded and said, 'Well done!' very quietly. She seemed almost as delighted to give me this mark as I was to get it.

Later she told me the work was almost perfect. What a shame, she said, that I left off that algebra sign, or she could have given me 100 per cent. Keep it up, Cecilia!

However, at school, I also kept coming across the kind of treatment I'd had from Sister John . . . the kind that fulfils the famous maxim of one of our politicians: 'Life wasn't meant to be easy!' To me it felt unnecessarily violent and quite uninspiring. The incident with Sister Geoffrey and the dentist appointment was an example of this.

I was in the intermediate class – third year – and the bell had gone for change of periods at ten to three, the last period of the day. It was the business principles class with Sister Geoffrey, who came bouncing into the room with short steps and heels firmly planted on the wooden floor as she walked. I had a dentist appointment in the city at 3.30, but didn't expect any problems as I had already handed in a note to the principal, Sister Raymond, asking permission to leave at 3 p.m. to catch a bus uptown.

Sister Geoffrey was going on about what she wanted the class to do. I was sitting quietly in the front desk waiting for her to draw breath so I could ask to go.

She said, 'All right then. Start work.'

I was about to stand up when she noticed my books packed neatly in front of me. Nothing was open.

She was aggressive. With a sharp intake of breath she took a couple of quick steps towards my desk, and I quailed.

'What are you sitting there for?' she snapped. 'Open your books and start work.'

I stumbled to my feet.

'What,' she bridled, 'do you think you're doing?'

'I have to go, Sister,' I stammered. 'I brought a note to go to the dentist.'

'Sit down!' she almost shouted. 'You're not going anywhere.'

My face was flaming. There was a deathly silence in the room except for the intake of breaths as the kids imagined the annihilation about to come.

I stood there, silently shaking inside, with my mind whirling. I wondered if I should just make a run for it. Would she grab me, or trip me as I went?

There was not a sound, and I could feel a breathless frisson of excitement in the room – awe mixed with fear, and anticipation of slaughter.

'Sit down!' she almost screamed again. She took a step towards me and puffed up. I kept looking at the floor, but I knew her face was red and her eyes were flashing lightning. I'd seen it before, but never at me. Now, I could feel the heat only a foot or so away.

She's going to hit me, I thought. My mouth was dry and there was a thundering in my ears. My knees felt like water, but I continued to stand. I said nothing, but I would not sit down.

Thoughts raced around my brain. Would I be expelled? I didn't care – she was the one who was wrong. But if I did make a run for it and left the room, something really bad would have to happen. Perhaps I'd never be allowed back to the school, or at least to this class. Right now that seemed a good idea. Then I thought, no – I've got to do this subject to get the Intermediate Certificate. What if I have to leave school without it?

Bugger you! I said in my mind, with anger surging up in me.

I could hear her physically fuming as she hissed again, 'SIT DOWN! I SAY, SIT DOWN!'

I swallowed my anger and distress, and folded onto the seat in helpless tears, head in my arms on the desk. I could feel the atmosphere in the room begin to melt.

'Well,' she said to the class, 'what are you waiting for? Get on with it.'

About five minutes later she banged me on the arm and said, 'You can go now.'

Still sobbing quietly, I collected my things and headed for the door.

The next day I went to the principal, Sister Raymond.

'Sister,' I said, quivering, 'I'm sorry for what happened yesterday.'

'And what was that?' she said.

'If you don't know, I don't want to tell you.'

She hesitated. 'Well,' she said, 'Sister did tell me about it. Don't you think you should apologise to the teacher concerned?'

'No, Sister,' I said. 'I think she was out of order.'

She looked at me for a moment, then smiled a small smile.

'Very well,' she nodded. 'I'm sorry it happened, too.'

Is it any wonder I remember Sister Raymond as one of the people I admired most in high school? I continued in business principles. The incident was never mentioned; I did all my work, but Sister Geoffrey and I largely ignored each other, in a polite kind of way.

On that day in 1952 my feeling of dread was real and not too much allayed by remembering the fair, just and kind teachers I had had. There was also Sister Anselm, who taught me English and history in the senior years, and brought out the best in me with her gentle encouragement. These people, and others like them, inspired me to emulate them I think, and join them in their way of life.

My sister Bet seemed happy enough after eight years with the Sisters of Mercy. But then again, when I visited her in various convents, and met her different superiors, I was astute enough to see some of them as tough old birds, without too much compassion. I thought life could be hard living with them.

But there I was, sitting on a grassy hill beside the road, having a picnic, and preparing to enter the Sisters of Mercy for the rest of my life.

# Part Two

Religious Life

# 6

## Entering the Convent

It was time. We packed ourselves back into the car and headed up the highway. The big impressive iron gates of the convent stood open and we drove in, up the red gravel path between lawns and flowerbeds, to the front door. It was open, so we didn't have to ring. One of the nuns was waiting to meet us and we were taken into the large reception room, where there were already several girls and their families. I smiled a forced smile as I recognised them from our brief meeting a month or so before.

Afternoon tea arrived on a tray. We were introduced to the novice mistress, Mother Cyril, and Reverend Mother Mary Augustine came regally to greet us. Then Mother Cyril suggested we might like to unpack the car. Three or four novices in long black habits and white veils appeared, smiled at me, and carried off the luggage through the big doors into the convent. I had a glimpse of green lawns and more garden as the doors closed behind them.

Other families arrived, and too soon we were rounded up and shepherded through the door to the cloister. Eight of us traipsed across the paths to the novitiate. Then we arrived in the novitiate community room and a sea of twenty laughing novices were flowing around us, kissing us and saying, 'Welcome!'

Sister Mary Paul of the Cross told me she was my 'Mother' and would help me settle in. She was small and friendly, and oozed encouragement. We went upstairs to change, and I found my luggage already next to a bed in one of several dormitories. Sister Paul drew the screens across and said, 'I'll wait here. Sing out if you need me.'

I opened the big suitcase to find what I needed. My little briefs were changed for voluminous convent undies that came to my knees, and I hitched the long black stockings to my suspender belt. My neat little bra was changed for a convent variety – white, too big, and designed with the intention of flattening the bust. Flat black shoes replaced the sandals I had been wearing, then I put on the copious black stuff.

I could hear giggles from across the dormitory as others struggled with the unfamiliar gear, and I reluctantly folded up my dress and underclothes, and packed them and my sandals into a bag for my mother to take home with her. I felt unreal. It was like being dressed up for a concert, except once Mum took my clothes I'd have nothing to change back into. This was weird, and didn't bear thinking too much about. I took a deep breath –

'I think I'm ready,' I said, and came out of the cubicle.

'You look really good,' said Sister Paul. 'Come downstairs now, and get your cap.'

There were eight frilly white caps with black tulle veils pinned to them hanging on the statue in the community room, and as each new postulant reappeared, Mother Cyril took one and 'capped' us formally. She put it on my head and fixed it by tying four inch-wide black ribbons under my chin.

I felt even more strange – done up like a cupie doll dressed in black – as we headed back to the reception room where our folks were waiting. My skirts were swishing around my legs, and I was conscious of my new sensible shoes, stiff and noisy on the polished floor.

There were photos taken with the family, and soon it was time for them to go. The goodbyes were teary and a bit fearful. Mum was practical about it, though – she gave me a hug, a kiss and patted my arm. Dad's hug was longer and firmer. I knew he was a bit upset as he let me go.

He's remembering my look on the road, I thought, and he's worrying about me.

Next, Jim gave me a kiss and that was it. My family went out the door and down the path to the car, and then they were gone. I wiped my tears, and Mother Cyril collected up the eight of us and we headed back to the novitiate. I went into some kind of emotional neutral just to cope with all the overwhelming events.

We went to tea with the novices at a long table in the big refectory behind the tables of the black-veil community. Everyone smiled at us. I guess they all remembered their own first day. Because it was a Feastday there was talk for tea, meaning we were allowed to talk during the meal, and we were officially welcomed. The novices told us there was usually silence at meals during Lent. Shit! I thought. This is only the beginning.

We had our first community recreation, sitting and talking around the long table in the novitiate. There was lots of brittle laughter. The night prayer bell clanged out at 9 p.m., when the novices went to night prayers in the chapel and our 'mothers' took us up to the dormitory to our beds, showed us where the bathrooms and showers were, and told us what went on in the evenings.

I put on one of those dreadful unbleached calico nighties made for me by old Sister John to the convent pattern. It was scratchy, barely reached to my knees and was very draughty, so I eyed with envy the soft interlock or cotton nighties that some of the others had. They hadn't had the doubtful privilege of having theirs made 'to the convent pattern'. Their mothers had bought them.

My black dress had to be worn over my nightie when I was walking around as we had no dressing gowns. We lined up for a bath or shower, giggled a lot, and were relatively quiet when the novices came up after night prayers. Then the Great Silence settled on the convent. I slept the sleep of exhaustion.

It was a shock when the bell rang loudly in the middle of the night – 5 a.m. – and there were sounds of quiet movement all around. The novices were getting dressed for meditation, but we had been told we didn't have to do the formal duties for the first week, and the only rule we had to keep was the Great Silence.

We were expected in the chapel for Mass at seven, so sometime before that we struggled out, got into all the unfamiliar gear, and began our first day in the novitiate.

We spent the next week finding out about life in our corner of a religious order, going for picnics down on the farm, laughing a lot and writing our first letter home to reassure our families we were okay. And we were.

I settled into the routine that was so different from the past. Silence, as it was Lent, was hard for me. Silence days were long. I'd only ever had a few days of retreat, and even then I went home in the evenings. The girls who'd been boarders at 'the college' – Saint Catherine's College, Singleton, on the same grounds as the convent – had more experience of this kind of thing. In some ways I felt a bit second-rate, not having been to 'The College' – it seemed that it was an unofficial juniorate and a breeding ground for vocations. The girls who were at the college had a familiarity with all of this that I sure didn't have: rising at 5 a.m. on the first sound of the bell to go to the chapel for meditation, Office (prayers in Latin) and then Mass. And this was all before breakfast.

The rest of the day was a round of duties: there was Office in Latin in the afternoon and evening also; study and lectures on religious life in the novitiate; private prayer and spiritual reading; meals in silence, sometimes with someone reading aloud from *The Lives of the Saints*; and recreation in the after-noon and at night.

It was all new and began to be an adventure for me. The novices and postulants joined the professed sisters in the chapel and the refectory, but were never allowed to talk to them. We had our own community life. Our superior was the novice mistress, Mother Cyril (who was soon replaced by Mother Francesca), who was responsible for our training. From time to time Reverend Mother Augustine came over from the convent to visit us, and these were special occasions as she was like a Mother Abbess, in charge of the whole Order.

I found myself in trouble for my exuberance early on. Religious life with so much silence and so many little rules got all a bit much for me sometimes, so I'd let off steam by sliding down banisters, climbing trees down on the farm, and acting the goat in silence times. Sister Denise, who was very serious about things, went to Mother Francesca and asked her if she would explain about the silence to the other postulants, as some of them didn't seem to understand. Mother took delight in telling us this – with tongue in cheek. She was secretly amused that Sister Denise had dobbed us in.

I found the demure eyes-down demeanour expected in religious life just about impossible. How could you know what was going on if you didn't keep your eyes open?

A very wise old Passionist priest, called Father Anthony, came to give the retreat to the whole community in the August I was a postulant. It consisted of silence and prayer, with three lectures a day from Father Anthony. I enjoyed the eight days of quiet with its atmosphere of peace. There was lots of free time to sit in the sun, do handcraft, or read – as long as it was a spiritual book.

There was also an opportunity to talk to the priest if you wanted to. He was a complete outsider, so you could speak to him with impunity. I went along. He was so understanding, that I poured out my tale of troubles to him.

'Look, girlie,' he said. 'I wouldn't worry too much about it all. There was nothing very wrong in the things you did. The worst thing you did was get caught. And if you're going to do them again, just don't get caught!'

Good, sane advice.

*It's Sunday and I am too small to join the family trip to Mass. I'm on the front verandah waiting for Dad to come home, watching for them to turn the Rutherford Hotel corner.*

*There he is! I run down the path to meet him. He opens his arms and swings me up to his shoulder.*

*'Did you see him, Dad? Was Farley Jones there today?' Farley Jones was a mythical character that Dad made up for stories.*

*'Yes, he was. Just as we came out of the door after Mass, Farley Jones came creeping around the side of the church and grabbed Mum's handbag!'*

*'Oh!' I gasp with delighted anticipation. 'Did you get it back? Did you chase him?'*

*'Oh yes!' he says. 'I shouted "Stop thief!" and Constable O'Brien started chasing him too!'*

*We're in the kitchen now, and I'm standing in front of him, with bated breath.*

*'We chased him out onto the street, and up the hill past the sale yards. But just as we caught up with him and I grabbed Mum's bag, we heard lots of bellowing and shouting.'*

*He pauses, and I shiver.*

*'I looked around and there they were! The bulls had got out of the sale yards and were coming up the road after us!'*

*He starts running on the spot, and waving his arms.*

*'I jumped over someone's front fence just as they caught up with us, and Constable O'Brien ran into someone else's yard, and all the bulls tore past with their eyes wild, and their horns waving as they mooed and bellowed.'*

*Now Dad is a bull, with horns, pawing the kitchen floor.*

*'And after they'd all gone by, Farley Jones had disappeared. But we'll catch the bandy swob if he comes next week. You'll see!'*

*I am nodding. Bulls are running in my head.*

*Mum is frowning and shaking her head.*

*'Dad! Stop filling the child's head with that rubbish! She won't be able to tell truth from nonsense!'*

# 7

## My Eighteenth Birthday

It was 14 February 1953, my eighteenth birthday, and almost twelve months since I entered the convent and became a Sister of Mercy (or a postulant, at least), and by then I had become a novice.

That day I rose at 5 a.m. when the bell clanged out. 'Lord Jesus preserve us in peace,' said the caller, after knocking on the dormitory door. The greeting was hardly 'Rise and shine, you lot!' but it was the traditional call.

'Amen,' I mumbled in answer.

I got up, but not with the leap exhorted in the novices' guide – 'as if the bed was on fire'. I struggled out, still three-quarters asleep, and splashed my face with cold water from the enamel dish on the washstand beside my bed.

My eyes felt glued together and my brain was still numb with sleep, but I got dressed as quickly as I could organise myself. Voluminous undies, a bra and singlet, black stockings fastened to my newly acquired lace-up corset. Then a long black half-petticoat, fastened at the waist with a button. I tied the separate pocket around my waist. It held my blue check handkerchief and whatever else I wanted to carry around. I could reach into it through one of two slits in either side of my habit.

So far, as required for the sake of modesty, I had been dressing under my calico nightie – called a tunic – though the screens were still closed around my cubicle. The one little candle lit by the caller (the person who rings the bell) and put in the centre of the dormitory ensured no one could see me in the early half-light anyway.

Next came the important garments – the religious habit. Each piece was kissed as I put it on. First, the long black habit – my everyday one, not my good one. When I wanted to wash my everyday habit, which was not a very good black because it was made out of pieces of material that were second- or third-hand, I had to ask permission to wear my good habit for the day. This was except for Sundays, when I always wore the good one, but everyone knew that nobody ever washed anything on Sundays.

I kissed the cross worked into the lining of the heavy serge habit with its regulation eighteen pleats, nine each side, and pulled it over my head. It opened right down the front to about eight inches below the waistband, which held the pleats together. I did up the hooks and eyes – two at the waist, and two holding the yoke above the pleats.

Next, I kissed the cincture – a long black leather belt around my waist, and falling nearly to the floor on my right side. There was a ring through which I pulled the cincture twice to hold it, then threaded through the ring the very large rosary beads with an ebony cross with white inserts – only worn by the Sisters of Mercy.

I then kissed the six-inch crucifix I received at my reception into the novitiate, and tucked it into my cincture. The cord I threw over my head. I tied the tapes of my starched guimp around my neck and stretched them behind me to pin the stiff ends together. It was white and starched hard, and covered me from neck to below the bust.

Then the coif and veil. The coif was starched white calico, with a forehead piece called a dimity ensuring I was visible only from the chin to the eyebrows. If the novices were doing the ironing in the laundry the dimity was likely to have a big scoop in it, hiding eyebrows, and even eyes, so that I had to pull the coif up hard just to be able to see. Then it cut me under the chin, and I found it hard to open my mouth to speak, let alone eat. But today it was all right. It was a bit smelly and stained with perspiration though, as the last few days had been hot and sticky in all this wool and starch. I only got one clean coif and veil each week.

I didn't have to worry about it covering my crowning glory because my hair was cut off the previous September at my reception as a novice. Eight of us, dressed as brides, were officially received into the order by the bishop in the chapel.

I wore my sister-in-law Lois's wedding dress with a billowing train, and her veil, kept on with a spray of fresh flowers Mum had the florist make for me. I had Lois's long white gloves too. There was great excitement in the novitiate as the eight of us got dressed. We were officially still in our preparation retreat, but it was too much to expect us to keep strict silence on such a day. When we were ready we all had photos taken out in the garden – eight brides all in a row. I stood proudly on the front steps of the novitiate in front of the statue of Saint Joseph while Sister Paul took my photo.

This was also when I got my religious name. During the preparation time for reception into the Order a lot of thought was given to choice of the religious name you would ask for, as you were going to have it for a long time. I quite liked Saint Ignatius Loyola, who founded the Jesuits. He was a strong man who did much for God, was very spiritual, and had a really interesting life story. There was a 'Sister Mary Ignatius' over at the convent, so that name was gone, but there was a 'Sister Mary Loyola' down in the little cemetery, so that name was available. I went down and absorbed it. It looked good on the headstone, and I substituted 'Cahill' for 'Gates' (which had been her family name). Yes, I decided, Sister Mary Loyola would suit me very well.

In my bridal gear, I knelt in front of Reverend Mother Augustine in a corridor of the convent on my way to the chapel, and said, 'Reverend Mother, may I have Saint Ignatius Loyola for my patron, as Sister Mary Loyola?'

She looked down at me kneeling there, gazing up expectantly at her and said imperiously, 'No, Sister, you may not. You will be known henceforth as Sister Mary Scholastica.'

My heart sank and my voice choked a bit but I said dutifully, 'Thank you, Reverend Mother,' as I was supposed to. I thought, why is she doing this to me? Scholastica is a terrible name! And then I was carried along by the exhilaration of the day.

Looking back now, why *did* she do it to me? It was rare to have a name refused, and then you were likely to be warned by the novice mistress beforehand. At this distance it's hard to read her mind. Maybe she was a bit like Sister John, and thought it would do me good to be frustrated – 'character building' and all that. I had come to her attention for various indiscretions. Maybe it was just a whim on her part that morning. Who knows? But Scholastica I was.

In the chapel we were presented with our habit and veil during the ceremony, then we retired while the ceremonies continued, so that we could don the religious dress. My hair was hacked off with scissors, then my head was run over with clippers. It would be too uncomfortable to have any hair under all that starch. I had dreaded that moment for weeks, but when it came it was just part of the rush and tumble of change.

Next, we went back to the chapel dressed as novices, in our black habits and white veils, for the rest of the ceremony. At the end of things the choir sang the traditional Latin song 'Ecce Quam Bonum' which meant 'How Good It Is to See Brethren Living in Unity', and we went up and down the chapel to be kissed and welcomed by the sisters of the community. It was all very joyful, and we left the chapel in procession to the lovely strains of the majestic 'Te Deum' sung with great exuberance by the choir.

There was always great interest in the community about the new names, and word spread quickly, so that when I met my sister Bet waiting for me outside the chapel, she kissed me and said, 'Oh, Ceal! Why did you do it? Scholastica is an awful name!' Why, indeed!

I got used to my name, though. In the end it wasn't so bad. Saint Scholastica was the twin sister of Saint Benedict, and lived from A.D. 480 to 543. Stories about her are thin on the ground, but she was a woman ahead of her time, personifying independence, learning and holiness in a time when women were mostly unseen. She founded, and was Abbess of, the Benedictine Order for nuns, following the rule of Saint Benedict. In fact, I *became* Sister Mary Scholastica for many years, and the generations of girls I taught will probably remember me as Sister Scholastica, or 'Sister Schol', forever. Eventually, in the relaxation of religious traditions after the Vatican Council, we were allowed to revert to our family names, and I was Scholastica no longer, but 'Sister Cecilia Cahill'. I was glad to claim my own identity again, but was still a bit nostalgic for the identity I had built as Sister Scholastica over the years.

But back to dressing on my eighteenth birthday. I kissed the little red cross worked into my veil, and pulled on the whole headgear. The veil was also starched, and had to be folded and pinned to shape in a rubrical way with a rubrical number of pins. (Lots of things were 'rubrical' – that is, laid down in the *Book of Customs* to be done in a particular way.) Under the veil there was a soft piece called a domino. This was both for comfort and for protection against the wind turning my stiff veil inside out.

I was now ready to leave my cell (a bedroom or cubicle) and go downstairs, change my slippers for shoes from the shoe press in the covered walk to the chapel, and go inside for morning prayers. I moved very quietly when I pulled back the screens around my bed and left the dormitory, as we were still in the Great Silence. This was a very solemn time from night prayers till the end of Mass when the whole house was in profound silence. Never a word was spoken unless there was an extreme emergency, like fire or illness. However, stories were told – perhaps apocryphal – of saintly nuns in the olden days who lay on the floor all night with broken hips rather than break the Great Silence.

As I left the dormitory, I turned sideways and held the sides of my starched veil so they would not be caught on the door-frame. I had become accustomed to moving this way through doors.

Most of the nuns were already kneeling in the stalls along the sides of the chapel waiting for the prayers to begin. There were about thirty-five or forty of us. I slipped into my place in the row of novices. We were kneeling half side-on to the front of the chapel. The stalls were designed to face the centre so that when we said the Office we were facing each other across the chapel in two choirs. That morning Reverend Mother started morning prayers, then I sat down in the stall on a little stool.

I faced the altar, and the folded high seat of the stall stuck into my back. It was uncomfortable – probably meant to be – but not uncomfortable enough to keep me awake at this time of the morning. Very soon I would be immersed in my usual struggle with sleep. My head would droop and I would sway sideways, till my head dropped and I jerked awake, sat up straight, and began the process all over again. Sometimes the sister behind me would give me a poke in the back when I looked in danger of rolling right out of the stall into the aisle.

I was supposed to be meditating, but I was not quite sure what that meant, so I was always glad when the 6 a.m. Angelus bell rang and I could kneel up for the Angelus prayer. Meditation was for half an hour morning and evening, and we had thick meditation books with a chosen meditation laid out for each day. My books were very old and had belonged to a dead nun. I often thought she must have had more success with them than I did, and I felt a bit of a failure. Each day had a short piece of the Gospel, then three points based on this to be considered and prayed about.

One I remember was the story of the Good Samaritan. I always liked this story because of the selfless goodness of this stranger, an enemy almost, who saved the life of the Jew who had been beset by robbers and left to die. The Samaritan even parted with his good money for this Jewish stranger. I liked the idea that everyone, irrespective of race or creed, was 'my neighbour', and I was his or hers.

The theme of the meditation in the book, however, was to consider how this Jewish man had gone down from Jerusalem to Jericho. How he had turned his back on the Holy City and the Temple of God to go *down* to Jericho, a foreign city looked down upon by the Jews of the day. What was Jericho for me? This man had fallen among thieves because of his infidelity – we must pray not to fall into the same pit!

All of this left me cold. I couldn't spend thirty minutes in this sort of discursive 'prayer'. I liked to think about the goodness of the Samaritan, not the infidelity of the Jewish man. In spite of lectures we had in the novitiate on how to pray on these 'points', I invariably succumbed to early morning torpor and slept instead.

After the Angelus we sat on the high stall seats, faced the centre and said morning Office – Prime, Terce, Sext and None – all in Latin. I had an Office book with an English translation on the opposite page, but so far I'd been too busy coping with the Latin pronunciation of psalms and hymns to take much notice of the translation.

When Office finished we filed out of the chapel – still in solemn silence – to the community room for a 'lecture'. This was a ten-minute or so gathering where the novice mistress could correct us for anything she had noticed and wished to bring to our attention. For instance, she might think we were not walking quietly enough in the Great Silence, or she might have noticed some sisters not keeping the 'custody of the eyes' (that is, eyes cast down at all times). Then she read stories to us from *The Lives of the Saints*, a very old book which was falling apart and had been mended. I liked storytime, and sat and listened with my eyes down, concentrating on my sewing. I'd be darning stockings, mending something or sewing some part of my habit, which I had to make myself.

When the big bell at the convent rang out we knew the priest had arrived for Mass. We put away our sewing and went back to the chapel with downcast eyes.

Mass in Latin was always the real beginning of the day, and on special feast days we had singing too. On *very* special days, such as Easter, or Our Lady of Mercy's Feastday, we wore our cream serge church cloaks over everything. I loved the singing. Some sisters, specially the music teachers, had exquisite voices and the harmony would swell to fill the chapel. My heart would swell and soar too. There were lovely Christmas and Easter hymns, Latin motets, classical sung Masses, and very beautiful psalms and songs that spoke to my heart.

There was no singing on the day of my eighteenth birthday, however, as it was already Lent – the season of silence and penance preparing for Easter, when my parents would be permitted to visit me. I saw them last on Boxing Day for three hours when they came by train from Newcastle.

After Mass I went back to the dormitory to make my bed and tidy up before breakfast. The bell rang and I took my assigned place in the refectory in silence. Breakfast was cereal and milk, which often tasted slightly off because the day's milk had been mixed with the day before's (though the sisters in the kitchen often tried to tell us it was because the cows had been eating weeds, and perhaps it was). Then there was cold toast and a little butter, shared between three or four people, and a cup of tea stewed in the large teapot and poured for me by a novice who was serving at table. Sometimes we had stewed tomato and onion, or scrambled eggs, but not today, because of Lent.

We ate in silence, and I would try to catch the eye of the sister opposite – or, if that failed, kick her under the table – to show her a sign I would make with my fingers above my cup, meaning 'Could you pass the milk for my tea, please?'

After breakfast I did my charge (chores I was in charge of). I was responsible for sweeping and dusting the community room. By nine o'clock we were ready for the proceedings of the novitiate to begin. There were talks by the novice mistress on religious life, study of the rule of our Order, meditation, and learning the customs to be observed. We copied these out to improve our handwriting as well as to become familiar with them.

We broke for 'lunch' (which was really morning tea) at eleven o'clock, and I walked sedately to the refectory again for a cup of tea and a piece of bread which I had to hack off the loaf with my own small table knife. I always hoped there'd be some butter left to put on it. No biscuits today, and Lenten silence was everywhere till recreation time at 4.30 p.m.

On the way back through the garden – on the path, of course – the silence sometimes got a bit much for me, and I might do a hop and skip to catch up with one of my friends. On this day I walked close behind Sister Julie and whispered, 'Today's my birthday!' as we went up the steps to the novitiate.

She half-turned to me and whispered, 'Happy birthday!' and we both had a quiet grin – till we ran slap-bang into the novice mistress. She said nothing but froze us with a look. I blushed and we slunk back to study class in silence.

Before the 1 p.m. dinner there were more prayers. When the dinner bell rang, Reverend Mother intoned a Latin psalm and we filed out of the chapel to the refectory reciting it and straggling along the cloister in what was supposed to be a crocodile of two by two.

It was my turn to read in the refectory – a real ordeal. I stood next to the rostrum at the end of the refectory opposite Reverend Mother. During grace I bowed and begged a blessing – all in Latin – then climbed awkwardly into the rostrum. At a sign from Reverend Mother – a tinkle on her small bell – I began to read from the assigned book. Today it was on the life of Saint Therese. She was a French teenager who entered the Carmelite Convent – a really strict order – and found it hard going. She kept a diary about it, got consumption and died by the time she was thirty years old. It was an interesting story.

I had practised reading out loud in the novitiate, but I still felt very nervous as I looked up the two rows of professed sisters – thirty black veiled heads bowed over their dinner plates.

What I didn't know was that they were all supportive and sorry for me undergoing such a formidable trial. They'd all had their turn at being a novice reading in the big refectory like me. All I saw were rows of black on each side, and Reverend Mother glaring at me from the top.

My hands were sweaty and my voice refused to come. After a couple of croaks it came out, and I could see Reverend Mother frown down at me. I flushed red, stumbled and picked myself up and went on reading until activity slowed at the tables. Reverend Mother rang the bell to end the reading. I gratefully fell out of the rostrum to stand beside it again, and grace was said.

The sisters all filed out, saying the Miserere in Latin, and I was free to have my dinner of chops and three vegies kept warm in the kitchen, a little the worse for the wait. With me were two other novices who had served on the tables, and we ate together in silence. Then it was back to the novitiate for the afternoon of study, music practice and private spiritual reading.

At 4 p.m. I went to have a cup of tea again. Today there was fresh bread and jam – a real treat for hungry young people. By 4.20 I was back in the chapel for Vespers before recreation, when Mother suggested a walk around the farm, and we were free to walk and talk as much as we liked. We sauntered along in threes – 'no twos, please!' – and at last I could legally tell people it was my birthday. We laughed and joked as we walked, and in spite of the stresses of silence and regimentation, life was good among my friends. Our friendships were meant to be general, however, not exclusive, so there were no 'best friends'.

Recreation was short but we always packed a lot into it, and let off steam. We went to Office again at 5.05. This time it was for Matins and Lauds, those 'hours' of the Office which are said in the middle of the night by the monastic orders, like the Carmelites. After Office we had a lecture again – another story from *The Lives of the Saints*. Some of the stories were a bit weird, though. For instance, there was one saint who had a bird in her cell in a cage, though I didn't think this was permissible, but we were always being told that 'you can do anything with permission'. So I presumed she had permission.

This bird was a linnet, and one day in winter a starving sparrow flew in and tried to take some of the seed from inside the linnet's cage. The linnet drove the sparrow away with great screeches, flutters and pecking. The saint lectured the linnet on charity to those less fortunate, and suddenly a hawk flew in and tore off one of the linnet's wings. The saint was very distressed as the linnet lay on the floor of the cage, bleeding and dying, so she turned to prayer.

'O Father,' she said, 'who desires more the repentance and conversion of a sinner than his death, have compassion on a poor ignorant bird.'

When she finished her prayer she turned and saw that the linnet had recovered and grown a new wing, more resplendent than the first.

I ask you – could you take this sort of thing seriously?

At study between six and seven o'clock we had set topics and time flew till the bell rang for supper. This was a simple meal of tea and bread and usually something else. I was hoping it wasn't just beetroot as it sometimes was, but was relieved to see bowls of salad with cold meat on the table.

I was out of luck with the reading: because it was Lent I had to read again at supper. When the meal finished the nuns all filed out to the chapel, and I had my meal before I joined them to struggle with evening meditation till night recreation began at eight o'clock.

This hour was my favourite time of the day. I'd talk and laugh with the others as we sat and did our sewing or some other craft. I was learning to do tatting (a kind of lace-making with a shuttle). I made lots of mistakes, as I loved to talk and laugh with friends, and tatting took concentration.

Promptly at nine o'clock the night prayer bell rang out and we all went into immediate and deep silence. We'd go back to the chapel for some more Office (called Compline) and a litany of the saints with some other prayers. By nine-thirty I was changing my shoes for slippers and heading up the stairs towards bed.

I pulled the screens very quietly, climbed out of my hot gear into my convent nightdress, and got ready for sleep. I fell into bed as fast as I could because I was always tired, and knew 5 a.m. would come all too quickly.

At 10 p.m. the lights went out.

*I'm five years old, and I'm waiting for Dad to come home from work.*

*Earlier in the day I jumped off the high front verandah wall at Waratah with an umbrella to see if I could fly. Dad brings his bike around the back, and I'm waiting as he comes into the dining room.*

*I throw myself into his arms, sniffling, fresh tears rolling down at the memory.*

*'That's terrible!' he says. 'Did you hurt yourself?'*

*'Yes!' I wail. 'I broke my heart and soul!'*

*Next day is Friday, pay day, and he arrives home with a bag of lollies – soft jubes shaped like orange and lemon segments – and he tells me they are 'heart and soul lollies'.*

*'I went to see the doctor,' he says, 'and asked for something to cure a little girl who broke her heart and soul. He said these would be very good.'*

*Recovery takes several weeks.*

# 8

## Mr Nickerson

It's spring and I'm walking the path from the rosary walk to the novitiate cloister, through the garden by the Calvary mound. The life-sized Christ is crucified in stone; Mary and John stand guard. I smell the peach blossom at the crook in the path, glorious in September, with the buzz of myriad bees in its pink profusion. There's a lightness in my step.

Mr Nickerson, kneeling beside the pansies, is straightening from his weeding stoop.

'Mornin', Sister. Have ya got the time, please?'

'Good morning, Mr Nickerson. It's twenty past eleven.'

'Thankya St'r,' says the old man, settling back on his heels. 'Flies are bad right now.'

'Are they, Mr Nickerson?'

I can never bring myself to put my eyes down and hurry by him as the rules of religious modesty say I should. He's a lonely old man, and I think he chooses to weed near the path at times when the young novices are passing. Like now. It's just after morning lunch (morning tea), when we are headed back to the novitiate for study of vows or teacher training school. It's a silence day outside – most days are – so everyone walks alone.

'Yairs,' drawls Mr Nickerson. 'I swallowed one this mornin'. Round the front.'

I shudder. I don't even have to pretend.

'Hmmm. And last week I swallowed two down in Maitland. One near the station when I got out of the train, and then I swallowed another one walking down High Street.'

'That's terrible, Mr Nickerson . . .'

'Yairs. Bad time o'year for flies.'

Here's my chance to get away. 'Goodbye, Mr Nickerson. Don't work too hard in the sun.'

That night at study time I join a queue to 'show up' to the novice mistress. She sits at the head of the long table and the novices and postulants sit along both sides of it in order of seniority. Each of us has a drawer in front of us holding our personal possessions: pens and pencils, maybe paints, art papers, a few holy cards and a small bundle of letters from home you can read again when loneliness strikes.

The novice in front of me is kneeling and speaking quietly. Oh-no, I think, Sister Mary Denise was late for the Angelus today . . .

Suddenly, over she goes, face to the floor. For some reason, 'late for the Angelus' is one of those faults with its own penalty: kissing the floor.

Sister Mary Denise gets up, face flaming, and walks to her seat. No one looks up. We all feel for her. We've all been there – and it could be any of us tomorrow.

It is my turn to 'show up'. I take her place and drop to my knees beside the novice mistress.

'Yes, Sister?' she asks.

'Mother, I was late for training school and I talked to Mr Nickerson.'

'And I suppose that's why you were late. What were you talking about?'

'He asked me the time, and told me he swallowed a fly . . .'

She smiles. 'Seems it's not unusual for him. But you're always talking to him. How many times is it this week?'

'Three.'

'Well, surely you don't have to stand around talking to him every time he asks the time. Specially if your duty is to be at training school.'

'No, Mother.' I am dismissed with a nod. As I get up and go back to my place I wonder, what's wrong with telling Mr Nickerson the time and talking about the flies? Why is it frowned upon? For him it's a way of making contact. He's an old man who lives on his own and works at the convent a few hours a day for a few shillings and to get out of the house.

Sister Jean is a postulant who entered in her early twenties. She had been almost engaged before she entered. She's an attractive country girl who laughs a lot and often has us all in stitches with her unbelievable tales, like the one about Dudley, a fifty-year-old parrot who had shingles and herpes, as well as having lost most of his feathers.

Mr Nickerson looks out for Jean with her bouncing step and bubbly personality, until Mother gives her such a bad time over him that it becomes a community joke. Even

Mother smiles when people tease Jean at recreation about her elderly 'boyfriend'.

Speaking to Mr Nickerson comes under the loose heading of 'secular intercourse' – an unfortunate choice of term. It's not permitted to have contact of any kind with people outside the Order. Even after you leave the novitiate, you are not supposed to have more than the briefest unavoidable contact with parents of children in your class, unless there is some special reason, and then you have to get permission.

The whole fuss about Mr Nickerson is like a lot of other things I find perplexing in the novitiate. I read about Jesus in the Gospels. He was never abusive to others, except to the buyers and sellers who were defiling his father's house. He was kind and forgiving to sinners, and treated people with real respect – even the Samaritan woman who had had seven husbands and the man she was with at that time was not her husband. Jesus went along to help friends celebrate at their wedding parties, and even helped with the wine when the supply ran out to save his young friends embarrassment. He had compassion on the multitude, and cried at the death of his friend Lazarus.

I'm sure HE would talk to Mr Nickerson.

# 9

## Leaving Home

By the time I was twenty I was already well settled into religious life. I was a second-year senior novice due for profession at Easter. Profession was the ceremony where you made vows of poverty, chastity and obedience, got your black veil instead of the novice's white one, and moved out of the novitiate into the community at large.

I should have been professed the previous September but was 'held back'. When I asked for profession, Reverend Mother said 'No'. She seemed to think I was out of place – didn't quite fit in – and decided the situation would be reviewed in six months. Then I would either be professed or sent home. This was devastating for me to hear at the time, as I wanted to stay.

I wanted this in spite of the trouble I was often in for defying the regimented life by talking and laughing in silence time and the attention I seemed to attract for small things, like being late for prayers in chapel, or breaking things. In

91

spite of the public or private humiliations I received as part of my training, I still didn't want to go home. I liked the singing and praying together, and I liked living with the other novices. Also, there was still my commitment to the dream that one day I would be out there 'saving the world' – helping others and teaching people about the Jesus of the Gospels whom I admired and loved. Besides, nuns didn't leave. If they did it was for health reasons, not because they didn't keep the silence. My father and mother were so proud of me. Leaving would be failure. *Especially* being sent home.

I made up my mind to conform more to the picture of the perfect novice always being held up to us. I'd keep the silence better, show more concern for custody of the eyes by keeping them turned down as I went around, and generally have a more staid religious decorum, not hurrying around the place or running down the stairs like I often did.

It must have worked for I was professed when the time came, six months later. No mention was made of my previous problems, and I made my vows of poverty, chastity and obedience in front of the bishop and the community in the chapel.

During the last few years I had seen little of Mum and Dad. It was leaving home with a vengeance. While we were living in the novitiate parents were only allowed to visit every three months, and I could only receive letters once in between, no matter how many letters arrived during that time. Mum adjusted to this and was very careful to always 'do the right thing'. So news of home was sparse. From living at home and coming and going every day, talking to Mum while we made the beds or did the cooking, sharing family meals, suddenly I was far away and out of touch.

This had been very hard on my parents too. I was just seventeen and the only child still at home when I left. Mary told me years later that Mum said the day I left home to enter the convent, they both came to Singleton with me and then went home to an empty house – just the two of them, as they had started long, long ago. When they decided to say the family rosary that night they were too upset to finish it.

When Mum and Dad came to see me it was a very formal visit. They travelled in an early train from Newcastle to Singleton, ate their sandwiches in the park and walked the mile or so to the convent. They could visit any time after 2 p.m. but had to leave before 5. Needless to say, they were on the doorstep right on 2.

We walked in the garden together and sat among the lawns and flowerbeds when it was fine. Wet weather meant we were cooped up in the reception room – all twenty or so novices and their families, perched on the antique Austrian chairs around long, wide polished tables.

Afternoon tea was provided on a tray – good china, little sandwiches and creamy fairy cakes. I was not allowed to eat with my parents and had to duck away if I wanted a 'cuppa' myself. They left by 5 p.m. to stay at a hotel in town and to catch an early train home the next day. Gone for another three months.

The first visiting day after I entered was Easter Monday. I had been in the convent six weeks. My 'mother' in the novitiate, Sister Mary Paul of the Cross, suggested it might be nice to put my hair up in rags to give it a few curls under the cap. I thought this sounded exciting, so I wore the makeshift curlers to bed overnight and she combed my hair out in the early morning Great Silence before Mass. Of course, I couldn't see the back, but the front looked pretty good in the small mirror above the handbasin in the bathroom corridor.

I had a good feeling about it all – Mum and Dad were coming, it was Easter time when there's a high in religious life and everyone's happy. Even the weather was glorious – crisp mornings and clear sunny days. I was dressed in my best long black dress and good shoes with a freshly laundered postulant's cap and veil, and my hair was curled. I had happy visions of myself sitting with my parents in the sun among the flowers.

There was a general thrill of excitement running in the novitiate community room after 1 p.m. dinner as we waited to hear the doorbell ring at the main convent building, announcing the arrival of visitors.

Suddenly, one of the 'black veils' from the convent (as distinct from the white-veiled novices) was at the door with a list of people who had arrived and Mother called us up. After reading out the names the novice mistress said to me, 'You wait here. I need to see you before you go over.'

I hopped from one foot to the other wondering what it could be. Surely it could wait! Mum and Dad were over at the convent waiting for me. I champed at the bit.

Then the axe fell. Reverend Mother had noticed my beautified hairstyle in the chapel after dinner and had sent me a message.

'The frill on your cap is folded and pinned too high,' the novice mistress told me. 'And she also said to tell you your hair is sticking out like turkey's tails at the back. You're to fix both before you go over to your parents.'

My religious mother was distressed for me and felt guilty that she'd caused the problem, so she took me off to the handbasin and mirror. She plastered down my acquired curls with water, re-pinned the offending cap and veil, and dried my hair off with a towel. I dried my tears as best I could.

All this took up precious time and I went back to the novice mistress looking a bit like a feather boa that had accidentally been through the washing machine.

'All right,' she said. 'You can go now, but you're not to tell your mother and father anything about this.'

I was happy to escape and made some lame excuse about having to do my hair when Mum wanted to know what took me so long.

Dad was very proud of me and glad to make the trip for these visits. He was warm and affectionate. Mum worried about me – especially when I wasn't allowed to be professed. She arrived once with a large green can of olive oil, labeled 'Olio Sassio', which someone had told her was very good for you. Apparently it oiled the whole system, relaxing you, and was beneficial in many other ways.

I wasn't keen on it, but Mother Francesca, who was now novice mistress, was very amused and said I had to take it if my mother thought it would do me good. For months I gagged as I swallowed a tablespoon of oil every day with water and a pinch of salt to take away the taste. It never occurred to me to tip it out, or otherwise secretly dispose of it, as it would nowadays. I had been told to take it, and I was learning to practise obedience. I took it all very seriously.

Mum's concern was very practical. She always arrived with a gift – a warm cardigan in winter, some new stockings, a pair of shoes she couldn't really afford. Another time it was a good pair of scissors she thought I might need when she realised I had to make my own clothes. However, most of these things I was not allowed to keep. Of course, I had to tell the novice mistress that Mum brought them. It was called 'showing them up', which most often led to 'giving them up' so they could be put in the community cupboard till I – or someone else – needed them.

Except the scissors. I was allowed to keep them. They travelled with me down many paths, and years later when I left the convent, I still had them, though they were rusted and blunt – not the precision instrument my dressmaking mum went to town specially to find and purchased all those years ago.

The time of family closeness had gone. Somehow the relationship with Mum and Dad had changed forever. I'd become 'Our Daughter Who Is a Nun' – proudly, fondly, but at some distance. I wouldn't be able to go back to see them in our home for many years.

I was the third of their seven children they had given to the Church. Bet had already been a nun for over ten years, and Maurice was away studying to become a priest. They didn't regard us as 'lost' to them, however, but as blessings God had bestowed on them and the family. Blessings who were distant from them.

Distant – that's how the Order wanted it. *They* were to be my new family.

# 10

## Initiation into Teaching

As a second-year novice I was officially promoted to teacher training with Mother Mary Calasanctius in the training room down the hall in the novitiate. This training was incorporated with our religious duties, and took up the whole year.

We began at 9 a.m., after the morning religious duties. Mother Calasanctius (Mother Cal, as we all referred to her behind her back right through the years) was a brilliant and spiritual woman in the widest sense, who graduated from the University of Melbourne in the 1920s. She and another sister began studying by correspondence when not too many women – let alone nuns – were on university campuses. Then they had to move from Singleton to live with the Melbourne sisters for their final year.

We had a general primary school teacher training, beginning with infants. We learnt all about Madam Montessori's kinesthetic methods in a day when Montessori schools had never been heard of in Australia. We did our practice teaching in the infants' classes of the local primary school. This was a nightmare for me as I'd never had anything to do with little people and had no idea how to talk to them.

My first lesson was a 'join the dots' session for newish kinders. It was a disaster. I prepared the sheets, collected the pencils and wrote out my spiel. On the day I handed out the papers, I began with my prepared line: 'Now, Sister [that was me] will give you a pencil and . . .'

Suddenly, a little five-year-old red-haired girl in the front seat called out, 'You don't have to give me a pencil. My mummy got me some pencils!'

'All right – er – Sister will give you a pencil.' This was now said firmly as panic was setting in. This interruption was *not* in the script.

'But you don't have to give me a pencil. Look! I've got lots. My mummy gave them to me.'

That was the end for me. I froze. I couldn't remember a thing. I stammered. I looked wildly round the room. All these little eyes were staring at me, expecting something to happen.

'Er – er . . .' I stuttered. Then I felt tears welling up and I turned away.

The regular kinder teacher came to my aid and took over. The other trainees (all smirking), Mother Cal and I all went back to the training room for the inevitable post-mortem.

The others said things to me like, 'What happened?' and 'Why was that so bad?'

I just winced and mumbled at them.

Teacher training was fun sometimes, though. We spent a

lot of time having our minds expanded by listening to Mother Cal read stuff like T. S. Eliot, or being taken on nature walks in the grounds. She had an amazing breadth of knowledge ranging from cultivated plants to Australian natives – 'You can't cultivate flannel flowers. You just throw them down, like this . . .' (On this occasion, however, the flowers did not obey her instructions, and died.)

As well as conducting study of regular teaching methods, she took us on tours of the convent rooms and corridors to see prints of early religious art, and enthused about each painter. She told us how Fra Lippo Lippi's Madonnas were capricious Florentine maidens, and how he had to have a religious excuse to paint them.

When we got to the primary part of the training it was easier. It was fun, too. We had excursions over to the reception room in the main convent building, where there was a wireless in a large floor-model cabinet of walnut. It was the only wireless in the convent. We sat in a semicircle, perched carefully on the good Austrian dining chairs with their woven seats and backs, and listened to the ABC broadcasts for schools. We took notes, then went back to the training room to see how we would use them, and what we could learn from them.

At other times, we found ourselves bounding with great enthusiasm around the Axminster carpet being kangaroos or plodding as elephants to the appropriate music. Other times we'd sway like pampas grass in the breeze.

At the end of the year, Father Thompson, Head of Catholic Education Training, came from Sydney and we had our exams. This time I didn't collapse giving my demonstration lesson to fifth class, and we all got our Catholic teaching certificate.

At Easter 1955, I was allowed to make my first, or temporary, vows, and I found myself out in the real world teaching first class at New Lambton. The day was very long. You had to change lessons every little while because the children got through them so fast. Sometimes we had finished everything I'd prepared for the whole day by eleven o'clock. That's when my woebegone face would appear at the little window in the door to the adjoining second class room. When Sister Mary Gonzaga came over to see me I'd bleat, 'I've finished everything! What else can we do?'

Hiding her amusement at the panic in my face, she'd very solemnly rescue me by suggesting things I could do with the children next.

Things didn't get any better the year after when I found myself and seventy-five kinder and first class children all crowded into one small room at Tighes Hill, an inner-city industrial suburb of Newcastle, full of post-war migrants from Europe. They were keen, and I was desperate. Seventy-five little children seemed far too many for one person to manage, but that's just the way it was. The sister next door with second class had less, so she took thirteen of the better kids to teach with her class. Almost before I'd noticed they'd gone, we got fifteen new kinders at Easter.

There was often pandemonium as I struggled to keep everyone busy. Sister Mary Ignatius, who taught the infants class in Singleton and was a brilliant teacher, came to my aid when she heard how bad things were. She designed a special daily timetable for my mixed class.

I spent the day running from one side to the other, in the recommended twenty-minute intervals. The timetable went something like this:

10.00 Set kinders to work colouring in, while first class copies their numbers from the chart.

10.05 Sums for first class. Work through the sheets I've given you.

10.20 Kinder – give out the boxes of sorting materials and put the contents in pairs on the desks.

10.25 Check on first class. Walk around, then correct the sheets.

And so it went on, for the whole day. It was brilliant. Sister Mary Ignatius provided lots of worksheets and little boxes about six inches by four which used to have reels of Silko cotton in them, but now had bits of material, pictures of fruit and other teaching aids to be sorted by kinders. She also suggested ways of using the little readers we already had.

'Iggy' (an affectionate name we all had for her) saved my life, but it was still a very long year. On top of all that, we had all the emergencies which happen with five-year-olds who have just started school – running away home, tearful faces and wet pants.

In the case of the all too frequent wet pants, I was lucky to be able to call upon a mother who lived a couple of doors down from the school, Mrs Sheehan. She had a large family and thus a good collection of spare clothes which she kept for this specific purpose. I would send a first class boy down to her with a distress call, and she'd magically appear, clean up the little person and put them in fresh clothes. She'd even bring back their own clothes all clean and dry before the end of the school day.

Some of these little people imprinted themselves indelibly into my memory. There was Reggie (who called himself 'Weggie') and was accepted at four and a half years old on compassionate grounds. His mother pleaded that she was desperate. She was a deserted wife, she told us, who knew no one in the strange city. She begged us to take Reggie as she was completely on her own. She had to work to provide for herself and her boy and had no one who could help care for him. We found out by accident much later in the year that she had actually put up his age by nearly twelve months – when he came into my class he was not even four years old.

Weggie was a big child for his age, though, stocky and with a thatch of fair hair hanging in his blue eyes. But he was lost as far as knowing what the rest of us were on about.

One day, not long after he arrived, I noticed Weggie in tears.

'Whatever is wrong, Reggie?'

'There's no toilepth in thith thcool!'

'Yes there are. You know, down the back where the boys go.'

More tears flowed. 'Yeth . . . but they're only thand-up toilepth. I want to thit down!'

'Dennis,' I said to a bright and chirpy first-class boy, 'run down and show Reggie where the sit-down boys' toilets are. Quick!'

A couple of minutes later, Dennis reappeared in the doorway.

'Sister, we went quick. But we weren't quick enough!'

When I went to look I saw what he meant. There was a brown trail from outside the door. Poor Weggie! I sent down the street for Mrs Sheehan, but as luck would have it, she'd gone down to the shops. I ignored the pandemonium in the classroom, and cleaned up Weggie the best I could. When I looked for something to put him into, all I could find was an old but clean short-sleeved woollen singlet that someone had sent along in a bundle of polishing rags. It came down to his knees and past his elbows, but did the job of keeping him warm till Mrs Sheehan appeared.

None of the children seemed to take much notice of his change in appearance, but at recess I couldn't help suggesting to the other nuns that we had the child Jesus at the age of four as he stood against first class wall in the sun in his long cream robe.

Another memorable child was Stanley. Stanley was at least six when he came to kinder. He was a big boy who managed to look slightly unkempt despite his new school uniform. Stanley had spent his early years in displaced persons camps in Europe, and couldn't speak English. In fact, he didn't speak at all for quite a long time. He only grunted at the other children, and grabbed anything he wanted. While I was aware of his difficult history, there wasn't a lot I could do for him among seventy-five other students.

One day Stanley had an 'accident', and Mrs Sheehan fixed him up. Afterwards, he refused to come inside the classroom and hung back at the door with her.

'What's wrong, Stanley?' I said. 'It's all right. Come on in.'

He kept shaking his head and pointing to his soiled pants.

Then he spoke for the very first time, searching for the words:

'I . . . mus' walk . . . wid . . . *dem* pants!'

His voice was guttural, but his message was clear. For him this was just one more strange country where things were taken from you, or lost, and there was no way he was going to be parted from those new pants – even if they were soiled.

Time took care of his fears, however, and in the end he became just one of the boys.

One day my friend Sister Margaret, who taught third and fourth class, came to the door for something. I was busy with first class, teaching them sums from the blackboard. I had just set the kinders to work on a sorting exercise. On their desktops they each had a little box of fabric shapes to be sorted into pairs according to colour, but this was not what was happening. Instead, there was a general buzz from them as they entertained themselves with other things. Weggie was sitting up, licking his playlunch banana from the outside of his fist. He had got it out of his schoolbag under the desk, peeled it and squeezed it till it oozed out between his fingers. He had it in his hair and all over his face.

Sister Margaret surveyed the scene, leant against the side of the door shaking with laughter, and with tears rolling down her cheeks.

'My God,' she said, 'how do you survive? And just what is *he* doing?'

I looked to where she was pointing and a little tiger called Chris, with pug nose, freckles and crinkly auburn hair, was busy moving up and down the aisles calling out, 'Boxes! Boxes!' as he collected up the little boxes I had just given out. His face was barely visible above several piles of Silko boxes. The rest of kinder was either lost in their own worlds, or just relaxing in their seats watching the shemozzle.

It was not always quite as bad as this, however. I got better at managing as the year went by, and somehow we all survived.

# 11

## Living in a Branch House

The year of 1956, during which I had my twenty-first birth-day, was spent living at Tighes Hill, an inner-city suburb with lots of migrant families. It was the decade when fathers worked in the industries, mothers stayed at home and struggled with English, and children came to school to mix with 'old' Australians and absorb a different culture. On weekends there were Italian classes, Greek school and long Orthodox Masses to maintain the old cultures.

My twenty-first birthday came and went. I got up at 5 a.m. as usual, went to meditation, prayers and Mass, had breakfast and went to school. As birthdays were not to be celebrated in the convent, it continued like any other day.

After school I found a parcel and card from my mother which the superior decided to give me, in spite of the general custom of non-celebration. I was lucky that, this year, my birthday was a few days before Lent began, or there would have been no such concessions.

When Mum rang up in the evening from a public telephone box down at the post office, some distance from home, I was allowed to speak to her, though it wasn't usual for young nuns to be allowed to talk on the phone between visiting days.

Sister Stephanie, our cook, made a special cake for afternoon tea (not a birthday cake as such, you understand), and we had it in silence because it was a silence day. However, we had talk during tea that night – a nice concession for my twenty-first.

There were six of us living at the convent in Tighes Hill that year – the four of us who staffed the primary school up the road, old Sister Francis who taught music all day at the convent, and Sister Stephanie who looked after the kitchen and laundry.

We had the same community life in our small house as we did in Singleton. We said our Office in the little chapel, with three of us in the stalls on each side, saying the prayers in Latin by turn. We had singing for Mass on Feastdays and for Benediction when we had it, and on Saturday evenings we sang the litany of the Blessed Virgin in parts. It got a bit thin sometimes.

After Vespers we had our afternoon recreation, sitting with our sewing or craft on the verandah in summer, or in the warm community room in winter. At night from 8 till 9 we relaxed in the community room, and went to night prayers and the Great Silence when the bell went. We cleaned and polished, mostly in silence, on Saturdays, and Sundays we spent in the community room, after we had finished our visits to some of the old and lonely people in the parish.

We didn't have a TV, and there was no radio in the

convent. We had a record player and a few records, though – classics or musicals. I remember hearing *Man of La Mancha* and *Oklahoma!*. We played these on Sundays as we did our school stuff or handcrafts, and chatted.

Life at school was pretty exhausting but rewarding too, in a way. There I was, out in the world, finally fulfilling my vocation. I loved the kids, and even enjoyed teaching them when I wasn't busy being overwhelmed by the sheer number of them. I taught them religion and told them stories about Jesus. I was a good storyteller, and all those little eyes were glued to me while I dramatised my favourite Gospel stories. I also enjoyed living a community life, praying and eating and recreating with the others.

Fluffy was also part of the community at Tighes Hill. Fluffy was a huge Persian tomcat, though I'm sure he must have been 'fixed up'. It would never have done to have the convent cat out roaming and moaning for a mate! Fluffy had a good life at the convent, and he knew it. He was a particular favourite of the superior and got the best food and treatment. He knew all the sunny spots and comfortable chairs to relax in and regarded the convent as his personal domain. When he had an abscess on his tooth he was taken to the vet, had antibiotics and left a trail of pus up the hallway and into the refectory when his abscess burst. Somebody just cleaned it up without complaint.

At the same time as this I had a middle-ear infection with a burst eardrum, but received no concessions. I was given two Panadol tablets and went to school. That day in kinder-and-first must have been chaotic as I struggled with the pain, feeling very sick with it.

I was too miserable to think that the cavalier attitude to my ear (as opposed to Fluffy's tooth) was because I didn't shed pus around the place. My ear was encased in a starched white coif hiding the globs of cotton wool stuffed into it. It lacked visibility. Also, there was no one to take care of my class.

Sister Mary Louise, who was school principal, insisted the superior send me to casualty at the Mater Hospital in the afternoon after school. So finally I got antibiotics too, and several days off school. The others rearranged classes, got a mother or two to come along and help, and reassured me: 'Don't worry, we'll manage.'

At the convent I was the junior sister in the community and therefore had lots of extra little charges. Because there was only one of me, a couple of the others also took turns at some of the juniors' duties, such as being the bell ringer for prayers and meals, and being the portress, answering phones and doorbells.

As a junior sister with only temporary vows I was technically still on probation, and so subject to some small restrictions. For example, I wasn't allowed to talk till 10 a.m. on Sundays, while the finally professed sisters were allowed to talk from 9.30.

On Sundays we always went to two Masses. Because at Tighes Hill we had to walk some distance to the church in all weathers it was decided that we should go to 7 a.m. Mass and stay for the 8 a.m. Mass, one after the other. We had late breakfast about 9 – in silence, of course. Sister Margaret and I did the washing up and cleaned the refectory. This would happen at about 9.30, when she could talk and I couldn't.

We arrived at a mutually agreeable compromise about this – she talked and I listened! When I laughed I tried to keep it quiet, and hoped the superior was busy elsewhere.

Tramps were a feature of life at Tighes Hill in the 1950s – homeless men who wandered the country and slept under bridges or wherever they could find shelter, and who were largely a legacy of World War II. There was no social security for them. They had no family, no roots, and were always moving on, often at the suggestion of the police. Mostly, they were honest and harmless.

When our boot-polish kit was stolen from a shoe press on the verandah we said 'Oh – the poor man must have wanted to clean his shoes' and bought another one. It also disappeared. We were mystified till someone enlightened our innocence: boot polish was used for flavour and colour in their methylated spirits!

The nuns said the men passed on the word through the 'tramps' network' that Tighes Hill Convent was always good for a feed. They got a good meal: a cup of tea in an old mug or a takeaway jam jar, a doorstopper sandwich of meat, and a piece of cake, pie or fruit left over from afternoon tea or dinner. Sometimes this was handed out in a paper bag to be taken away, or on an old enamel plate on a tray. There was also a stool on which they could sit while they ate their meal on the back verandah.

'Leave the tray at the back door, please,' Sister Stephanie would say.

One Sunday Sister Stephanie popped a chicken into the oven when she was preparing Sunday midday dinner. The idea was for a cold salad for tea and she left the chicken to cool inside the fly screen near a window. When she came back the chicken was gone.

Where did I leave it? she wondered. There, near the window. Perhaps I put it in the fridge? (Quick look.) No. Did I move it? No, I put it there – near the window. No sign of it. Then she asked, Did anyone see it? No, we hadn't seen it.

We started to hunt.

The mystery deepened till someone found the empty plate on the back verandah, and a trail of chicken bones out the back gate and down the street to the empty lot next door, where the rest of the chicken had been eaten in seclusion. An enterprising, hungry (and less honest) tramp had come to the back door and realised that someone had left the latch off the laundry screen door. He let himself in and happily made off with Sunday tea. That night we had a slice of cheese with our lettuce and tomato, and were more careful with the door in future.

One last glimpse of Tighes Hill.

It's a glorious day in September. The sun is shining and the sky is blue. In the garden everything is in bloom and the perfume of a myriad flowers floats on the air. I am perched high on a stepladder by the trellis on the side verandah, cutting sweet peas to decorate the chapel for Sunday.

It's a silence day but I'm singing at the top of my voice while I work: 'Oh, what a beautiful morning – Oh, what a beautiful day . . .'

Sister Margaret's face appears over the edge of the balcony above me. She is concerned and amused. She uses a stage whisper: 'You're having a good time! I could hear you from upstairs. What are you singing for?'

''Cos I feel like it!'

'Mother'll hear you and you'll get into trouble. *Again*.'

'I don't care! I'm sure God never meant us to be silent on a day like this!'

It is a Sunday night in summer and just about all the family are home except Bet, who is in the convent.

They've been playing five hundred round the big dining room table. Mum has come in from the kitchen, and she has been watching the game with Maurice and me.

'What did you do that for?' Dad fairly bellows. 'You trumped my ace!'

Mary goes red, and is very quiet.

Dad wins the next trick, and the next. Then the last. No one else has any trumps left.

'A-ha! Gotcha!' says Dad. 'We've won!'

Everyone is smiling, especially Mary, and joking and starting to pick up the cards.

'I'll put the kettle on,' says Mum, 'for a cup of tea.'

Dad starts a post-mortem of the last few hands, everyone stands up to stretch, and Jim winds up the gramophone. He puts on a record – 'The Colonel Bogey March'.

I run and get Dad's 'bones' from the windowsill behind the curtain and he starts to play them. He holds the two of them somehow in the fingers of his right hand, and they spring to life.

Feet are tapping, and we're swaying to the beat. Dad is stomping his foot, and waving his arm in the air. The 'bones' are doing a wild clickety-clack in perfect beat with the record, and everyone is laughing as it finishes.

'Put on another one, Jim,' says Dad.

And we do it all over again till Mum bustles in with the teapot and biscuits, and we get the good cups and saucers out of the sideboard.

# 12

## Teaching at Hamilton

Fortunately for me, the next year someone died, or got sick, and they needed a fifth class teacher in New Lambton. I was promoted. This was much better, as I had more idea of what to do with these older children. Also, if I said 'Open your maths books at page 57' the students knew what I was talking about. So I happily taught fifth class for a couple of years.

But it was not until a year or so later, when one of the high school staff at Hamilton collapsed and went to hospital for an indeterminate stay, that things really changed. They needed a new teacher in the high school, and my education roughly fitted what they needed, so I was promoted again, at the age of twenty-four.

Suddenly from packing up and moving each year – twice in one year – I found myself at Saint Aloysius Girls' High, Hamilton, where I would happily teach geography and commerce (and a few other odds and sods) for the next fifteen years. I loved the high school atmosphere and the teenage girls who, in spite of the agonies of finding themselves, were so friendly and responsive.

I had found my niche.

It was Friday morning, and we were all lined up and packed in on the concrete back verandah of Saint Aloysius Girls' High School. The whole school – 450 of us, including teachers. It was a school assembly, 1961 style.

Theo – Sister Mary Theophane, the principal – was just visible above heads, standing on a tier of green steps used for choir practice, ready to address the school. She was talking into a hand-held megaphone which doubled as the PA system, as it was the only thing we had, but we couldn't hear her. We knew she was talking because we could see her mouth moving, so the girls delighted in calling out loudly, 'Can't hear you, Sister!'

She was flustered, called for help from a staff member, examined the buttons on the megaphone, and tried again.

'CAN YOU HEAR ME NOW?' suddenly boomed forth to deafen everyone as she got the buttons right, and the sound bounced back off the nearby primary school wall. The echoes hung in the air, and the girls called out 'Yes, Sister!', enjoying the pantomime.

They remembered the day she actually fell off the steps and were always hoping for a repeat performance. She was a dynamic speaker, waving her sheaf of papers about to emphasise a point with her starched coif and black veil nodding and tossing. That day as she was reading the riot act over some indiscretion committed by the students, she stepped backwards, lost her balance and toppled.

Black veil went over, and those in the front were also treated to a view of black skirts and petticoats and flailing black-stockinged legs in black shoes. There were those who later claimed to have seen flashes of white underwear, but this I couldn't vouch for.

There was a stunned silence as the school realised what had happened, and then gasps of concern. Theo struggled to her feet, recovered her dignity and came back around the front to climb the steps and continue her tirade. When the girls realised she wasn't hurt, everyone saw the comical side of it and laughter set in. It began as suppressed giggles, spread through the throng and surged up to the roof in gales of unrestrained mirth.

Theo just stood there at first, then began to smile.

'All right! All right!' she said. 'I'm not dead! So I fell off the steps – is that a reason to lift the roof off? Settle down, now. Settle down.' She waved her papers for silence. 'As I was saying . . .'

But the moment for continuing the tirade had passed, and she knew it. She was always the first one to enjoy a good laugh, even at herself, and often kept us amused at recreation with tales out of school.

But today she was not going to fall off the steps, and dismissed the students to their classes.

'Betty Jones and Pam Casey, you stay behind. I want to see you.'

Two fifteen-year-olds in pigtails turned pale, and lined up with a few other girls who had some business to transact. There was no office, so Theo reigned from her small science room. Inside there was a clutter of textbooks, official

117

documents, syllabuses and examination entry forms on a side table. Betty and Pam waited their turn. The girls liked and respected Theo, but they also knew she could be a bit of a dragon when she thought it was called for.

'And you two!' she fairly bellowed. 'I've heard you were seen down the street on sports day when you should have been at the park. Without permission! *And* I believe you've been using bad language. Where did you learn such words?' There was no response. She glared at them. 'I don't want to hear another complaint about either of you, do you hear?' She thrust her face close to theirs. 'And if I do, you needn't expect a reference from me at the end of the year when you leave school.'

There was a mixed chorus of 'Yes, Sister. No, Sister.' They began to shuffle uncomfortably away. As they went, Theo patted the closest one on the shoulder and said, 'Go on, then – back to class. And behave yourselves.'

Theo turned to me and said, 'The scallywags! They'll be all right, though. Their mothers were just the same. Best friends right through school, and always up to mischief. But they've turned into fine women.'

She continued, 'Mary,' (she called all the nuns 'Mary' as an abbreviation of our names) 'you don't have a class now, do you?' My heart sank. My class had gone to PE and I was hoping for some unaccustomed free time for corrections, but I smiled and said, 'No, Sister.'

'Well – would you just check those Leaving Certificate entry forms for me? I think they're all right, but I need to be sure. The girls' own forms are here. Just see that they match.'

I sat down among the rubble on her desk and began to

check, feeling a bit ashamed of my reluctance. Theo ran a school, taught and did the necessary administration. She had no secretary, so she depended on us younger folk for help when she needed it. Meanwhile, her small science class filed in and settled themselves at the benches. Theo was demonstrating an experiment for them.

She held up a beaker of grassy-green liquid and said, 'There you are! A purple reaction.'

I joined the class, looking in disbelief. She looked at it too. Then she added, 'Well, purplish, anyway. Can you see it?'

There were a few half-hearted murmurs from the class, and I smiled to myself as I remembered tales told by the nuns who had been her pupils in the past: tales of similar wrong colours or strange smells or loud bangs that weren't supposed to have happened.

'There,' she said. 'I think it's going purplish *now*.'

More half-hearted murmurs. Then she grinned at the girls and said, 'Well, I wonder what I did wrong this time?' and everyone laughed.

The students loved her for her honesty and her directness, and between them – Theo and the class – they usually worked out what went wrong. They enjoyed science and, on the whole, did well.

When they left she said to me, 'Thanks a lot, Mary. I've got the envelopes here somewhere.' She opened a cupboard and we were inundated by a landslide of papers, books and official-looking documents. We picked them up, she shoved them back in and handed me the envelopes. I marvelled that she kept track of so many things with so little space, so little time, and such a haphazard filing system.

Later in the evening, three of us sat around a small table in the community room helping Theo count money, as it was Friday – the day when we added up the accumulated fees for the week. We opened the scraps of paper, pages torn from exercise books and the occasional envelope, recorded the names written inside and put the coins into a heap on the table. There were lots of coins, as fees were five shillings a week, and everyone paid weekly. Of this, Theo got sixpence to run the school, and four shillings and sixpence went to the convent to pay for our keep. It was a pittance, and I marvelled that Theo made ends meet somehow with the help of raffles, an occasional stall and the sale of potato chips alternating with Paddlepop iceblocks in summer. We didn't have a tuckshop, so some trusted senior girls sold them from a classroom window.

As we were opening envelopes and notes, I came across one from a mum apologising that she couldn't pay school money this week because she had two boys at the Marist Brothers' School, and you *have* to pay there. I was indignant, and said, 'Listen to this!' and I read out the note. 'All very well for them, getting their fees and we're not. Just because they're MEN!'

Theo said, 'Don't worry. Poor woman would pay if she could. Her husband's been sick and nearly lost his job. It's a hard time for her, with four kids, and all of them migrants in a new country.'

We counted, we wrapped, and we had little jokes on the side. It was silence time, but things were a bit relaxed because it was Friday night, and we enjoyed this little ritual of counting the money with Theo.

* * *

By the age of twenty-six, I'd been teaching at Saint Aloysius for several years and had been really enjoying it. The girls were fifteen – not such a big age difference. Classes were huge by today's standards, so corrections were almost impossible to keep up with, but the kids were great. Seventy-five in 3B, and a few less in other classes.

I was on duty for eight periods a day, five days a week, because that's how it worked. You did the best you could, and enjoyed the students. I'd never been keen on correcting mountains of books, setting and marking endless exam papers and writing up all those reports, but the actual teaching and relating to the girls was really enjoyable.

Maybe I wasn't always ready for teaching the lesson, and sometimes I'd be only a few pages ahead of the class, but we always (well, mostly) enjoyed being together. However, the syllabus might not get completely covered, and proposed end-of-term exams sent me into a panic.

My biggest anxieties were when someone suggested across-the-form religion exams. There were certain slabs of Church teaching, liturgy and doctrine laid down to be covered, and we – my class and I – never managed to cover it all. Interesting things always cropped up to disrupt systematic course work.

We had a class question box where lots of the girls' concerns were aired. Was it wrong to kiss a boy? Should you be allowed to wear shorts? If not, why not? What was wrong with *Blue Lagoon*? – it was a good movie. Why shouldn't we be allowed to wear shorter uniforms? There was also a lot of conflict about whether the Seekers' song 'A World of Our Own' was about a rich relationship or a couple opting out of life in the Christian community. Some of these questions challenged my own thoughts and opinions. Given my lack of experience, however, I wasn't a good one to pontificate. Sometimes I'd try to say what I thought I should, or what *The Catholic Weekly* said, but the students would challenge it all. Somehow common sense won through, and I learnt a lot weighing up their opinions.

The Beatles burst upon the scene, and everyone had a photo of their favourite member stuck inside the top of their lift-up desk. Orders came from Theo to remove them, and resentment loudly followed. (Not that Theo would have cared to make such an edict, but she would bow to the pressure of disapproval by the senior sisters on the staff.)

'All right,' I said. 'I've told you now. You'll get into trouble if some teachers see your photos, so take them out, or keep your desks closed.' (Echoes of what Father Anthony had told me: 'Nothing very wrong in what you did – just don't get caught!')

We spent ages discussing these and other matters of not so great theological significance. I found myself listening to what the girls had to say, rather than pushing the 'party line', and I think some of my expositions of the Church's moral teachings were, at best, half-hearted. I often felt guilty, though I don't think I did any real harm – but then, I did hope no one was listening at the door.

Sometimes things got a bit riotous as the girls from the traditional right-wing Catholic homes clashed with the more progressive in the class. I'd try to shush the commotion. Someone would get up and close the classroom door to keep in the noise, or the closed door would open suddenly and in would burst a senior nun. She might hesitate and then say, in a very frosty voice, something like 'Oh – I'm sorry, Sister. I thought there was no teacher in here!'

The kids could be really protective of me on these occasions. They'd go quiet until someone in the front would chirp up with 'Oh, Sister, we were just discussing one of the pictures we've seen. We're sorry for the noise.'

The interloper would withdraw, still frosty, and we'd all go 'Sh!' as the argument started again, and we tried to keep it quiet.

Sometimes there were challenging encounters in the classroom. Someone might be caught out passing catty notes, or would answer back to me, or just wouldn't do any work. On rare occasions I'd lose my cool, but on the whole it was enjoyable and rewarding.

The kids – as kids always do – gravitated to a young teacher. The year before, I had charge of form 1B classroom which had a glass partition up onto the stairs, so that anyone coming down the stairs had full view of whatever happened to be going on in the classroom. As the school had no money for cleaners, the girls had a weekly roster of 'charges' for cleaning the classroom and other areas. Sometimes during the after-school clean-up we'd all finish up at the front table on the platform. As like as not, I'd be trying to mark the roll for the day from the collective memory. The clean-up detail, plus anyone else still around, would all be gathered at the table with me. We'd laugh and have fun as we did it. However, you could bank on it that one of the senior sisters would be coming down the stairs and peering in, looking like a thundercloud. You were not supposed to talk to the girls outside classes. Perhaps no one talked to these sisters. I didn't know. One thing I was sure of – they didn't like to see girls talking to me.

Maybe they worried about the effect I might have on them. I don't think any of the girls would have actually dobbed me in for not toeing the party line, so they wouldn't actually *know* what I said, but I guess they *suspected* that lots of my opinions were not quite 'kosher'.

It was not unusual for the superior to send for me in the evening to tell me she'd had another complaint I'd been seen skylarking with the girls after school – *again*. She'd say I had to learn to keep my distance from them and act with religious decorum. There were certain things you didn't discuss with the girls. Matters of sex, for example. They knew enough about these things already. She wouldn't be surprised if some of them knew more than she did. When she was growing up, your mother told you what you needed to know before you got married, and if you were going to enter the convent you didn't need to know, so she didn't tell you. And that's how it ought to be.

I never understood why I heard this particular tirade from the superior. Did she think *I* knew too much about sex? She needn't have worried. I was largely self-educated from literature and science manuals. My mother hadn't told me very much, but I had a growing appreciation of the concept of sex, its power and its role in relationships. I listened attentively to the superior, nodded, and kept my own counsel.

Some girls sought to talk to me in private. They waylaid me on the playground or in a classroom, or offered to carry my mountain of exercise books for correction just for the chance of a few words. There was no school counsellor for them to talk to.

There was Jane, who'd just found out she was adopted, and was having trouble coping with the news. Helen's dad was in prison, not away working interstate, but she wasn't supposed to tell anyone. Maria's dad bashed her mum last night, and they all had to climb out a window and go to their aunty's house. 'I couldn't do my homework,' she said, 'and I can't tell the other nuns.'

One girl told me she was pregnant and had to leave school; another came back after she'd left to talk to me about the abortion she'd had. Mary came from a Maltese home where she had nowhere to study for final exams because there were so many in the family. She started home-work in the kitchen after school, then sat on her bed when the table was needed for the evening meal. At 7.30 p.m. the little kids had to go to bed in that room and the light went off. So she'd go and sit on the toilet seat in the bathroom. But whenever anyone wanted to use the bathroom, she had to go out. Her father always came home late for dinner in the kitchen and read the paper there, so that table wasn't free again till very late.

I had no solutions for Mary. I could only listen, and feel concerned for her. She ended up solving things by going to bed early when the little ones did, and setting the alarm for 3 a.m. when she'd have undisputed use of the kitchen table . . . and we wondered why she wasn't paying attention in class.

I discovered there were so many things going on in the girls' lives that no one knew about. These things had never gone on in my home. Yet the kids sat up in class in their uniforms, mostly did their work, were polite and obedient, and only occasionally went off the rails. I began to understand much more about life, and to feel that my stable background made me inadequate to cope with it all. But they still wanted to talk. I could only listen, hear their pain – and maybe learn.

I enjoyed living in the convent at Hamilton. There were about thirty of us in the community – some old, but quite a few young ones too. Friends have always been oil to the wheels of my life. Grassroots women. We've always got on well. We had lots of laughs, good stories and sharing together.

As a junior in the community, one of the things I often got a turn to do was to lock the gates. The two juniors were responsible for unlocking the gates each morning at 6 a.m. and locking them at 5 p.m. each evening. I shared this job with quite a few nuns over the years.

Recreation was at 4.30 p.m., and this meant sitting around sewing and talking in a big circle on the back verandah or in the community room in winter. Sometimes the 'young ones' played basketball down on the high school courts. We tucked up our habits behind us with big safety pins so we could run and move more freely. But whatever we were doing during recreation, come 5 minutes to 5 it was time to ask leave to go and lock the gates. We would collect the gate keys and set off around the grounds.

At this point the superior was supposed to remember if anyone was out after school – at the dentist or doctor or anywhere else. The back gate, a door tucked away under the primary school stairs, would be closed but not locked so they could come in, and you had to go back later to lock it.

There was a car gate in the corrugated iron fence at the end of the high school playground, and the high school gate closer up to the convent in the same fence. Each gate had a large iron bolt and padlock, except the back gate under the primary school stairs, which was a wooden door with a modern-looking key. The others often had very big old padlocks, with corresponding big old keys.

After you'd locked the high school gate, you'd go up along the fence to the music studio gate. Sometimes you had to wait there for the music teachers to finish teaching at 5 p.m., and they were often a bit late.

We never minded waiting. It was such a carefree time; two of us off on our own with no one checking up on us as some of the senior sisters were wont to do. We'd laugh, tell stories, and sometimes had to lean against the fence under the gum trees until we recovered from laughing so hard.

One of my gate-locking companions was Sister Mary Henrietta of the dimples and laughing blue eyes. Another youngish sister – Sister Mary Paul, who had been my 'mother' in the novitiate and was a good friend – had charge of the little tuckshop set up through the window of a storeroom, and often asked us to lock up for her. She might have had a late delivery, and it would be frowned upon if she asked to go and lock up herself. Paul also sat at the same table as we did for meals.

When we had to lock the tuckshop we'd run our fastest to get there, raid the lollies, chocolates or chips, and have a picnic on the rest of the way round the perimeter of the convent. We weren't supposed to eat outside the refectory, so this naughty behaviour would set us off giggling as we stuffed our faces and rushed to make up time.

From the music room gate we'd go along the front of the main building and lock the small gate to the church, and then the main imposing iron front gate of the convent. After that, round to the little tradesmen's gate behind the kitchen (where we'd have a few words with Sister Marie Elizabeth preparing supper in the kitchen), then out again to the back gate under the primary school stairs.

All this usually went smoothly, and we'd go back to recreation – sitting sedately, and grinning at Paul as we passed her the keys. She'd know very well what we'd been up to! At the end of recreation we went to the chapel for Office.

Often in the middle of Office or study, or sometimes even later, there'd a commotion at the back gate. Someone had been locked out! Mother had forgotten they had gone somewhere. There'd be banging and shouting, and a couple of desperate figures would appear halfway up the primary school stairs, waving and calling to get in. A kind of *I Leap Over the Wall* in reverse, only they couldn't leap. It was too high.

We'd have to leave Office, study or supper to get the keys and let them in. It wasn't *our* fault if Mother forgot they were out, but that didn't make them any sweeter when we eventually let them in. Especially if they were senior sisters, and expected consideration from the superior and deference from the rest of us.

These were good times, even if they were hard times, and the friendships made endured across the years, both with those who stayed with the Order and with those who left. By now the rot had set in, and nuns were beginning to go. Mostly we never knew who was planning to leave, and we'd only find out when an announcement was made after they had gone. Sometimes they'd be at school all day, and then absent from Office in the afternoon. Later – sometimes at recreation or supper – the announcement would be made: 'Sister Mary So-and-so has chosen to leave religious life.'

Some of my good friends went, and I missed them. Margaret, who slept beside me in the dormitory for years, told me she was going and said goodbye, but was not supposed to tell anyone. There was rarely a chance to say goodbye, but one young sister who had been obviously unhappy for a while – crying and moody – sought professional help and was advised to leave.

Attitudes were changing about all this and she asked to come to recreation to say goodbye and thank us for our support in the last difficult months. She went around one by one and kissed us. We all said a few words of good wishes, until she came to Sister John, who refused even to take her hand and said loudly, 'You know what Our Lord said about those who put their hand to the plough and turn back.'

I curled up inside. We all knew the end of the quote: 'It would be better for him if he had never been born.'

I felt upset and embarrassed. This was a terrible thing to say to a girl who had been so unhappy, and had been advised to leave. It was unnecessarily rude and cruel.

Looking back, I can only say that Sister John *was* old and came from a different era when people *never* left, no matter what. Hers was a hard spirituality. The girl who was leaving coped pretty well with it, I thought. There were tears in her eyes but she finished her round, and most of us had tears in our eyes as well.

I could understand their reasons when my friends left and I missed them, but I never wanted to leave myself at this stage. I was still inclined to fall foul of superiors, and sometimes things would seem so unfair and harsh to me that I'd cry in the chapel or into my pillow. But the rest – my grassroots friends and the kids – made it seem all worthwhile.

On a Saturday five or six of us would often have an afternoon of sewing. Saturdays were generally silence days – lots of days were – but as the dressmaking room of the high school was an old army hut bought years ago and put at the very end of the playground, we didn't take the silence too seriously. The laughter and talk was subdued, though, and we kept an eye out for anyone who would be too critical of our relaxed arrangements.

The day was generally arranged by Sister Mary Eveline (Evie), who was a free spirit and good at sewing. Evie was in her forties, though very young at heart and supportive of us young sisters.

We would all sit around at sewing machines or the big tables, struggling with bits and pieces of our habits which custom demanded we make ourselves. Let me tell you, this was a pretty tall order for some of us! Evie lessened the pain by being always ready to help with pleating a habit, measuring a hem, getting the darts in the right place or by getting a coif to fit so that when it was starched stiff it didn't come down over your eyes like a knight's visor.

Pleating a habit was quite an art, as everyone had the same yards of black serge whether they were like Twiggy or Miss Piggy. All of us were meant to have the same number of pleats and the trick was getting right the width of the pleats and the amount of material you hid behind them. Evie was a magician. She also kept us entertained with very funny stories, and she had plenty of them.

She always had a large tin of sweets in her sewing press to help us through the day. God knows where she got them (friends? family? none of us had any money to buy such things), but the tin was always full and available to any of us who felt a desperate need of food or comfort. She would say life was demanding enough on young people so she did her best to ease the pain. I was not too sure about this philosophy – how did she come by the sweets? And eating regularly outside the refectory! – that was forbidden. So I had the occasional pang of guilt, but found myself able to go along with it.

Someone would look out the door and see a disapproving senior sister walking up and down the playground, saying her rosary – 'Sh!' she would say. We'd all grow very quiet and intent on our sewing for the next quarter of an hour, while the sister walked up and down till she finished her prayer and went back to the convent.

I would look across the room at Evie in the silence; Evie with her warm heart and ready smile. She had helped to keep me sane in this busy inner-city school and convent. Classes were big, teaching loads heavy, and I got very tired trying to keep up with 5 a.m. rising, the rigid schedules of prayers, teaching, playground duty, preparations and corrections.

I was always behind with everything. I used to think, thank God for Evie!

Evie had not had it easy in the Order, though. Her unorthodox ways always got her into trouble with the powers that be. Her laugh was too raucous, her voice was too loud. She flew around the place 'with unreligious haste'.

One day in the main front garden in Singleton, Evie had her photo taken without permission, *and* holding a baby. The sisters were never supposed to hold a baby. The only rationale I can imagine for this rule is that it was supposed to be some guard against becoming 'clucky', and regretting never having children.

Evie had always been very popular with the pupils and parents, and when a new child or even grandchild arrived in the family, it was often brought some distance to the convent to show Sister Eveline. What was more natural than to hand the baby to her for a nurse, and to take a photo?

On this particular occasion nobody saw her, and she initially got away with it. Her sin caught up with her, though, when her friends sent her copies of the photos in a letter. The superior slit the top of the envelope as was the custom, and out they fell! Like Queen Victoria, the superior was 'not amused', and Evie was placed under special restrictions for quite a while.

Evie was always full of energy and a zest for life. While I found it hard to get up at 5 a.m., Evie was often up before that, had put her washing on and would be saying her rosary while it was washing. She had often even hung it out on the line before I staggered into the chapel, just in time for meditation.

One afternoon when I watched Evie bending over someone's sewing on the table, I thought, she is truly a treasure in an earthen vessel. When she finished, I called her over to check my pleats.

On those sewing days I couldn't see the years ahead. I couldn't anticipate the day that some depraved mongrel would lie in wait for her when she came to put her laundry in the machine in the half-dark, and assault her. The nuns found her inarticulate on the laundry floor.

Sewing days are over and the years have rolled on. The Hamilton convent has closed as numbers of nuns decreased. It was too big to maintain, and too empty for a few nuns to rattle around in. Evie recovered and went on living her religious life in her own way, but I guess there were times when she woke in the night with her heart thumping and her mouth dry, ears straining into the silence. The years have passed, and now she has gone on to her reward.

In spite of the passing of those years, the closeness and companionship I experienced with my friends created warm memories which will endure as long as I have the capacity to remember.

*The wireless is on, and we're all in the dining room. Dad's reading a book. So am I, and Maurice is working on a plan for a letter rack he's going to make. Mum's mending something.*

*Bing Crosby comes on, singing 'White Christmas', and Dad says, 'Turn that up a bit, Ceal. That's a good song, and Bing's a decent family man. Not like some of those others in America.'*

*Later, the announcer says, 'And here's Frank Sinatra, singing his latest . . .'*

*Dad doesn't wait for more.*

*'Turn that thing off!' he says, pointing at the wireless in its cabinet, standing in the corner. 'I can't stand that man! He's been divorced. Twice!'*

# 13

## Dad's Death

I was twenty-seven and living at Hamilton Convent when Dad died in October 1962.

A year or so before his death the doctor sent for Mum and told her that Dad's heart was enlarged and he could have a heart attack at any time. Be prepared, he said.

But what we weren't prepared for was that it was Mum who had a heart attack and landed in the Mater Hospital at Waratah. It caused much anguish in the family. No one had expected Mum to be the one to give us a fright this way. We had a family conference with Dad and suggested he go and live with Mary for a while, so she could look after him.

He eyed us calmly and said, 'Look, I know you're all concerned about me. But if I'm going to die, I'll die just as well here on my own as I would if there were twenty of you with me!'

So he stayed at home where he could easily walk up to the hospital to sit with Mum, who had a number of setbacks. Eventually he did give in and went to Mary's to live for a few weeks. He settled there pretty well, reading his paper or a book, and waiting for Mum to recover.

One morning in October, about 5.30, Mary heard Dad calling from his room and went in. She could tell by the look of him that something terrible had happened. Bill went running down the road to fetch a doctor from his home, and then to the phone box across the road to ring the ambulance. Mary stayed with Dad. I'm sure it seemed a long time before the doctor arrived in his pyjamas and dressing gown, but when he did come, Dad had already gone.

It was an ordinary morning at the convent. We were all in the chapel at meditation just before 6, and I was sitting down in the bottom of my stall in my usual morning stupor. I can't remember the phone ringing, or anyone going out to answer it. The first thing I knew was that someone came in and told me Mother wanted to see me upstairs.

My heart sank and I had an empty feeling in the pit of my stomach as I went up the stairs and round the corridor to the door of the superior's cell. It had to be bad news at this hour. I thought the bad news would be about Mum. There were noises of hurried movements from inside and when Mother opened the door, she was still hurriedly pulling on her cardigan.

She said, 'Your brother-in-law is on the phone. Your father had a bad turn this morning and unfortunately died before the ambulance arrived. Go down and talk to Bill.' She paused. 'You may need to ring your sister and tell her, too.'

I went downstairs to speak to Bill who was patiently waiting for me in the phone box down the street from their home, when he wanted to rush back to the distressing scene he had left. He told me the sad story again, and asked me if I would ring Bet. I rang the Nelson Bay Convent and asked to speak to her. Any calls coming at that hour of the morning could only be bad news, so Bet had already prepared herself by the time she came to the phone. She was composed, though shocked, and I had a sense of everything being unreal. There were no tears yet.

Back in the chapel, I sat down. Mother had obviously told the community the news because I could sense the feelings about me. Sympathy, distress, fear for their own parents and pain for the memory of their own losses all flowed around me, though I was numb myself.

Father Terry Williams arrived to say the Mass and I could see him putting on his vestments. No one went to tell him about my father and to ask him to say the Mass for the repose of my Dad's soul. I couldn't believe it, as it was the custom to say Mass for the repose of a deceased relative's soul, so I went out of the chapel, round the back to the sacristy, knocked and went in.

'My father has just died,' I said, choking a bit on the words. 'Can you say Mass for him?'

Terry was distressed. Distressed that I was there telling him myself, that no one else had come to tell him; distressed for me and my loss, so raw and fresh. He struggled to find what to say, and was very kind. I had no feelings yet, and went back to the chapel and knelt for the Mass.

After Mass the sisters came and kissed me, hugged me, and told me how sorry they were, and at last my tears began to fall copiously.

Somebody drove me over to Waratah to the hospital to sit

with Mum. She was still quite sick herself, was dazed, and seemed almost too numb to talk. Bet arrived during the day, and Mum perked up a bit. I was very pleased to see Bet too and we cried as we clung to each other.

No one had told me to stay at the Mater or to come back home to Hamilton. It just hadn't been important. The Mater Hospital was run by our sisters, so when the superior of the Mater Convent asked me if I was staying, suggested I should be with my mother, and arranged for a change of clothes and a bed for me, I was grateful. It seemed right and I took it for granted that I should stay, if I stopped to think about it at all.

Bet and I sat with Mum for the next few days, and the rest of the family came and went according to the demands of their own lives. Mum talked about Dad a lot. About how she thought he was a bit of a wag on that first evening when he walked her home after Benediction at the church. The fellow walking in front of them had a hole in the heel of his sock, and at every step his heel slid up out of his shoe and you could see the hole. Dad pointed it out to Mum, and they laughed all the way home. She told us how they laughed a lot during their courting. She talked about their first home, too – and many other things I'd never heard before. It was easy to encourage her to talk.

On the day of the funeral Bet and I decided to split up. Reverend Mother Alexius came down and went to the church with Bet, and they sat with the family. I stayed with Mum. Nuns were not allowed to go to the cemetery in those days. Sister Leonie, a good friend who worked at the hospital and had been very good to Mum over the weeks, doing her washing and visiting her each day, came in to sit with Mum and me while the funeral service was held down in the parish church. I was feeling lost, and glad of her company. It was unreal to be sitting there while my father's funeral service was happening without me down the road. When Leonie saw the funeral procession going past the hospital on its way to the Sandgate cemetery, she quietly began to say the rosary. I looked out to see the hearse and the coffin, and couldn't believe that all that was left of my Dad was disappearing forever up the road, and my tears began again. Choking, I joined in the rosary. The prayer flowed about us, oddly comforting, and tears flowed as well. Mum knew and understood, and she put her hands over her face and cried quietly herself.

Family and friends gathered briefly outside the church; some – I can't remember who – followed on to the cemetery, and then the family came back to join us in Mum's room. At last the dreadful day was over. The doctor suggested giving Mum a sedative and offered something to the rest of us so we would get a good sleep. The staff were wonderful to us. They had put Mum out of the public ward and into a small private room out the back, and opened a sitting room close by for the family.

We said goodbye to each other, the family went off to their homes, and Bet and I went back gratefully to the Mater Convent. After tea with the community, we were thinking about going to bed when someone came and said I was wanted on the phone. It was my superior from Hamilton.

Instead of having concern for my wellbeing, which I thought might be the reason for the call, she was really phoning to ask why I hadn't been in touch with her in the last few days. Why hadn't I sought permission to stay at the Mater, and when was I coming back to teach my classes? In fact, she said, I should be home by now, and she would send a car for me in the morning.

To say I was devastated would be too weak. I hung up and cried all the tears I thought I didn't have left. I cried until exhaustion at last drove me to sleep. It just seemed too much to lose my dad, to have my mum in hospital so sick (and with the possibility that the shock of Dad's death might trigger a further heart attack), and then to get into trouble for not seeking permission from my superior to be there with her.

In my innocence, I had presumed that staying with my mother was the right and proper thing to do. The superior of the Mater Convent had encouraged me to do so, and I guess I took her encouragement as permission, if I thought about it at all. It had not occurred to me that anyone would see it differently and to imagine their illusory rights as having been transgressed, or that they would feel so strongly about it they could abuse me in a time of great distress.

My mother was surprised I had to go home, but accepted it as she had done so many things over the years. She was glad Bet could stay with her. I couldn't even promise when I would see her again.

I went back to Hamilton a sadder and wiser girl, but with a flint in my soul that hadn't been there before. From then on I did everything I was supposed to do, asked all the permissions in accordance with the superior's requirements, but a quality of respect for her had gone, and some of my gentleness, softness and ingenuous innocence as well.

I had changed. I put coolness and distance into the

relationship with that superior deliberately. I guess that in some way I was reacting at last to all those other slights and humiliations I had swallowed for so long.

All my little floutings of silence and silly rules over the years meant nothing in the big scheme of my vocation. I was called and was living it out, but by Father Anthony's maxim of 'not getting caught'.

*This* was different. It was a kind of serving notice: 'Beware! I am beginning to become my own person at last!'

# 14

## University and Other New Things

When I was a postulant and had my cry on the shoulder of the wise Father Anthony, one of the other things he said to me was 'Girlie, the wheels are always turning. This year it's someone, next year it's someone else.' He made circles with his hand. 'Turning. Always turning.' He meant that the superiors I had upset by non-conforming would not always be in charge, and that the next superior would not necessarily see me the same way.

In 1964 I had been at Hamilton Convent for some years, and Sister Mary Theophane (Theo) had been appointed superior of the convent as well as principal of the high school. Now she was *Mother* Theophane.

In the 1960s, registration became an issue for Catholic schools. There were government guidelines laid down for minimum requirements for things like a toilet/student ratio. These could be costly for the Catholic community to meet, and the Catholic schools in Goulburn protested by closing and sending all the pupils to the local state schools. This brave protest against what was believed to be an unjust situation helped to change things. Why, Catholic parents thought, should they have to fund a parallel school system – from 'after tax' money – when they already paid tax to support the state schools? Some of this money should go to the schools of their choice, they believed.

Some of us began agitating quietly for change. We didn't have enough toilets for the number of students. We had a lot of business expertise and know-how among the fathers of our students, though. Why couldn't we harness this to make drastic changes to the situation? We put out an SOS for a fathers' meeting which resulted in the forming of a men's committee who undertook to raise the money required through functions and subscriptions, and applied for a Government building grant. These had by now become available to Catholic schools, and we were able to acquire four new classrooms, a small library, some offices, an assembly hall and tuckshop as well as the new toilet block. The men's committee planned and oversaw all this down to the small details. (We were particularly amused by their research and discussion at their meetings as to whether the sanitary disposal units should be inside the toilet cubicle or near the washbasins, and what type would be best. However, no one consulted us! I guess it was not the sort of thing to discuss with the nuns, who sat quietly in the meetings.) One of the fathers who was an early electronics whiz personally installed cables with the latest technology for sound and television in every classroom.

Theo now had her own school office and a secretary, and she revelled in it. She also had some free time to sit in the office and administer justice there. One day when I came in she was standing there before the control centre of our new PA system and about to make an announcement to the school. I held my breath as she threw switches and pushed buttons.

'Can you hear me?' she boomed around the school. 'Would someone in 2B come down and tell me if you are hearing me there?'

Several girls turned up at the door to report 2B *could* hear, but 1A said they *couldn't* hear in their room, so Theo started the button and switch process again. She then turned to me. 'Mary,' she said, frustrated, 'just have a look and see if you can see what I'm doing wrong.'

Theo's proficiency with gadgets had not improved, but she still loved them.

The Provincial Council in Singleton soon decided that the two jobs were too much for Theo. She reluctantly resigned from her job as principal, and gave more time to her role as superior of the convent. She continued to take a few science classes, though, as she'd miss teaching and the students too much to give it up completely.

As the school had been a happy, if busy, place to work, so too the convent became a happy place to live while under Theo's administration. She set up a TV room and the daily timetable began to be relaxed. We rose at 5.30 instead of 5, and Theo suggested we might like to say night prayers privately. Night recreation was more informal, and we could go to bed early if we wanted, or watch TV.

The news was popular, as well as current affairs programs. I remember there was a Sid James comedy a few of us liked to watch after the older sisters had retired which had some delightful naughty bits. Theo would come and watch it with us, but I doubt she was laughing at the same things. Dave Allen, who I thought was clever and very funny, was a cause of controversy, as some of the more conservative sisters were offended by his sketches about religion.

Gradually the regimentation of our lives was breaking down, but the introduction of more personal choice and responsibility was causing insecurity and some discord across the liberal/conservative frontier in the community.

When I went into the office to tell Theo I had a heavy cold and felt quite sick with it, she was attentive. Often the superior would not take too much notice of such a thing, and you'd be lucky to get two aspros and a sleep-in till six o'clock the next morning. But Theo was all concern.

'What do you need, Mary?'

She threw wide open the newly replenished medicine cupboard and I left five minutes later with a whole packet of Panadol, cough mixture, Vicks to help with breathing at night, lozenges for my sore throat, and some Sudafed to help dry things up.

'Anything else?' she asked. 'And you'd better go to bed straight after tea and sleep in till breakfast for a few days till you feel better. Your eyes are dull and you have a temperature. Let me know if you're not well enough to go to school tomorrow.'

This idea, though, was beyond the pale. We never missed school if we could possibly cope as everyone taught full-time, and there was no one to fill in for sick teachers. So I'd get up and go to school dosed up on all my medications, but at least feeling cared about.

The provincial superior (that is, the Reverend Mother) in Singleton had also changed. ('The wheels are always turning.') Mother Mary Alexius was kind and thoughtful. When she came on the first of her annual visitations to Hamilton Convent, she said to me, 'Sister, it's time you thought about study. You're a bright girl, and should do a degree.'

I took a deep breath. 'Oh!' A bubble of excitement began to build inside.

'Mother tells me you're doing very well at the high school.'

Just like Theo to give me a good rap!

'Thank you, Reverend Mother.'

'What would you like to study?' she asked. 'Arts or Science?'

We agreed on Arts, with emphasis on geography, because that was the main subject I taught.

'You should also fit in some English,' she said. 'You'd enjoy that.'

Yes, I would!

'Write to Armidale,' she added, 'and get enrolment forms for next year. Singleton will look after your accounts and books.'

My heart sang. It might not be English at Sydney, but Arts at Armidale was pretty good.

The usual route to a degree for the nuns was through the Department of External Studies at the University of New England in Armidale. So I enrolled and was quickly inundated with thick packages of notes and assignments. I started to look for the mail with both excitement and dread. Study occurred after school, in the evenings and at weekends. Students who were also teachers still had to manage lesson preparation, teaching and corrections. If you were lucky, and the principal was a bit of a magician, you got a slightly reduced teaching load and didn't have to do playground duty. You were also excused from the evening Offices, but had to come to the recreation times, unless there was a real crisis. In this case you could ask permission to be let off, and Theo was often sympathetic.

I worked upstairs in a specially designated study in one of the spare bedrooms. As an extra concession I didn't have to be in bed by 10 p.m. This was a mixed blessing. When an assignment was due I'd regularly find myself working a few nights till midnight, or later. The house was quiet then and I had an uninterrupted run of time. This was good for the assignment, but not so good for me in the mornings. Study seemed like a course in crisis management as one assignment ran into the next, and school went on relentlessly. I guess anyone who has studied part-time while holding down a job has had the same experience. However, assignments did get done and posted away on time (mostly) and returned much later, when you'd completely forgotten what they were about and were immersed in some other crisis. They generally came back with good marks and encouraging comments from lecturers, and this made it all seem worthwhile.

There were residentials in school holidays when I had to go to Armidale or some other venue and live in for a week or two to cover practical work and have tutorials. Because of the problem of needing to go everywhere in twos, Sister Mary Aquinas and I both did geography and English.

On our first residential in Armidale we spent an agonising week trying to map the uni campus with a surveyor's dumpy level and measuring tapes. Our output didn't much resemble reality until one of the fellows with a complete lack of moral scruples borrowed a small map of the campus from a girl who was an internal student. After that everyone's map took on a much more realistic appearance.

It was good having the fellows around. I'm not sure what they made of us in our long black habits and flowing veils tramping around the countryside, but they were friendly and often really helpful. They offered to carry heavy equipment or gave us things they'd sussed out, like the little map. They had a much more cavalier attitude to the whole process, and that was good for us, as we took it all a bit too seriously.

When the evening came, the other students gathered in the recreation rooms or bedrooms and grogged on till the wee small hours. Sister Mary Aquinas and I retired to our rooms early and refrained from these particular extracurricular activities. I sometimes thought they might be fun, but they didn't quite fit in with religious decorum.

After two years of external studies with Armidale, I transferred to the recently established campus of the Newcastle University at Shortland and attended the lectures in person. I found this much better. Theo suggested I learn to drive, and when I got my licence she tried to make the convent car available for the university students (there were several of us by now) whenever she could, to make life easier.

I liked meeting lecturers and other students and being in

the university atmosphere. Once I had left the convent and school behind, it was much easier to leave behind whatever else was happening there – exam corrections, fetes or fundraising functions, and the inevitable ups and downs of a shared existence in a community. Some of the other students were girls I'd been teaching a year or so before, like Fran Doyle, who is now my solicitor, and I enjoyed many cups of coffee, deep and meaningful discussions and good friendships down in the union building. The place was abuzz. There were romances and broken hearts, bad subject choices, failures and conscription to the Vietnam War by ballot. The questions raged among the students: what exactly was a just war?

I loved campus life. It shed a new light on my religious vocation. I was in full habit, so I stuck out like a sore thumb round the place. I became aware I was the public face of the Church and religious life, which could be wearing when I wanted to sit in the union with a scotch to recover after an exam. However, it also opened doors to new friendships. Patrick began to sit near me in English and talk. First of all it was about the course, then life in general. After a few weeks he told me his father was in jail, and life was tough for them all.

There were a couple of priests also doing my subjects, and we got together with some of the students who wanted to have a campus Mass at lunch time, or a religious discussion. We had some days which I was able to organise for prayer/discussion at our convent at Toronto, by the water at Lake Macquarie.

One of my bad subject choices was geology. I thought it would be a good extension of my geography, but hadn't counted on the amount of science involved. I was definitely an Arts student, overwhelmed by the chemistry involved and glad to scrape a pass, though I made great friends in the course. They are friends I have had for many years, like Michaela and Brian Gilligan, who married after studying three years of geology together.

English was my recreation subject, and I lapped up lectures on the novel, drama and poetry. Delving into Blake's poetry with lecturer Norman Talbot didn't seem like study, and I *had* to read so many really good books. I revelled in it all. Study was part-time until I reached my geography honours year. I was on campus a lot more then, as I was technically a full-time student. At the other end there was no one else to take some of my classes, so I was also teaching a little more than half a full-time load. It was a struggle to fit everything in, but the effort seemed worth it for the experience of the honours year.

Then it was all over. I graduated in full habit in the Newcastle Town Hall, had my picture on the front page of the *Newcastle Morning Herald* and went back to teaching all day, sometimes before and after school as well.

We are all in the dining room. Dad is reading his paper at one end of the table and Mum is pinning up the hem on my new school tunic for the start of high school. I'm up there on the other end of the table, standing on a sheet of newspaper so as not to scratch the polished wood.

'It's too long!' I say.

Dad is listening. I can see we've disturbed his reading, but I persevere.

'Mu-um . . .'

'Room to grow,' says Mum, through her mouthful of pins. 'I don't care about the other kids. Their mothers can have their tunics whatever length they like.'

Dad pauses in his reading and looks at us over his glasses.

'Aw, Mum,' I say, 'all the other kids have bought tunics, with narrow hems.' I'm getting close to the edge, I know, but I keep going. 'I'll look silly . . .'

That's it. Dad takes off his glasses and puts them down on the table. I glance at him briefly and then look down, waiting for the storm.

'You do as your mother tells you!' he snaps.

I can feel the heat in his tone and I know he's glaring at me.

'Don't dare answer her back, and be grateful that she's taking all this trouble to make your clothes!'

# 15

## My Mother Dies

The year after I finished my honours degree at Newcastle Uni, 1969, was the year my mother died.

I am sitting with Mum in the Mater Hospital. It is so much easier to spend time with her now that I can drive the car, and Mother Theophane is generous with its use. Mum has had several trips to hospital and become more and more frail, till we wondered how much longer she could live at home on her own. My sister Mary and my two brothers who live in Newcastle have taken turns to have her at their places till she was well enough to go home, but this has only raised the question: what happens when she can't go home and live on her own any more?

None of them really has the space to take her, though all would willingly look after her if they could. Even having her for just a little while has been difficult. No one has the spare room in which to put a sick lady without disrupting their family. I've been able to drop in and see Mum often on the way to and from uni in the last year or so, and do things for her. I would like to be able to go home with her and look after her there, but that's not even a possibility, and I feel the frustration. She is my mum, for goodness' sake! Rules have changed, but not that much. At least I am able to call in often, and here I am sitting beside her bed in the hospital.

She opens her eyes and sees me there. I smile and take her hand and she drifts off again. As I sit holding her hand, my mind goes back to the early days in Waratah. Pictures come and go, floating through my head. I am there.

Mum was always sewing, cooking, mending and making beds. Her sewing machine was her most prized possession, and she made lots of our clothes. She wouldn't often talk about her time in business, but as a young woman before she met Dad she was a seamstress, and had trained as a cutter in the work room of Winns Store in Newcastle. It was a big concern making *prêt-à-porter* and made-to-measure clothing for the well-to-do. This meant travelling by train every day from Maitland to Newcastle, and must have been quite adventurous for a young woman in the early 1900s.

After this, she and a friend from the work room, Mamie Masterton, set up a business in a room above some shops in High Street, Maitland. She even hired herself out to sew for country women in their own homes. She often reminded us that on one of these country visits her hostess on a cattle property taught her to make the delicious scones she was always so proud of.

The scene in my mind changes and now it's evening. She's sitting in her corner of the settee in the breakfast room and, as usual, she's got something to sew. The news is on the wireless, or Dad is reading his paper. I have my book and the fire is sputtering in the corner. Mum is just there, peaceful and creating a haven of peace for the rest of us. She never had any hobbies apart from sewing which, despite its practical nature, gave her a great deal of pleasure. She also learnt to knit woollen socks on four needles and to turn the heel, so she always had one of these on the go for Dad for work, or for one of the boys, especially when they were in the army. I can never remember her reading or gardening. She was always too busy. Books had no appeal for her at all. I recall a few years earlier when Mum wasn't well and the doctor suggested she should put her feet up and rest for half an hour or so after lunch each day. This nearly drove her silly until she discovered the *Women's Weekly*, and after that she happily lay back and read about the exciting goings-on of the royals, real-life stories, recipes and household hints.

My reverie now slips further back to when I was small. When Mum would be fed up with Dad or with all of us, she'd threaten, '. . . I'll put on my hat and go out that door to town!' Sometimes when she was *really* cross she'd do just that, and I'd have to go too, because I went everywhere with her. We'd go on the train into Newcastle. Mum loved the shops – the big stores in particular, where she'd wander around and look at dresses, kitchen things, sheets, towels and materials. As we reached the hat department my heart would sink. I'd think, we'll be here for hours while she tries on one hat after another! Mum always loved hats. She'd primp and preen in front of the mirror, turn this way and that. Then she'd say, 'I do-o-n't think so! It's not quite what

I'm looking for.' I'd peer out from under a counter. Maybe we're going now?

'Perhaps –' she'd hesitate, 'something with a brim?' and the hapless girl would go to fetch a few more hats for Mum to try.

While my mum was busy 'finding herself' again on these trips, I'd be busy getting lost. Left to my own devices, I'd explore the shop, find the 'Ladies'', look for a drink of water, and play behind the dress racks. For her it was sheer escapism. If ever she bought a new hat for some very special event like a niece or nephew's wedding, she'd carry it home in triumph and store it in the hatbox on the top shelf of her wardrobe. The hat would come out when she was feeling flat and be tried on in front of the mirror again, Mum turning this way and that, until it was worn to that big family event.

I remember Mum getting me out of bed early, even during school holidays. There was never a good reason to lie in bed, Mum thought. After she came in and woke me up she would return to the kitchen and bang on the wall to ask if I was up yet, and announce the time – not always accurately, either. When I discovered John O'Brien's poem 'The Little Irish Mother', I reckoned Mum was a good second to her:

> *'Up ye childer – late 'tis getting'*
> *Shook the house beneath her knock.*
> *She wasn't always truthful*
> *And she tampered with the clock.*

I think of the rush of school mornings when Mum plaited my hair. This was a special time when I had her to myself and could talk away while I had her complete attention. Of course, if I was in disfavour we didn't talk, and she wouldn't be so gentle with the plaits! When I was ready to go she'd hold open the door and say, 'Have you got a clean hankie?' I'd get a quick peck as I dashed past. 'Goodbye. Learn all you can!'

I'm sure it was a relief when I'd gone, as I was the last to leave the house and the last in a long line of kids Mum had gotten off to school. She'd then sweep the kitchen floor, wash up the breakfast things and run the carpet sweeper through the breakfast room and hall.

When all the jobs were done she'd have a little time to herself. She'd go inside to say her prayers. She had a special book with prayers in it that she liked, and she'd sit with it in a big chair in the lounge room (which was rarely used, except when Father Ford called or we had special visitors). Opposite her chair was a big picture of Jesus known as the Sacred Heart. It half-filled the wall and had an ornate frame from which Our Lord looked down kindly. One hand was raised in blessing, and the other pointed to His heart, which you could see through His clothing. It portrayed God's love for us. This was a special picture of which Mum was very proud. She won it in a raffle she didn't even know she had tickets in. She had bought some tickets from some little Catholic magazine like *The Far East* or *The Messenger of the Sacred Heart* that she used to get at the church, and they had missed putting her tickets in the draw. With a great sense of justice, the magazine entered her in a raffle for a much better prize, and the first she knew about it was when the picture was delivered with a letter of explanation.

Mum's prayer time was her way of maintaining peace in her soul. She'd sit quietly before her picture in the presence of the Lord and pray for each of us and whatever 'special intentions' she had at the time. In the hot summer weather she worried about Dad laying bricks in the sun and she'd drag us – Maurice and me in the Christmas school holidays – into the lounge room to kneel down and 'say a decade of the rosary for poor Dad out in this terrible heat'. I remember the special barrel of sweet biscuits – like little date pillows – that were specially for him when he came home from work. Mum really loved and worried about Dad.

I think of her going down to the shops. A butcher, a fruit shop and a small general store were in the group of shops down at the corner of our street, and Mum would put on her hat most days and walk down there to get what she needed. There was no refrigerator, only the old ice chest, so she needed to buy things fresh. During school holidays she always sent me to get things – a pound of chops, some firm tomatoes or a few nice apples. If they weren't to her satisfaction, she'd send me straight back with them. I hated turning up again at the shop to say 'Mum said these are too ripe' or 'They have too much fat'.

Every now and then she would put on her little hat at just the right angle, hang her bag over her arm and set off up to the school to see the nuns – my teachers. One of the main aims of my life during primary school was to keep Mum and my teachers apart. I had an idea that if they combined forces, life could become intolerable for me. There were no parent–teacher nights in those days, so eventually the time came for the dreaded encounter. Sometimes I would hover and listen when Mum arrived, or I might be banished to the playground while they talked. I guess the teacher told Mum all about how untidy and careless my writing was, how I didn't learn my spelling or my *Green Catechism*, and that I was careless with my sums and often got the wrong answer. Sister didn't have to complain about my behaviour, though, as I was generally good.

Mum would tell Sister just how hard I was to get out of bed in the mornings and how she had to hound me to be on time. She would say how she had to repeatedly tell me to tidy my room and do my jobs about the house – like cleaning the bath and feeding the chooks. About how careless I was doing these jobs, or perhaps how I answered back and was not completely truthful all the time about homework and such. Then the persecution would start. Mum would say, 'I'm going to come down on you like a ton of bricks every time you . . .' She'd be on at me about learning spelling, the catechism and doing my homework neatly. I'd have to show her, and do it again sometimes. Then at school, Sister would say, 'Your mother told me . . .' and put her own pressure on me. Their combined efforts quite destroyed any comfort zone I'd managed to build up, and I'd find myself hounded from both directions to do things I'd rather dodge or let slide. Eventually it would wear off, and I could settle back again into my comfortable mediocrity.

While I could keep Mum and the nuns apart I could be what I wanted to be at school without Mum destroying my school image, and I could be what I wanted to be at home without having my peccadilloes paraded in that other arena, destroying another image I might be carefully nurturing. It was sort of a 'street angel/house devil' role.

I remember the days I stayed home from school when I was sick. You had to be *really* sick to be allowed to stay home from school, so you were usually pretty miserable. But it was also nice. Mum made me little sandwiches with the crusts cut off, or a bowl of soup with toast cut into little squares so you could drop them into the soup. In winter she'd sit me near the old fuel stove, swathed in rugs and pillows in her special cane chair. She'd sit at the table near me doing her jobs – peeling vegies or mending something. She'd listen if I wanted to talk, or she'd just sit.

I slip back in memory to the little hall inside the front door. Every now and then the doorbell would ring, and there'd be a rush to see who it was. I always hoped it wasn't Father Ford come to pay us a visit, or we'd all have to sit in the lounge room and talk polite talk. Sometimes it'd be the Rawleigh's man with his suitcase of aromatic creams and lotions, or maybe Mum's sister-in-law, Aunty Elsie from Maitland, who was always like her real sister. Aunty Elsie was an English war bride from World War I and was soft and gentle and had a lovely accent. Mum loved to see her and they would talk for hours.

Sometimes when I opened the door there was Aunty Beat looking like a big brown bear, with her skinny legs sticking out under her fur coat. Mum would hear her voice and there would be shrieks of delight on both sides. Aunty Beat was Mum's oldest and best friend who lived in Sydney. Her husband, Uncle Wally, was an engineer who sometimes had to drive to Newcastle on business. He'd drop Aunty Beat off while he went away to see people. Mum would usher Aunty Beat in to say hello to everybody. Then she'd make a cup of tea and they'd sit down to talk. I wasn't really supposed to be listening, but Mum would get so absorbed with Aunty Beat's stories she wouldn't notice me. Aunty Beat had a way of conveying that the story was quite juicy. She'd lower her voice and pat Mum's arm confidentially. Mum would sit transfixed, with her eyes glued to Aunty Beat's face. Sometimes – I think it was when the story was too lurid for my ears – Mum would take Aunty Beat into the girls' room where her sewing machine was and shut the door. If I went in on some pretext to see what was going on, I'd find Mum sitting with a piece of hand sewing on her lap, gazing spellbound at Aunty Beat, who'd be nodding and rolling her eyes mid-story. Too soon the doorbell would go again, and Uncle Wally would come for Aunty Beat, still busy with her storytelling. They'd say goodbye, and Mum would be sad to see them go. She'd be quiet and wistful all evening.

Today as I sit here with Mum in the hospital, I am sad to think about how few times something enjoyable for Mum like Aunty Elsie's and Aunty Beat's visits happened. Mum never had a holiday, except when she went to visit Aunty Beat when I was little, and even then the holiday was spoiled when she broke her ankle by slipping on a wet path with me in her arms on the day we were coming home.

Life has been hard for Mum with seven children to raise right through the Depression and War, with a husband who went to work outside in both the hot sun and freezing cold. But perhaps it was harder when it rained and he didn't go to work for weeks. There'd be no money coming in, but the baker still needed to be paid for the bread he delivered in his big basket, the insurance man still rang the doorbell regularly, and Mum still had to find meals to feed us all. I think of the box in her dressing table drawer with its little compartments, all labelled with words like 'Food', 'Insurance', 'School money', and so on, and I imagine the juggling that must have gone on to keep up with all those bills.

I remember fondly the fresh bread and dripping with salt and pepper that I loved eating after school. Goodness knows what it did to my cholesterol, but it was nourishing and cheap. Sometimes there was damper with golden syrup that she had made in the fuel stove, or 'apple' pies made from the prolific chokos hanging from the fowlyard fence. I smile to think how she conned us into thinking these were all delicacies, and not just a way of stretching the budget in lean times. We had blancmange flavoured with a peach leaf, and stewed fruit from the trees up the backyard, or lemon sago and custard. They were all nourishing and filling, and available when money was scarce. Sometimes, in earlier days, Grandfather Edwards (Mum's father) would arrive on the train with a sugarbag of vegetables and fruit from his garden. We would have delicious hot gramma pies then. Mum always said she would never have fed the family through the Depression without his help.

Yes, life hasn't been easy for my mother, but she made a good fist of it. But now she's had yet another heart attack, and this one has left her weaker than ever. We have all agreed that the time has come when Mum can't go home. This time she will have to go to a nursing home. We all know she'll hate it and I wince at the thought, but we don't see any alternative. Mary has found a place and today we're going to tell Mum about it – Mary, Bet and I.

When we do, she nods and agrees it's the only thing we

can do. It's sensible. She sinks back on the pillows, and we are relieved she is taking it so well.

The next day I am sitting with her when lovely, soft Auntie Elsie arrives, Mum's very close sister-in-law with her lilting English voice. She has shrunk, doesn't walk too well, and looks like a faded rose. It has been a tremendous effort for her to get here. She and Mum hug each other, and I can tell they're both crying. Then I hear Mum's first words, which tear at my heart.

'They're going to put me in a home!'

They are both clinging and crying, and I turn away to leave them with each other. I look out over industrial New-castle with its curtain of smoke over it, and I can hardly see anything for the tears pouring down my face as well.

Within the week Mum is transferred to the nursing home by ambulance, and I go to see her after school. Mary is with her. When she sees me she starts to cry quietly. I kiss her and feel the tears well up into my eyes at the sight of her distress.

Mary is encouraging her to eat the bowl of soup sitting in front of her. She pushes it away disdainfully and says, 'Bar-ley soup! It's full of barley and nothing else.'

'Come on, Mum,' Mary pleads. 'Give the place a chance.'

Mum's face is full of misery, and I am aware of the pall of disinfectant smell hanging over everything. She doesn't eat the soup, but nibbles the bread and butter. We kiss her good-bye, and leave with our own pall of misery.

That night I can't sleep. I want to gather Mum up and run away with her, but where to? There's *nothing* I can do! In later years, nuns were given leave to go home and look after their mothers in such circumstances as this. But not at this time. The helplessness of not being able to do anything for Mum is overwhelming, but I accept that this is the way it is. I have chosen to enter religious life, and this is part of the cost, no matter how bad I feel.

In the morning Mary rings. 'I'm going out to get her!' she says. 'I couldn't sleep. I can't see her like this!'

My heart sings. 'Thank God!' I say.

'We'll rearrange things,' she says. 'Someone will sleep on the lounge.'

When I visit after school, there is Mum, smiling broadly, relaxed and comfortable against her pillows at Mary's place. We are all relieved, and so grateful to Mary, who spoils her with tempting delicacies – no barley soup! – and Mum begins to pick up. But not for long. Within a week or so she is back in hospital, gasping and struggling for breath. We sit with her for a week as she wheezes, chokes and drifts in and out of consciousness. She's restless and vague.

'Whose orange juice is that?' she asks at one time, as her eyes focus on a glass. Then she's gone again – not with us. When she next comes to herself I am sitting with her, and she's quite lucid again.

'What day is it?' she asks me.

'Monday,' I say.

'And what day is Dad's anniversary?'

'Thursday,' I tell her.

She nods and closes her eyes again. I have a lump in my throat at the thought she knows she's dying and is trying to pace herself to be still with us for the anniversary of Dad's death. Or perhaps to be with him.

But at five o'clock on Wednesday morning there's a knock on my bedroom door at the Mater Convent where I've been staying to be near Mum, and Bet comes in to tell me that Mum has died. She just couldn't wait till Thursday.

It's hard to believe she's gone forever, and we weren't there when she left us. After sitting with her for so long, we were persuaded by the ward sister to go home and sleep, as it didn't seem she was so near death.

We all say to each other, 'Thank God she had that week at Mary's!'

It is all so different from when Dad died. Everyone is caring and there's no pressure on me to rush back to Hamilton. But there's a vacuum where my feelings should be. I am surprised I am feeling nothing. Is this what it feels like, I think, when your mother dies, and you're going to the funeral?

We go down to the Waratah church where I had been to Mass so often as a child. My brother Maurice says the Mass, and I begin to find my tears. Bet and I don't go to the cemetery, but when everyone comes back to the house – Mum and Dad's house – we have the kettle boiling. We are all there with our family and friends. There's no need now for Bet and me to hide away in the lounge room to have our cup of tea. We sit and talk and eat our sandwiches with everyone, and the first small beginning of healing happens.

We are having dinner in the kitchen – Mum and Dad, Maurice and I – when Mum starts one of her 'genealogy' trips.

'I met Judith Brown down the street today. She lives in Waratah now.'

Dad grunts in a noncommittal way.

'You remember Judith Brown, Joycie Parrott's daughter?'

'No,' says Dad. 'Who's she?'

'You know – Joycie Parrott. From over Lorn.' Mum is patient.

In Mum's genealogy trips everyone seems to come from places with mysterious names like 'over Lorn', 'down the bend' or 'outside Morpeth'.

'No. I don't know,' Dad says again.

'Yes, you do, Dad. Joycie Parrott from over Lorn. Her mother was a Bull.'

Maurice looks at me and says, 'Her father must have been a fair cow!' He and I get the giggles. Mum glares at us.

Dad is concentrating on his baked dinner, not terribly interested. 'No. Don't know them.'

'You do!' Mum's patience is wearing thin now. 'Jim Parrott, her brother, was the SP bookie at the pub for a while.'

'O-oh! Yes,' says Dad. 'I remember him. What about him?'

'Ah!' Mum gets up in disgust.

# 16

## Falling Apart

I've seen people wearing t-shirts saying things like 'I was wrecked on Great Keppel' or 'I survived 'Frisco 88'. And I've seen slogans like 'If you remember the 1970s, you weren't really there'. I could use my own variations of all these: 'Wrecked in my thirties', or 'I survived Burwood Psychiatric Hospital'. In a way, I could claim I wasn't really there. I don't remember a lot about it all.

Of course, there was the exhilaration following my graduation from Newcastle Uni with an honours degree; the sense of achievement in producing a very good thesis – an in-depth study of a sector of inner-Newcastle city – which was highly praised within the department and by the external examiners. But the years of study and teaching at the same time, urged on by an outsized sense of responsibility and need for perfection, took their toll. I was burnt-out, and when the final exams came I was tired, stressed and plain weary. The facts were squeezed out like sausages, with no flair. I passed, but the weariness dragged on. It didn't lessen with time, and a worn-out heavy cloud hung over me.

Also, Mum's death was a shock. She had come to my graduation in the town hall and was very proud of me, but deteriorated gradually till her death threw us all. Eventually we went back to normal, but Mum's death drove me further into the weariness. I was barely surviving.

My superiors thought that maybe a move would help. Fifteen years in one place was a long time, they said. So I packed up and went back to Singleton to teach at Saint Catherine's College, which was in the throes of changing from a day/boarding school for girls to becoming a regional coeducational high school. I was deputy principal that year, and taught geography up to year 12. The year dragged by. The heavy pall hung on. I felt helpless to shift it, constantly tired and often in tears. I asked for some help, and went each month for an hour's appointment with a psychiatrist in Sydney. Drug therapy didn't help, and certainly spending an hour each month crying in Sydney didn't help either.

Of course, this was bad depression and I think I knew it. What I was really sure of was that I just wasn't coping. Looking back, of course, I can postulate that it was grief over Mum's death, mixed with the stresses of study and who knows what else. Whatever the cocktail, the result was just plain burnout.

By October – twelve months after Mum's death – things were still just as bad, and my psychiatrist suggested some time in Saint John of God Psychiatric Hospital in Burwood. I agreed to go, and there I spent the next five months.

I am sitting in the dayroom of Saint John of God Hospital, Burwood, where I have already been for several months – I think. It's all very vague – just one day of emptiness opening into the next. This morning when I woke from my drug-assisted sleep my first waking sensation was a sinking 'clunk' in my tummy as I thought, 'Oh God! Another day. All those hours and minutes before I can sink back into the oblivion of sleep.' Maybe it wasn't in as many words, but that's how I felt.

The hours and minutes hang heavily. Nothing rouses me from the emptiness. I can understand suicide, I think, I really can. It would put an end to this heavy emptiness. I look out the window to the gardens. The sun is shining on the trees and flowers and plants, but I feel nothing. And it is the nothingness that is so heavy.

I had shock treatment this morning. I've had it before and I hate it. Well, perhaps 'hate' is too strong a thought. I don't even have the energy or emotion to hate. The nurse came in and hung a sign on the end of my bed, and I was told to stay there. I was to have no breakfast, as I was having 'treatment'. This was ECT – electroconvulsive therapy. I don't remember much about it, but the accounts received after I eventually went home were for sixteen lots of it, which seemed to be very high when I learnt the usual dose was eight.

The nurse turned back the sheet at the bottom of the bed so that my feet were just peeking out, and then pulled away the rest of the covers. The sheet hung loose around the bed. Then they came in. A flurry of them, talking. Even a laugh. Nurses and doctors – with a machine rattling along, trailing cords. I was numb, so I submitted to whatever . . .

When I woke, I had a headache and they were gone. A nurse checked on me and said, 'Oh – you're awake.' She disappeared and came back with a cup of tea and a plate of little sandwiches. I ate them, and rested a while till the headache went. Then I got up, got dressed and came here to the dayroom.

I have a book with me. I've been reading it for ages. Often when I get to the end of a page I don't know what I've read, so I go back and read it again. The 'treatment' has scrambled my brain so much I don't know what I read yesterday. I know I must have read it because this is where the book-mark is.

Someone comes in. I look up. A man. He looks at me with bleary eyes that don't really see me and stands facing the window. After a few minutes he turns on the TV, and sinks into a chair in front of it. I'm aware of voices on the TV going on and on . . . talking, talking. Occasional words penetrate my numbness: 'Australia . . .', '. . . perform', 'next month . . .' I sit holding my book.

Now it is lunch time. We both get up and head for the dining room. Other patients are appearing from rooms or the garden, and we sit around the tables and eat. No one has much to say. I finish, pack up the dishes and leave. I can have a rest after lunch so I head for my room and bed. If I'm lucky I may fall asleep for a while and escape this numb, heavy nothingness.

While I was at Burwood there were drugs for sleeping, 'happy' pills and ECT. I lived in several 'lady bowler' dresses which were supposed to make me feel more 'normal' than wearing my habit in a mixed psychiatric ward. They were hardly secular dress as they were stark white and nearly to my ankles. I'm not sure who they were 'normal' for. My memory of it now is all a bit of a blur between recollections of being drugged, 'shocked' and deeply depressed. I felt nothing except heaviness and a kind of despairing absence of feeling.

Sometime in January a new brother arrived to take charge of the ward, which was really a wing of rooms and amenities. He was Brother William Marshall – Bill – and I owe him my sanity. After a few weeks assessing my situation he came by one morning when I'd been prepared for yet another shock treatment.

He stopped at the end of the bed, looked at me and asked, 'What are you doing here?'

'I'm having treatment.'

He snorted. 'You don't need shock treatment any more than I do! Go and have your breakfast and they won't be able to give it to you.'

That memory is clear, and from then on things improved. Nobody ever talked about it to me but there was no more shock treatment. I had long talks with Bill instead. His reassurance that this was only a bad patch and there would be life on the other side of the patch helped me greatly.

Bill asked me if I was sure I wanted to stay in religious life and go back to Singleton. This was a surprise. Perhaps it shouldn't have been, but the idea of leaving had never occurred to me. Perhaps it was tucked away there, underlying my inability to cope and the deep depression I was in, but it had never surfaced. I realised I had to work through this idea. I thought no one would blame me if I left. I'd been through a lot. I wouldn't have to blame myself. I'd had a nervous breakdown – a perfectly valid reason for changing my life. Mum and Dad were both gone, so I wouldn't be upsetting them. I thought Bet would understand. But I wondered what the nuns would think.

Whispers like 'You know, they're never the same again!', which I had heard said by nuns in the past about others who had had a breakdown, rose up to haunt me. Would I 'never be the same again'? Would others think that anyway?

And if I left – what would I do? I could move to Sydney, and get a teaching job. I'd get a place to live, and earn my own way. I knew I was a good teacher – at least I used to be, before all this. The thought was scary, but there was a certain relief in the thought of not having to face it all by going back. But another thought kept recurring. Do I really want to do that? The answer seemed to be no.

I talked to Bill some more. The image that kept coming into the conversations was that I was on the bottom of the barrel, in pieces. I was as low as I could get. I was shattered. I'd lost my 'self'. I didn't want to go back to my old self, either, as she had never been acceptable. I had just never felt 'good enough' to meet the expectations of others. Or perhaps my own expectations.

Somehow I had to get those pieces back together. I began to believe Bill's words that I *would* get it together again, but I also decided that I would not be the same. I would stop striving to be the perfect nun they all wanted me to be. It had never been very successful. I was going to stay in the convent, but I would be my own person. I would be the kind of person, the kind of nun, *I* wanted to be.

My mother had a saying, 'You can't make a silk purse out of a sow's ear'. I had no idea where it came from, but there was never any doubt what it meant. Things always complied with their intrinsic nature. They didn't pretend to be something else. A dog was a dog and acted like a dog. He didn't try to be a horse. It was the same for people. You have to be yourself, whatever that might be. No amount of wishing by other people can change you, and it may be just as futile to wish you were something different. It was better to accept things just as they were. My mother had a lot of practical good sense.

So that's what it was to be for me. No more trying to make a silk purse out of a sow's ear. I would be comfortable being a good sow's ear, and they could like it or lump it.

I struggled back to life, aided yet also hindered by the heavy load of drugs still prescribed. It would be dangerous to go off them suddenly, said the psychiatrist. They should be phased out over twelve or eighteen months after I went home.

I had survived, and by March it was time to go home to the convent.

# 17

# Home to the Convent and Changing Times

I'm in my bed in the corner of the small dormitory with the friends I had shared with before Burwood. It's late at night – after midnight – and it's dark in the dormitory where four women sleep in curtained cubicles. There are no street lights, as the convent is out of town. But it isn't quiet. The sounds of very unmusical heavy breathing and snoring are mixed with exasperated conversation in whispers.

'Maybe if we wake her up she'll stop snoring till we get to sleep.'

'That didn't work the other night. She just went straight back to sleep.'

'She never used to snore like this before . . .'

'It's all those tablets she has to take. She's drugged.'

'Ugh! Listen to that one . . .'

'Well . . . Maybe we should wake her up and ask her to sit up for a while till we get to sleep.'

The first I know of all this is when I feel a gentle shake on my arm, and hear Judy's voice penetrating the fog.

'Ceal! Ceal!'

'Mmmm?'

'Sorry to wake you, but . . .'

'Oh dear,' I mumble. 'Was I snoring again?'

'Yes,' she says. 'Could you possibly sit up for a while till we get back to sleep?'

'Okay,' as I struggle to sit as upright as I can.

'Thanks.'

The next thing I know Judy is shaking my arm again.

'It's okay, Ceal,' she says. 'For goodness' sake lie down. You're still snoring, and you're going to fall out of bed any minute.'

I lie down gratefully.

When the call bell goes at 5.30 a.m. I am oblivious. There's another whispered conversation. It's still the Great Silence. I don't hear anything, but it goes something like this:

'Should we wake her?' says Pat.

'No,' answers Cathy. 'It's cruel to wake her out of such a drugged sleep.'

'But she'll only get into trouble again,' says Judy.

There is another gentle arm shake, and 'Time to get up!'

'Thanks,' I mutter.

I crawl out of bed. I'm groggy. After I've splashed cold water on my face I'm not much better, but somehow I drag my clothes on and head for the chapel and prayers.


Day after day I struggled with sleep and stupor. They were right about me getting into trouble. It did happen if I slept in, even though I had all those drugs in me. My superior was well-meaning but unimaginative. When she asked the doctor how they should treat me when I came home, he was casual.

'Nothing special,' he said. 'Just let her get on with a normal life.'

I didn't know this at the time, but heard it later. Meanwhile, I just struggled on and wondered why she expected so much of me.

I am sitting at my desk – my space above a drawer at the long community room table – preparing a lesson for my year 12 geography class. They are behind as they missed having proper lessons till I came home from Burwood. There is no one else who could teach them at year 12 level, though people filled in as best they could.

Books are spread out around me, and I'm taking copious notes. I get out copies of the notes I handed out last year, and look at the program I had then. It's vaguely familiar and I have the feeling I knew what it was all about then. But now I'm confused. I can't seem to get my brain to work, and I can't pull much about the program from my memory.

I sigh. It's all new work again. Did I learn all this at uni? I have an idea I did, but the shock treatment at Burwood has scrambled my brain so much I only have brief recollections and recall just fragmented snatches of what I know I must have learnt. I go back to the textbooks, pick up my biro and start again on the notes for the lesson tomorrow.

We are studying the formation of river valleys. I collect last year's sheet of diagrams and copy them in the library before school so that when the class starts I have them ready to give out. Then I begin to explain to the class, except my mouth is constantly dry from the drugs, and even more so when I'm anxious. And I'm anxious now. I turn aside and pop a piece of chewing gum into my mouth and chew. This gets the saliva going again, and I can speak.

But now I can't remember what I was going to say. I grab my lesson notes and begin to read them out. I try to talk without them, but I stumble and can't remember what to tell the class. I end up reading the lesson notes aloud.

The next day I prepare an overhead transparency of the diagrams, project it on the screen and write the information on it as I go along during the class. This way I can read from my lesson notes as I write, and the students can copy it all onto their diagrams. This works much better and is not nearly so stressful.

Then there are days when it is all too hard and I feel I just can't cope. I hide at the convent and cry. Then I pick myself up and begin again. On bad days I just want to go to bed and sleep for a week. I struggle out in the mornings, sleep my way through prayers and pick up a bit after I've had breakfast. I think, I can't keep going! – but I do. Life is tough, but again I survive.

Gradually, over the months, things improved. I came off the drugs bit by bit, began to sleep normally again and was able to prepare and give lessons more easily. All this time the support of my friends was warm and encouraging. I found out later that a couple of them had spoken to the superior, saying they thought it unreasonable to expect me to get up early every day and go to all the morning prayers. But the superior told them how I should be 'getting on with a normal life', as instructed by my doctor.

When I heard about it I was distressed that she thought all this had been 'a normal life'. I really should have been in a room on my own, for my sake and that of the others in the dormitory too. I knew I snored and made noise in the night, and I felt very distressed about the nuisance I was, but decided to stoutly deny it all.

'No, no,' I said. 'Not me. I'm sure I don't snore.'

'Oh, come on,' they said. 'You do!'

So, one night, in the spirit of the game, my friends brought home from school one of those black, flat rectangular tape recorders and recorded the nightly cacophony. I was oblivious to the recording, till they brought it to afternoon tea the next day. Everyone laughed and laughed till tears rolled down their faces.

'Well – now do you believe us?'

I shook my head. 'No.' I said. 'That's not me. I don't know where you got it – you must have taped some old man in the park.'

Within two years, I had fully recovered. I was more surely myself than I had ever been. I was a happy 'sow's ear' and people accepted it, seeming to like the new me. Today people sometimes ask me didn't I feel anger? Regret? Conflict? When I think about it, I wonder myself why I didn't. I was busy surviving. To cope, it was a matter of 'batten down the hatches', do the best I could, and move on. I began to enjoy teaching again, and taking part in school and community projects. My thirties receded until they were only a bad memory. There was truth for me in the saying 'Life begins at forty'!

After the Second Vatican Council in the 1960s, changes began to creep up on religious life with the slow pace but overwhelming power of an ice sheet. The rate of change was initially gradual, though in the long term and viewed over the last century or two, it was quite meteoric. Just as a huge wall of ice gouges its way across the landscape, cutting a swathe through hills and valleys alike, leaving whole areas changed and devastated, and dragging large boulders along irresistibly to deposit them in a faraway place, change came to our convent.

We had all gone back to using our own names, as in Sister Cecilia Cahill instead of Sister Mary Scholastica, as I had been known for all those years, both in public and at the convent. We even called each other by shortened names or nicknames, and didn't bother with 'Sister' any more. The silence was beginning to break down too, and there was generally a more relaxed atmosphere. We still had Office, but now it was in English. Mass was in English too. We had our meditation and prayers in common, though we didn't start quite so early. This was the home I went back to, for my re-entry into life.

At first, there were many who couldn't see the need for change at all. Our way of life had been perfectly satisfactory for the 140 years since Catherine McAuley founded the Sisters of Mercy in Dublin in 1831. There was no need to change anything, they felt.

During this time there were meetings and, every few years, Chapters, which were election and law-making assemblies. Changes were mooted and discussed by the august members of these assemblies. Nothing much happened, though. For years

I had had this vague uneasiness that a lot of the way we lived religious life was out of step with the times, and even with the Gospel. It seemed to me that nothing would ever change while decisions were being made by this group dominated by ultra-conservative senior sisters. I remember thinking a lot about this and devoting one school and uni holiday period to exploring ways in which the method of election could be changed to give a greater representation to the community at large.

I sent this research off to the major superiors at the Generalate in Canberra, and heard no more of it. I also sent a copy to the major superiors of our province, but heard nothing more from them either. I suppose I thought, what else do you expect? Some years later when I was helping sort, clear and relocate old papers from the provincial offices, I found a copy of my research accompanied by a letter from the Generalate in Canberra directing that the superiors consider the implications of this research when deciding on voting methods adopted in each province.

There was no acknowledgement for the person who had written the paper. By then things had begun to change anyway, so I felt some satisfaction that I had contributed to the process, but perhaps a little sadness and frustration that my efforts had never been acknowledged at the time.

The discussions and changes initially concentrated on externals. Religious habits were to be modified. Hems crept up by inches. I remember the discussion of whether they should be a regulation number of inches from the ground and our realisation how ridiculous this would be. We had women who were five foot nothing and some who were nearly six feet tall. Eventually a decision was made on the

American choice of half-calf length, or 'haaaf-caaaf', as the Americans said.

Our headgear was simplified to show the whole face but no hair, and after a while it was permissible to show a small piece of hair in the front. The question of changing the colour of habits from black was hotly debated. It was after years of much discussion, many changes and lots of meetings that the religious habit was modified to a simple dress of any colour worn with the Mercy Cross – a small silver cross of a particular design which became the distinctive emblem of the Sisters of Mercy in Australia. For some time before this the wearing of the veil had also been debated with vigour and declared optional.

The problem with all of this change was that the value of the externals had to be separated from the intrinsic values of religious life itself, and this was where the real agony occurred. Was the wearing of those long black habits and veils, which declared to the world that we espoused a different set of values, really an essential part of our calling? Was the covering of our heads, with the loss of women's crowning glory, their hair, really an important statement of celibacy and commitment as a Bride of Christ? Would the people of the Church, and others, understand that we were not abandoning intrinsic religious values if we changed any of these things? And what about all that outmoded 'secular intercourse' being 'in the world, but not of the world'? Were the religious really demonstrating that it was possible to live a dedicated Christian life if we opted to live it on the mountaintop (that is, locked away in our convents and monasteries) and not in the marketplace – that is, where ordinary people had to live their lives in the hurly-burly of ordinary existence? And what purpose did all that silence serve in our spiritual lives, when we were teachers, nurses, social workers, psychologists, parish workers and chaplains in hospitals, universities and even jails?

Though the Vatican Council had been held in the 1960s, things didn't really change much till the 1970s, so by the time I had had my stint in Burwood and recovered it was 1973. I found myself in the thick of these discussions. As part of the process of discernment we had discussions in the local branch houses and we had provincial days where everyone was encouraged to come and think about things together. Sometimes there would be a facilitator – a priest or nun from outside – who would present us with points for consideration and discussion.

At this time I felt rising within me again those feelings which earlier superiors must have seen in me and tried to eradicate. Those feelings I didn't know I had: my questioning nature, my uneasiness with the way things were, and my feeling free to break laws which I thought were inappropriate or just silly. I now found I had the ability to articulate these things.

In the Old Testament there were prophets. Today we use the word loosely to mean a person who is able to look into the future and predict things, but the original sense of the term did not mean that. The prophets weren't people who foresaw the future. They were those who saw the present clearly and who told it like it was, whether people wanted to hear it or not. Life tended to be unpleasant for these prophets because people usually didn't want to hear their truth and the prophets often ended up being stoned, put down a well and left to die, or pushed out of society.

Often they didn't like their role. They didn't want to say the unwelcome truth and be stoned for it. They would rather have lived a quiet life. The story of Jonah is an allegory about a reluctant prophet who tried to run away on a ship but God wouldn't let him go. The ship was wrecked, Jonah was swallowed by a whale and spat back out to say his piece. The thing was that prophets had to speak. They had to call it the way it was, no matter what.

So it was with me. Eventually that drive inside me which I didn't know I had surged up and broke out. I found that there were things I *had* to say at community meetings. There was a truth inside that had to come out. It was not comfortable, because often what I said would polarise the community. I found the sow's ear spoke out, irrespective of the consequences, and my words were sometimes quite abrasive in the way they came out. I didn't care any more.

There were those who would say to me, 'I didn't know what I thought until you said that. Then I recognised the truth of it.' And then there were those who didn't want to hear anything I said and closed their minds as soon as I stood up to speak. They didn't agree with me, found it upsetting, and were very threatened. It's hard to remember now what I spoke out about, but perhaps I may have been questioning whether the length of our habits or wearing a veil or not really said anything about the dedication to Christ in our hearts. I tried to say that these things were outmoded forms of dress or customs from a former age that could really be an obstacle in relating to people. Others were also saying the same kinds of things as I was.

Anyway, the group discussion would split in two. I would be on one side and my sister Bet, who was also part of these discussions, would be on the other. She worried about the things I said – the 'unpopularity' they might cause me and the discomfort they caused her, clashing with what she herself thought.

We had always had a very warm and affectionate relationship, though she worried when things happened to me, like when I was held back from profession. While I was studying, I saved up all my mending for her and would send her a bag of undies to be patched, stockings to be darned, and other pieces of clothing that needed attention. Maybe a hem or a seam had come undone, or I needed a half-made garment finished. The bag would return via someone coming my way, with everything fixed.

After uni exams there were usually a few days' 'holiday' to recover, and I always went to stay with Bet, in whichever convent she was living at. We never lived in the same convent, which was probably just as well because we thought so differently about most things. She was accepting, I was critical. She was a conformist, while I had these revolutionary streaks. She was gentle and obliging, and I could be very direct and abrasive. I was inclined to say the odd 'bloody', 'shit' or 'bugger' on occasion, and she would get very cross about this.

Consequently, Bet was given responsibilities in the Order. She was a school principal very young, a superior in a local branch house early in her religious life, and was elected to the provincial council for a term of office. I was proud of her and I loved her deeply, but I could never be like her. I think she would have said the same about me.

So, very slowly and inevitably, the changes came. Much more responsibility was placed on each of us for our own prayer life and spirituality. The regimentation of the daily timetable was relaxed. All those small permissions we had to ask went by the way – for instance, we could write letters anytime and to whomever we chose. An allowance for small things like stamps and toiletries was introduced to allow us to get used to handling our own money again. Eventually this was extended to cover items of clothing and involved budgeting, so that life became much more 'normal'.

Sisters who really couldn't face the changes were allowed to continue to wear the old long black garments and starched headgear for as long as they chose, and an emphasis on tolerance and understanding became the norm. Most of the sisters came to more or less accept the changes, and the exodus of young people from the congregation which had been taking place slowed. We had entered the post-Vatican II stage.

*After the first time we go on holidays, we never take Dad again. It's at Christmas that all builders have their holidays. Except there are no paid holidays. Dad works till Christmas Eve, and then has a few days off till New Year, without pay.*

*Dad likes to spend his days off sitting on the back verandah reading the paper, or listening to the cricket. Since Jim rigged up a speaker in the front room from the big wireless out the back, he likes to sit in there in the cool. He reads a lot and Jim keeps him supplied with Zane Grey paperbacks. He likes the racy style.*

*This year Mum borrows a holiday house up in the Blue Mountains for a week from Aunty Beat in Sydney. We pack and then trek by several trains and taxis to Leura. We unpack.*

*We sit out under the huge old pine tree in the front of the little 1880s stone cottage and read our books, or go for walks down to Echo Point and watch the mist rise out of the valley. But not Dad. He pads around like a caged lion and after only one day, he packs and treks home again.*

*Mum is disgusted with him. For the rest of the week she swings between worrying about what he's eating and being cross with him for being so pig-headed and 'spoiling things'.*

*When we arrive home the next week, he is sitting there in his big chair on the back verandah reading Zane Grey. Happy. So we don't take him any more.*

ABOVE My parents' wedding day.
Joe Cahill and Alice Edwards, Maitland, 1919.

ABOVE LEFT  Me outside our house at Rutherford in 1938, age 3.

ABOVE RIGHT  Mary (far right) and me at Bet's Profession Day in Singleton in 1946.

ABOVE  A backyard snap taken by my brother Jim in 1940. Clockwise from top: Tony, Maurice, me and Bet.

ABOVE  A family portrait, 1949. Back row (from left): Tony, Joe, Maurice, Jim and brother-in-law Bill (Mary's husband). Front row (from left): me, Dad, Mum, Mary with baby Michael. Inset: Bet before she entered the convent.

BELOW  Me as a bridesmaid with Mum and Dad at Joe and Lois's wedding, 1951.

LEFT 'Bride of Christ' on my reception day as a novice, September 1952.

BELOW Later the same day in my novice's habit (second from right) with Bet, Mum, Dad and nephew Michael.

TOP  The family celebrating Bet's Silver Jubilee in 1971 at
Tighes Hill. From left: Mary, Jim, me, Maurice, Bet, Joe and Tony.

ABOVE LEFT  Sister Mary Scholastica at Hamilton, 1965.

ABOVE RIGHT  Graduation day, Newcastle Town Hall, 1969.

LEFT  Our wedding day at
Royal North Shore Hospital
chapel, March 1986.

BELOW  Cutting the cake
at our wedding reception.

LEFT  Graduating with a master's degree in psychology at Sydney University, 1987.

BELOW  In the office of my psychology practice in Chatswood, 1989.

RIGHT At my birthday
dinner in 2000 with
grandsons Reuben (left)
and D'Arcy.

BELOW Bruce and me,
seventeen years on, 2002.

# 18

## *The Fruity Melodrama*

One evening in 1974, when I was quite recovered, I was standing in the wings of our college hall in Singleton waiting to go onstage. Outside the curtain I could hear the busy hum of lots of people having a great night out: the chink of cutlery and of plates being collected or passed around, movement and much conversation.

I was there because I was Sir Herbert, Lord of Hardrow Hall, and I was about to plunge onto the stage to commence *The Fruity Melodrama*. I was dressed in check plus-fours, multi-coloured socks, a shirt and tie with a sports jacket, and an English country squire's cap on my head. Things had certainly changed in the convent over the years!

Make-up (one of the mums) had given me a ginger beard and moustache and bushy eyebrows. I was feeling stimulated and pleasantly nervous, but I'd done this part many times before. Looking around, I could see the others in the cast all dressed in character thanks to the St Vincent de Paul shop, the school playbox and Sister Raphael's skill with scissors and a needle. My 'son', Hilary, was managing to look lovelorn and gangling. Pansie, the mill girl, was suitably poor – all tattered and torn. Murgatroyd with his black beard, hat and cape looked really villainous, and Sybil, his daughter, most unattractive. Bags the butler looked like a butler should in his black evening suit.

It was an ordinary cast waiting to perform, except we were all nuns on the staff of Saint Catherine's College, Singleton, and it could easily have been any one of a dozen community concerts where I had played Sir Herbert. But this was different. Tonight the happy audience was made up of college parents and townsfolk who had come to be entertained at the music hall, organised as a fundraiser by the Parents and Friends group at the college.

We always had concerts; big ones and little ones. Concerts to which the whole congregation came, and concerts in the little branch houses with our limited talents. They were part of a way of life; celebrations of who we were. They drew us together, both participants and audience. Concerts created community spirit – a sense of belonging and camaraderie. They were fun. Looking back, they were important in cementing friendships, getting to know each other better, and fostering a sense of belonging. We had them for all sorts of celebrations but particularly for silver and golden jubilees of profession. Once a year all the sisters of the whole community came together in Singleton for the celebrations. The day consisted of a Mass at which the big choir sang in heart-stopping harmony, followed by a community meal prepared by the best of our cooks and equal to any five-star restaurant. As the jubilarians came in to dinner, the whole several hundred of the rest of us spontaneously burst into the joyous theme song, 'Jubilate in Aeternum!'

Then after dinner came the concert. Often this was a musical like *Brigadoon* or *Finian's Rainbow* (adapted, of course), or a program consisting of a humorous play and musical items. All of these had been practised long and hard all around the region – sometimes for months – whenever and wherever small groups of the performers could get together. The tradition was introduced early in religious life. In the novitiate we had impromptu singsongs, and our own little concerts. At least once a year the novices and junior professed sisters had to entertain the whole community who were 'home' in Singleton for the Christmas holidays. These were big occasions for which we practised well in advance.

The novitiate concert I remember best was *The Mikado*. Sister Mary Stanislaus, who was very musical, adapted the score. We practised in the laundry. With all the sisters 'home' for the holidays, the laundry was mountainous. As novices, that was our job. While some of us folded, some ironed, some sorted, some starched, and Sister Mary Stanislaus moved about teaching us our songs and parts.

Sister Mary Euphrasia was an excellent pianist and did most of the accompanying, when she was not onstage as the Mikado. There were quick changes at the piano as Ko-Ko, the Lord High Executioner (Sister Mary Stanislaus) raced off, so the Mikado could race on. For the one scene they were both onstage, someone else had to practise the piece very hard in order to fill in.

We had the full complement: Gentlemen of Japan, the

Three Little Maids from School and Pooh-Bah – the Lord High Everything Else. Sister Jean the singing postulant had become Sister Mary Bede the novice, a very successful Yum-Yum, in spite of shaven head and white veil under her costume. And Sister Val did a truly awesome job as the old scheming Katisha: 'There's a fascination frantic in a ruin that's romantic!' In those days none of us could take off any part of our habits, so costumes from the school playbox were voluminous and covered all. I was Nanki-Poo. Sister Mary Stanislaus cut my repertoire to the bone, and I managed to be a big success. To this day it is still very satisfying to think I was once the hero in a Gilbert and Sullivan opera.

The real tests of inventive talent were the concerts in small convents for jubilees or a superior's Feastday. Once at New Lambton, there were nine of us in the community and we had a silver jubilee among us. The jubilarian, Sister Mary Casimir, was to be entertained so that left eight. Two sisters were old and so were excused. That left six. The sister preparing the meal was too busy and that left five. The jubilarian could invite a number of her friends to dinner and the concert, so we were assured of an audience.

We reviewed the talents of our friends and called in favours. The parish priest Monsignor Vince Casey, who was not invited to the community function, nevertheless took a great interest in proceedings and made up a poem. Sister Casimir had been teaching in his school for some years. We dredged up a couple of skits and managed to practise them between school, prayers, preparations for lessons and helping get the meal organised.

In the end, we all had a great night. The community room

was the only place large enough for the dinner, so we set the tables up there. After dinner we got rid of the tables, lined up chairs for the audience and made a 'stage' where we could get on and off easily, and changed in nearby bedrooms. We had musical items too: there were violin solos from a visiting musician, a couple of solo songs from other visiting talent, our own little 'quartet' who sang some songs appropriately altered for the occasion, and we had our skits. Our sister jubilarian was thrilled. You'd think it was an Opera House performance!

But back to the music hall. When the Parents and Friends Group at our college decided to have a music hall-style dinner they insisted the sisters take part, and suggested a mixed octet with the army camp barbershop quartet. We went into a huddle and then said, 'No, thank you. We will take part, but we will do our own item.'

Consternation! There was real concern at the army camp outside town that we would be performing before lots of people and maybe couldn't cope. The male president of the Parents and Friends – a captain from the army camp – went so far as to take one of the lay teachers aside to ask him to find out what the sisters were going to do. He said the P&F didn't want the sisters to make fools of themselves. However, this was kindly meant, I believe.

Meantime, we dug out one of the hoary old chestnuts which had been performed many times over the years with a variety of cast members: *The Fruity Melodrama*. We knew it would fit well in a music hall.

I had always been Sir Herbert. By this time the rule about wearing habits under costumes was gone, so my plus-fours were a neat fit and the country squire's cap sat on my own hair. These were the best costumes we had ever had, as we were determined not to let the side down. As it happened, we brought down the house. Most of the audience knew the nuns personally – most were parents and helpers. At the end of the performance some were still trying to work out just who was who in the play.

The epilogue to this particular music hall performance was due to the leftover red wine. The chairman of the Parents and Friends organising committee – the captain from the army camp – had 'volunteered' several other officers to help with the committee job. Before the big night they went out to the Rothbury Estate Winery and stocked up on good red wine. They also procured cases of white Porphyry Pearl, a favourite with the mothers at the college. Two or three chefs from the camp were imported and took over the big college/convent kitchen. It was strange to hear the men's voices floating around the cloisters as they produced several hundred 'chicken in a basket' dinners.

In the huge clean-up after the event the men discovered some bottles of Rothbury's red left over, and insisted on giving them to a couple of young nuns from the cast of the melodrama, to be shared with adventurous friends. That night we gathered in the largest of our bedrooms, which was long and narrow and had a couple of spare beds pushed down one end. Everyone brought a glass, but we came and went very quietly because this room happened to be beside the superior's. It was a bit like a midnight party in a boarding school next to the head prefect's room. Someone had a box of chips and we opened a bottle of wine. One sip was enough.

Porphyry Pearl – yes. But this stuff tasted vile! We decided it was an acquired taste and we would never have the time or opportunity to acquire it. So we went to bed.

The next day someone went down the street on some pretext and came back with a few large bottles of Coca-Cola, lemonade and more chips. So we had another quiet assembly in the long room next to the superior's bedroom that night. It was BYO glass, make a shandy with your preferred mixer and perch wherever you could find a seat. People in dressing gowns sat on chairs, beds or just the carpet, sipping a much more palatable brew this time. Pass around the chips and keep it quiet!

The quieter we tried to be, the greater the impulse to giggle. The sight of maybe a dozen women in dressing gowns all sipping this potent brew of Rothbury Estate's Gold Medal Cabernet-Shiraz and Coke or lemonade just set us off. The idea of what the captain and his lieutenants would think – 'Sacrilege!' – made us more uncontrollable. As the effects of the wine took over we became helpless with subdued laughter and tears rolled down our cheeks.

We all slept very well.

So, you see, religious life was not just about teaching school, prayer and spirituality (which it undoubtedly was), but also about a sense of belonging, and of having fun together. It was about community and about living this way of life with these people, enjoying the experience at all of these levels.

# 19

## Time for a Change

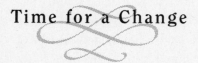

In 1976 I was working at the college in Singleton, mainly as the geography and commerce coordinator, but also as a careers adviser. For the last year or so I had been administering a grant I received under the Commonwealth Innovative Teaching Program. The idea for my project was new and I got it from the sisters who ran the infants school. They had introduced new and different concepts into their little school. My program put together two year 8 geography classes and teachers, and reorganised the syllabus into chunks. Each chunk was then put on a 'learning station' with lots of activities for students to work through, till it was time to change stations and go on to the next exciting lot of new material.

Students worked in small groups and teachers circulated round the groups to act as resource people when needed. At some stations one of the teachers would give an old-style 'lesson' to teach skills such as map reading. It was hard work for me because I had to keep finding or creating new activities, but it *did* keep the pupils busy and interested. And the federal government paid for lots of the resource materials we wouldn't otherwise have had, like videos, audio tapes, sets of topographical maps and expensive learning 'games'.

Careers advising had a very different pace. I had an office with all sorts of folders about possible jobs, and I sat and talked with the senior girls about what they wanted to do when they left school. I discovered that they loved this opportunity to talk one-on-one about things, and more often than not I found myself listening to sad stories. Stories about what was happening at home, family rows, trying to study in the family room with the TV on full-blast. Added to this were their personal study problems and I found I was being a de facto school counsellor – and finding it very satisfying. I also went to 'in-service' programs to help with the counselling aspect of my job.

Life was pretty good. I had recovered from my sojourn in Saint John of God at Burwood and those bad years. I was enjoying community life and finding it satisfying. My decision to be myself had been satisfying and, to my surprise, I had been elected to various committees organising things and thinking about the future of the congregation in the time of change. I'd also helped to organise some weekends for women, and these had been good for the participants as well as for me. These were weekends of reflection, discussion and prayer for Catholic women, who were often mothers of children in the schools. They were advertised in some church bulletins, so we also had quite a range of participants. We had discussions about religion, family life, and difficulties of relationships. I think some of these women revelled in the satisfaction of being listened to, and the feeling of being important enough to be heard. I found I had an ability to listen and to relate well to their concerns which they found helpful and sometimes healing.

Towards the end of the year I found myself having an interview with the provincial superior about what I would do the next year, in 1977.

'I think it is time for a change,' I said to Sister Dorothy. 'I'm not sure what.'

'How about some time to think about it?' she said. 'Maybe a year at Assumption Institute in Melbourne?'

The applications were made, and eventually I found myself on a plane for Melbourne.

What a great year 1977 was! Fifty nuns of many varieties from all over Australia, New Zealand and other parts of the region, all on a live-in sabbatical year at the Institute in Rosanna. It was called a course of personal renewal, and the wise administrators built into it tremendous freedoms which none of us were used to having. It was quite challenging to have to make decisions about our own prayers, our dress and lots of our activities. Most tried out how it felt not to wear a habit or a veil – and liked it! Every Wednesday we had a day off and we could go to the city to shop or to the pictures – and we took to going in secular dress; that is, 'mufti'. For me it was the first chance I'd had for many years to step outside a religious role, and wander anonymously along a street.

One day Anne Hughes and I found ourselves caught up in a protest march outside the movie theatres. Joining in was one way of getting along the street, so we took delight in our anonymity. We climbed onto the end of a row and went along joining in the chant:

'What do we want?'

(The response we couldn't quite discern.)

'When do we want it?'

'NOW!'

We had no idea what we 'wanted'. We amused ourselves with the thought, what if this is televised back home and our superiors see us marching along with this crowd, who were a bit scruffy and aggro.

During our time at the Institute we had lectures, did projects, and made retreats, which were times of quiet reflection of about a week's duration during which we thought about, and made our own, all the ideas we had heard, and the changes in thinking and acting we might want to make. I met up with Father Frank Wallace SJ, among other stimulating people, and I learnt from him what meditation was really about at last. After all my years in the Order this was a revelation to me, and life was never the same again. I learnt to empty my mind and float with my breathing; to use a mantra and to enjoy guided imagery. To be at peace with God, and with myself. It was like kneeling beside my bed with that little lamp alight all those years ago, just 'being there'.

In all, it was a year of new experiences, discoveries, and a deeper awareness of myself and others. It was also disturbing in that it opened up new horizons, gave me lots of answers and left me with some new questions.

1978 brought more change: I was appointed superior of a branch house convent at New Lambton in Newcastle, was asked to do some research for the province, and became more involved in adult education and weekends for women. No more teaching.

When I was asked to go and work at the Generalate House in Canberra in 1979, it was another new adventure. There was a small community of just eight living in a large house opposite the War Memorial. It had originally been designed as an administration headquarters for the Order in Australia, and a house of studies for young nuns.

At this stage, we had a venue that turned out to be a cross between an ashram and a conference centre. I arranged for priests to come and we held retreats for nuns and lay people, who stayed in the wing originally built for student sisters who were no longer coming to Canberra. Father Frank Wallace visited several times, and I was able to work with him and share with the participants the discoveries I had made through him in Melbourne.

People in trouble – mostly women – just seemed to find us and come to stay. Sometimes they sat in the chapel, or out in the sun with a book or their knitting, and sometimes they just wanted to be part of whatever was going on. They might fold letters for the office staff, collate pages or help with the housework. I was always more than happy to let them loose in the kitchen, as I seemed to do lots of the cooking. At some stage most wanted to talk, and I was the one who was there. Again, I did lots of listening to all sorts of sad tales.

One day Anne, one of the national councillors who came from Perth and was a very creative thinker, came home with a brochure she'd found somewhere.

'Look,' she said. 'There's a program on in Goulburn you might like.'

I looked, but was unsure. It was a clinical pastoral education program being run at Kenmore Psychiatric Hospital outside Goulburn. It was only one day a week, and Anne pointed out it could be a good break from my job in Canberra.

Still uncertain, I rang the organiser – the Anglican chaplain at Kenmore.

Reverend Robert Hockley said, 'We're meeting on Wednesday. Why don't you come and have a look? See what you think.'

When I got there I found a small group of men: Rob with two Uniting Church ministers who needed a third person to make the group viable. I was in two minds still, but got sucked in by the situation, and the evident pleasure of these men at the prospect of having me join them. It *did* sound interesting, so I decided to join in. And so began an eighteen-year relationship with Rob Hockley, which ended only with his death.

The next week we started. We needed to bring a written copy of a pastoral encounter (really a work situation) we'd found ourselves in, and it was to be discussed in the group. Maybe it was an interview with a guest I had staying at our convent or a visit to a parishioner by one of the ministers. Questions were asked, observations made, and Rob directed the traffic.

We learnt a lot of pastoral skills and a lot about ourselves in the process. It was enlightening, sometimes confronting and difficult, but always rewarding. I learnt more and more about counselling, and about myself as a counsellor. I found

I could 'own' my weaknesses, but more importantly that I also had a lot of strengths I didn't know about.

One of the ministers in the group once said I could fasten onto a weakness in a reported interview with the alacrity of a black widow spider, but was also very good at coming round with the pot of soothing ointment. He added that I was a very strong woman. All these comments were surprises to me, and I wasn't at all sure about that black widow spider. I also became aware that the listening I did at Saint Anne's was very helpful to people, and this deepened my commitment to religious life and my sense of doing God's work for His people.

There was also a personal interview with Rob every two weeks, and these filled a need in my life for my own counsellor. I found Rob so comfortable to talk to. I could acknowledge how I felt about anything. I found myself gradually opening up to feelings I never knew I had, about lots of things. About anger at the way I was treated in my early religious life; about my inexperience in matters of sex; even my doubts about where religious life was going, and whether I fitted into it any more.

Everything I said was okay by him. He had the kindest, most understanding eyes I'd ever seen, was good-looking and laid-back. His sense of humour showed in his twinkling eyes and a ready appreciative laugh. In the group and in private he could be quite confronting, but always in a gentle, accepting way which made you feel comfortable to be where you were. 'Maybe you'd like to think about an alternative?' he would venture. Nothing was black or white, right or wrong – there were just alternatives and possibilities.

When the end of the year came and we had to close the programs I'd been running at the Generalate, we were sad. Not that it hadn't been successful – it had just grown too big to manage, and we didn't have any more staff available.

In 1980 the question of 'Where to next?' came up, and I asked to go to Goulburn to work in a parish and continue with Rob at Kenmore in the full-time pastoral care program. Once there, I lived with the Sisters of Mercy in North Goulburn, and worked for the parish priest, Father Joseph.

Joe was easy to work for and became a friend. It was a good year, during which time I made many friends, both in the convent where I was living and in the parish, especially among its women. I became involved with the Solo Parents Group, which often had special functions, and I went on weekend and day trips with them.

Situations arose that I never thought I'd find myself in.

It is 6.30 in the morning and I'm in bed in Sue's little fibro house. She had to go to Sydney unexpectedly for a specialist's appointment with another child and she had no one to mind her two little boys – Matt, six, and Jon, four. Sue is a widow, and a member of the church's Solo Parents Group. It seemed a good idea at the time to offer to stay at her place and mind the kids for her.

So far, so good. The house is quiet. Sue said they get up about 7 a.m. to get ready for school. I climb out of bed at 6.30 in my convent pyjamas and sneak out to the bathroom. I'll get my shower over before anyone else stirs, I think. In the bathroom I see there isn't a curtain on the shower alcove, but there's no one about who might need to use the toilet. I undress and hop under the warm jets.

What's that? Voices! Someone's coming in the door!

It opens. I can't reach my towel or clothes, so there I am, starkers, with only the washer I've been using. I panic. Where should I put it? It's very small. I opt for the lower end and stand there in full view.

'Hello.' Six-year-old Matt stands in front of the shower, eyeing me, while his little brother, Jon, stands shyly just inside the open door.

'Hello,' I manage to say. 'Did you have a good sleep?'

Matt: 'I can see your nippies.'

'Well, I suppose they're the same as everyone else's,' I say, trying to sound as if this is something that happens to me every morning.

'No,' he eyes me thoughtfully. 'My mummy's are only little ones. You've got big fat nippies!'

'Okay, that's enough of that! Go on, clear out now while I finish my shower!'

They go. I move the washer, then collapse against the side of the shower laughing.

I'd have loved to be able to share the story, but could hardly do so with the nuns, who were great people to live with, but fairly insulated from family life with small boys and, understandably, a bit straight-laced. I had misgivings about telling Joe, the parish priest, lest he have visions of me in terms of 'big fat nippies' forevermore.

The amusement kept bubbling up all day. I'd never really bared my breasts to anyone but the occasional doctor, which had been a source of enough embarrassment. As for 'big fat nippies' – I'd never have thought so, going by the large-busted women I'd observed, fully clothed, of course. I'd never seen bare breasts of other women with which to compare.

Out at Kenmore there were three of us full-time, and three part-time people who came in for one day each week. The full-time people were all nuns of different orders, backgrounds and personalities, while the three part-timers were ministers. Two were the Uniting Church men I knew from the part-time year before, and the third was from the very evangelical Church of Christ. This third man was pretty chauvinistic, and had lots of problems fitting in with the group. Some of the things he said about his encounters with women in his parish stirred a feminist imp in me.

'She was just talking a lot of rubbish!'

'So you don't think women's opinions are worth anything?' I asked.

'Well – hers wasn't!'

'Are any women's opinions worth listening to?'

'Probably not!' he snapped.

'Have you ever worked in ministry with a woman who is your equal?'

'Come on! What's this all about?' He sat straight in his chair, eyes beginning to flash.

'It's just that I think you probably don't see women as equals, ever –' I paused. 'And what about celibate women – nuns? Where do they stand?'

'If you must know, I think they're a bit weird. It's certainly not for me!'

Which all made for entertaining times in the group sessions. Our smaller weekday group with just the three of us nuns and Rob for an hour or so each morning was intimate and more friendly. Sharing was personal and open, and there were lots of laughs. Rob was constantly amazed at the sense of fun religious women had, and at our store of 'Catholic' jokes. He thought it was healthy that we could be so loyal to the Church and yet laugh at its foibles and faults. He said that his Anglican Church tended to take itself more seriously, and didn't have Anglican jokes. Then one day he came along to the meeting very pleased with himself. He'd found an Anglican joke.

The minister of a village church in England, Rob told us, met his friend from an adjoining parish once a week for a get-together. One day he complained that someone had stolen his bike, which was his main way of getting around.

His friend suggested, 'Next Sunday preach a sermon about the Ten Commandments, and when you get to seventh – thou shalt not steal – mention the bike, and look about the congregation to see who looks guilty. If someone seems very uncomfortable, then he's the one who stole the bike.'

The next week the friend asked the bikeless one if he'd preached on the Ten Commandments as he suggested.

'Yes, I did.'

'Did you find the culprit when you got to the seventh Commandment?'

'No,' he said. ' When I got to the sixth Commandment – thou shalt not commit adultery – I remembered where I left the bike!'

I learnt lots about psychiatric illness at Kenmore, and had a great deal of sympathy for the patients. Just working in a psychiatric institution raised the ghosts of my own days in Burwood. I was uncomfortable, and discovered I'd pushed it all under the carpet for years. I'd never thought about it, and certainly never talked about it.

When I realised this I tried talking to Rob about it, and then admitted in the group that I had once had a 'nervous breakdown' and had been in a psychiatric hospital. My voice shook in the telling, and I was shivering and cold all over for some time after I'd finished. But once I admitted it and talked about it openly it lost its power over me, and instead became a source of understanding and compassion I could use with others, and would not have been without.

At the end of the year I went back to Singleton, the Mother House, where I became the superior of the convent. We had about twenty sisters living in the community there in 1981, and a huge house to live in and look after. My provincial superior suggested that perhaps I could explore ways in which we could use the convent more for the benefit of the Singleton people. Maybe we could do there some of the things that had been so successful during my time in Canberra.

We discussed things in the community and made decisions as to what we could do. I ran some discussion groups for the parish in the reception room and we had some prayer days for the parish in the convent chapel. These changes were welcomed by the town people, but some of the sisters found the opening up of our convent difficult to cope with. When a couple of the new teachers at the college asked if they could stay at the convent there was even more distress for some.

The teachers came from Newcastle, or even further, and thought it would make life easier if they didn't have to spend so much time travelling. We had plenty of spare beds in an unused wing of the convent where they could sleep. When this was proposed at the community meeting, there was agreement. It seemed a good way to use our space, and be helpful to the teachers. There was no dissent, but later it emerged that a few of the sisters were quite upset at the thought of having seculars sleeping in the convent.

I went down to the Royal North Shore Hospital Chaplains' Department one day a week and continued the pastoral program with Rob Hockley, who had moved from Goulburn to become the Director of Pastoral Care at the hospital. There were more students and more groups, and by now I was a trainee supervisor helping to run the training groups. The supervisors had our own group, and these sessions with the group and Rob became a lifeline for me.

In the group there were two Anglican ministers, two Uniting Church ministers, one Catholic priest and a Catholic sister from St Vincent's Hospital. In this supportive atmosphere I could talk about the difficulties of my situation as superior and my efforts to bring change to the convent, looking at the alternatives available. Then I would go home with some new ideas and try a fresh approach. And so the year went on.

*It's quiet in the dining room when I come out of my cold bedroom where I've been doing high school homework. Mum is sitting in her corner of the settee doing some sewing and Dad is at the table. The coke fire is burning in the corner and the room is warm. Before I go and warm myself, I stop to look at Dad. He has his book – Frank Clune's* Wild Colonial Boys *that Jim gave him for Christmas – propped up on something in front of him, and he is reading. I can smell the vile-smelling stuff he's rubbing into his hands which are hard and cracked from the lime in the mortar he uses, and the bricks he spends all day handling.*

*As I stand there I feel sad. He's looking old, and I think that the cold and frost have been getting into his hands now for forty-five years, deepening the cracks. I look at the creases in his face and my heart aches for this father of seven who has laid bricks year in, year out, to feed his family. He smiles as he reads, and sometimes laughs out loud at the funny bits. He's lost in the tales of these early colonial rascals thumbing their noses at authority.*

*His hair is still dark, with two curls carefully combed into place on his forehead, one each side of his hair part, and I smile at his one slight affectation. No-nonsense short back and sides is his choice – that's my Dad.*

*He's relaxed, concentrating on his book.*

*He's sixty years old and must keep laying bricks in the heat and cold for another five years at least before he can lay aside his trowel and float, and get the aged pension for him and Mum to live on.*

# 20

## Countdown

On 19 October 1981 I was sitting in the little upstairs prayer room at the convent in Singleton, and I wrote in my journal:

*It has been a wearing, weary and heavy year. Wearing here in the house situation – feeling alone with no one with whom to share how it's been for me. Wearing in the situations I have found myself in.*

*Weary in the sense of being tired of all the struggle to be what I believe in. Tired of being a 'prophet' – having to come to grips with the truth inside me and articulate it for myself, then having to articulate it for others precisely because it is inside myself.*

*Weary of crawling around in a dark basement helping people to light their little candles and enjoy the light when I know there is sunlight and bright air outside, and that I have the wings to soar and fly. I am weary of folding my wings and groping in the dim interior. I am weary of seeing it as it is, and trying to say it.*

*All this has raised very heavy issues for me. How long can I cope? How long will I want to cope? How can I stay on here? What hope is there of things ever changing?*

It is clear I was feeling isolated and burdened. Of course, there were others in the Order who also felt the need for change, and who were helping to row the boat along in the direction I wanted to go. This was in the direction of more openness, more involvement in the life of the Christian community, and allowing that community to take part in, and benefit from, the way of life and the lovely buildings and grounds we were privileged to have. But many of the sisters where I lived and lots of members of the Order did not see the need for this change. Changes were happening slowly, but it seemed I was in a hurry to move along. I also felt very lonely and tired of struggle. I longed for peace and some sense of closeness of mind and heart.

The Church itself was in turmoil. There were progressive priests and parishes and perhaps progressive bishops too, but these were thin on the ground and as new bishops were appointed, they were being chosen from the ranks of the conservatives. They were those who would support the status quo and not rock the boat. It felt as if I belonged to something big and sluggish, with some vibrant cells here and there, but not enough to drive it along.

Compounding my unhappiness was the fact that during the year I had not been well. A series of infections and allergies had me visiting the doctor several times, and it was here I admitted to being run-down, strung-out, overtired and 'down'. The doctor suggested a holiday, a change of occupation or an anti-depressant – or all three – but I was not ready for any of them. Nor did I know in what direction I should move. Instead I just wanted to cope with what I was doing. He prescribed some drug therapy as an interim measure.

By the middle of the year a number of alternatives began to become clear to me. First, I could hang in here, and hope that either things would change or I would cope better. However, it didn't seem likely things would change quickly, so I would just have to cope better. This was what I wanted to do. If this failed, the second option was to resign all positions of responsibility and withdraw to the periphery of the congregation and just live my life as I thought I should. No responsibility for others, and no need to endeavour to keep trying to bring about a new way.

The last, and most drastic, outcome was that I could withdraw from the scene altogether, and go and live my life in a different context as a lay person. This was scary. It meant living life outside the community, but it also offered the possibilities of peace of mind, and perhaps the closeness and intimacy I seemed to be craving.

Still, I felt no urgency to decide. From time to time it all welled up and submerged me temporarily, but then things would seem more manageable again. A priest who came to run a retreat in August was sympathetic. He said he could see the situation for himself, and thought I should move out in some way before it destroyed me. He suggested you can 'hang in' for too long.

On a return visit to the doctor, he said he would give me a certificate for 'leave' as I was no less strung-out than I had been months before. I resisted and instead took a few weeks' holiday at a country convent at Scone where the nuns were welcoming, the atmosphere was stress-free, and I slept. I walked. I relaxed.

I came back. Everything was the same, but I seemed to be different. More rested. A couple of mornings later, I was sitting in the little upstairs prayer room when everyone had gone to school, as I had formed a habit of doing. The morning rush was over, and this was a quiet time before starting my work for the rest of the day. I sat at peace with myself and God, and began to meditate in the way I had learnt by emptying my mind and concentrating on my breath. In and out. In and out. Gradually the realisation dawned on me.

Somewhere along the line in the last week or so of peace, the decision had made itself. I would leave the congregation and would probably never come back. It was a shock to realise how much at peace with this decision I felt. The weight bearing down on me for so long had lifted. There was no plan yet for what I would do or where I would go. I knew that would come. I just sat at peace with the decision.

In a few days I went back to the doctor and accepted his offer of the certificate suggesting leave. He wrote it willingly. I went to Newcastle and talked to Sister Evelyn Woodward, a wise lady I had spoken to several times during the year. Sister Evelyn was a psychologist and a spiritual director. She concurred with my decision – probably because of the sense of peace it had brought me – and talked over the alternatives with me: stay in the convent; go, and if so, where to? Then she wrote a letter of support to my superiors.

Armed with the two documents – the doctor's certificate and Sister Evelyn's letter – I wrote a formal letter to my provincial superior: 'On the advice of my doctor, and after consultation with a spiritual director, I would like: 1. To resign my position here as superior of the convent; and 2. To seek leave from the congregation for at least six months.'

I put this letter, with some pages from my journal and the other two documents, in an envelope and left them on Sister Patricia's desk. I knew the contents would be a surprise to her, and distressing, but I was sure it was what I needed to do. My main feeling, however, was one of unreality as I waited somewhat anxiously for her response, and mentally made plans for leaving.

# Part Three

A New Path

# 21

## Into the Deep End

Two months after I turned out of the convent gates and headed down the New England Highway towards a new life, I was as settled as I could be in a house in Roseville on Sydney's North Shore.

The past eight weeks had been horrendous. When I told my supervisors' group at the Royal North Shore Chaplains' Department that I was going to leave the convent, they understood. One of the ministers offered me the use of a lovely little house for a few months. It belonged to his deceased mother-in-law and was sitting empty, waiting for probate to go through. Empty houses are always a bit of a worry, he said, so I'd be doing them a favour if I moved in.

Rob Hockley suggested I might like to keep coming to the chaplains' department and be part of their summer program. I could stay as long as I wanted, he said, and leave as soon as I found something else. So that gave me somewhere else to live later when I left and something to do, among people I was comfortable with. I'd work out the rest as I went along.

My first night 'in the world' as a secular person I spent with my sister Bet at Branxton Convent, just a few miles down the road from Singleton. Branxton Convent was an imposing old building – now falling apart, with a perennial lake in the cellar – but the people in the small community there were very friendly. Bet had dinner ready for me when I arrived, and was full of concern for the day I must have had packing up and leaving Singleton. She knew the struggles I had been through over the months, and her deep caring for me enabled her to understand my decision. She knew it would never be her choice, but accepted it was mine.

After the others had said hello, they left us to ourselves, and Bet and I sat over dinner for a long time. I don't know what we talked about. I felt numb and exhausted. I had often stayed there but before tonight I had always belonged. Now I didn't. I had ended that 'belonging' and was taking a new path. I didn't know where it would lead me.

When we said goodnight, I went up the stairs for the last time as a member of the community to the sparsely furnished visitor's room. I fell into bed and slept.

After breakfast the next day we said goodbye, and I set out for Sydney with my belongings in the Singleton convent station wagon, calling on the way at my brother's house in Newcastle. Tony and my sister-in-law Peg also knew of the struggles I had been going through and my decision to leave, and were expecting me. They were pleased to see I had made it; they made me coffee, and saw me off to Sydney.

The little house in Roseville was waiting and I unloaded my stuff there. Suitcases, apple boxes, some food Peg had packed for me. I even hung some of my clothes in the empty wardrobe. It all seemed unreal, and I felt like an alien in someone else's world. I had the sandwich Peg had made, locked the door behind me and returned to Newcastle with the convent station wagon the same day. Then I went back to Tony and Peg's place for a few days. The effects of all the stress I had been under began to tell, and I went to bed there with the flu for about a week.

When I felt a bit better they took me back to my new place in Roseville. Tony drove and Peg had packed lunch, so we had a first meal there together. All too soon it was time for them to leave. I had looked forward to being on my own in my first house, with no one depending on me or telling me what to do. Now the reality had arrived and I had a moment of plain panic. I didn't want them to go. I stood forlornly on the small front porch to wave them off and thought, I am really and truly on my own.

The next day I caught two buses and went in to the chaplains' department at the hospital, more for company than anything else. The flu had never quite left me and it came back and hung on, so I went to a local doctor, who sent me to a specialist. It turned out I had full-blown glandular fever. Rest, the specialist said. Have good food and no alcohol. Take things easy. No stress and come back in a month. If it's no better we may have to put you in hospital, he advised.

No stress? I thought about running back to Tony and Peg, where I knew I would have been welcome. No, I told myself, I've come this far. I've made a beginning, and there's no going back no matter how bad things get. I'll survive. I *have* to make my own way.

'Don't just sit at home!' said a friend, Mark, when he rang. 'Get out and enjoy yourself. You've got all of Sydney to explore!'

I sighed. 'All very well for you. Where would I go? What would I do?'

'You need to get out and meet new people. Go dancing. Or how about a nightclub?'

'I can't . . .' I tried to answer, feeling myself sinking into depression and despair. 'Well, I'll think about it, I guess. Thanks for the call.'

I hung up and stared at the phone. This good friend I used to work with was concerned enough to ring me. We'd had long talks over the years, and been close enough to share our troubles. I knew he was unhappy where he was too, and thinking about leaving, so I'd even harboured the odd fantasy about having him for myself one day. But no, he wouldn't leave. In the end I knew he'd stay right where he was. So it was all very well for him to be telling me to go out! I did want to meet new people and do interesting things, but apart from having no idea where to find dances and nightclubs, I felt I wasn't managing well enough on other levels of my life to be trying new things. As for exploring Sydney as Mark suggested, it was as much as I could do to get my vegies, bread and milk home from the shops up the street, and to get in and out to the Royal North Shore Chaplains' Department. Even after I used my fast-depleting resources to buy an old green Toyota bomb from one of the nurses for a few hundred dollars, and transport was therefore easier, I still felt exhausted most of the time. Above all, I was isolated and lonely. I missed my friends in the convent.

Where could I go? How could I meet new people?

I turned on the radio. 'That was Julio Iglesias,' the announcer said. 'When you hear me play Englebert Humperdinck with his 1967 hit "Release Me" – the song for the next hour – phone in. The third caller will receive two tickets to . . .'

I spent a lot of time listening to 2CH. The style of music appealed to the conservative side of me, and was comfortingly familiar. It was a pleasant background sound to my depressed hours.

This time I heard the announcer saying '. . . lonely folks out there, remember you can always ring . . .'

Without hesitation, I picked up the phone, dialled and found myself talking to a retired minister as part of a counselling service the station offered.

'Good evening,' said Tom. 'How can I help you tonight?'

My whole story poured into his receptive ears. Eventually he told me about an evening for singles held on Fridays at a place called Wesley House, and suggested it might be a good place to start. Not too wild, and a protective environment.

'They're not all young,' he said. 'Quite the opposite, really. More inclined to be mature.'

So I gathered up my courage and my tired self and went into the city by bus to the gathering at Wesley House. I'm certain Tom had never been there himself, or he wouldn't have sent me.

There was a talk by someone about finances, and borrowing to own a home. I found this interesting, but the majority yawned their way through it. Then we were 'released' for the social part of the evening. A cheerful, outgoing minister appeared carrying his guitar, and we had a singalong, jokes and some chivvying of the regulars he obviously knew well. I began to relax.

After that came the dancing. Music blared from a ghetto blaster and weirdly gyrating bodies, with lots of angular elbows and legs, swayed to the beat. One girl of about thirty made a beeline for me and stuck to me like glue for the rest of the night. I think she may have had some sort of physical and mental disability, because her body was quite twisted. She was small, with bright eyes and had a bird-like quality. I found her hard to understand even when the music didn't drown her out.

An older man, a real roly-poly, swayed his way towards me. He had a vague look in his eye and a dribble of saliva hanging from one corner of his mouth. He asked me if I wanted to dance. At least that's what I thought he was saying. I said, 'No, thank you,' and turned back to my companion.

'I don' like 'im,' she said. 'I wouldn' dance wif 'im eiver.' She waved a crooked hand dismissively. 'Supper now,' she continued. 'Come 'n' 'ave some cake.'

I had cake and coffee, then said I had to go. She was disappointed and asked me to come next week. Out in the cool night air I found my face was burning and my heart pounding. I felt humiliated by the whole evening. Surely this wasn't what I was reduced to? All the way home in the bus I felt flat and slightly desperate. The only person there that night I felt I could relate to was the cheery minister. Were there any people out there like me? I had no idea where to find them.

This was my first – and very unsuccessful – venture into the Sydney social scene.

The flat feeling hung around all weekend. During Monday lunch time in the chaplains' department I mentioned the Friday night outing to Keith, who was a Uniting Church Minister, and knew the Wesley Centre well.

'What?' he said. 'You didn't go to that!'

I nodded meekly.

He laughed loudly.

Suddenly we had the attention of the others.

'What's so funny?' asked Anglican Chaplain Russell. 'Where did she go?'

Keith could hardly speak for laughing. He was doubled up and spluttering, but he told them.

'It's awful there,' he said. 'Terrible. Poor pathetic people.' Then he turned to me. 'I just can't imagine you there.'

As he described the scene the others began to laugh too, and my self-esteem began to rise slowly from the depths of my depression. I thought, they don't think I belong there! Thank God!

Soon after that episode, people I knew from the past slowly began to appear. The auctioneer who pontificated when we sold a lot of old stuff in Singleton was in town from Canberra, and took me to dinner. Father Joe, the priest I worked with in Goulburn, came to see me and we had a meal out. He asked his friends, Carol and Tom Walsh, whom I'd also met in Goulburn, to look after me, so there were invitations to come to Watson's Bay for dinner, good conversation, lots of laughs and staying the night.

Several people I had worked with in parishes rang or turned up, and were very encouraging and sympathetic. My nephew, Tim, studying to be a priest at Saint Patrick's College in Manly, came to see me, and took me to meet some of his many friends. Other nephews working or studying in Sydney came to visit. My friend Elaine Prest took me shopping at the Sheridan warehouse to buy sheets.

Slowly I recovered from glandular fever. My time at the Royal North Shore Hospital finished, and my Roseville house was ready to be sold. With Uniting Church Minister Keith's help I enrolled to study psychology at Macquarie University, and I found a small two-bedroom place on the top floor of a block of units at West Ryde.

The only thing I couldn't find was a job, and that search went on . . . and on.

I began applying for jobs in December 1981, shortly after I left the convent and was still in the throes of glandular fever. The *Sydney Morning Herald* seemed the best source, so every week I culled the jobs I knew I was qualified for and could make a good fist of. Just copying my CV and references and posting them off put a strain on financial resources. I didn't even hear back from most of these applications. Where I could make a phone call to follow up the application, the answers were always the same. Either I was overqualified for the position, or I lacked the necessary experience in the field. No one was willing to see that administration, adult education or personnel management in a convent setting were in any way relevant in the real world.

Added to that was the prejudiced idea 'The last thing we need here is a bloody ex-nun!' which a contact in Corrective Services assured me was common, and not only in his organisation.

Even the Catholic Family Welfare Bureau, where I would have thought my expertise and commitment would be valued, was not interested in employing me. A priest friend gave me an introduction to the director, who was enthusiastic. I was just the kind of person they needed, he told me. Surely a place for me could be found there. A deputy did the hiring and firing, he said, and he was out of town till the next week. He'd give him my particulars and get him to ring me. My spirits lifted and I began to feel better. Here was someone who valued my years of dedication, my obvious people skills, and my administrative experience. I walked in hope for the first time in months. But there was no phone call. After three weeks of silence I took my courage in hand and rang the deputy's office. He was cold and dismissive. Yes, he had been told about me. I was the one who had second-class honours in something or other, he said. No, they had no place for me in their organisation. If I liked to ring next year there might be a place in one of their training programs for volunteer counsellors.

It was devastating. I felt very second-class, and sank into near despair. Didn't anybody want me? As for the training program next year – a volunteer! What did he think I was going to live on? I didn't need that kind of training. I could *run* such a program! I felt totally flat and empty. No one was ever going to want me. I was, after all, an unemployed 47-year-old woman as well as an ex-nun.

But I persisted. I had to. I went for an interview for teaching at the State Correspondence School, where my friend Mary had lined up a job for me. The head of the department offered it to me, subject to official clearance. An inspector responsible for interviewing prospective Department of

Education teachers was welcoming, told me my experience and qualifications would make me an asset to the department, and shook my hand. The medical went well. It looked as if I finally had a job and my spirits took an up on the roller-coaster ride I had been on. But then my application reached a clerk who rejected it, in spite of all my years of teaching, because my 'teaching certificate pre-dated the year when Catholic qualifications were accepted'. So I hurtled down the dip on the other side of the ride.

Money had dwindled so I was forced to apply for unemployment benefits. I went hesitantly into the door of the Commonwealth Employment Service, took a number and lined up with a variety of the flotsam and jetsam of society to explain why I needed the dole. The others there were mainly young people, boys with long hair and earrings, untidy-looking girls in long, daggy dresses, and mostly none too clean. They all looked uninterested as they wandered around the boards titled 'Jobs Available'. It looked as if this was mainly a way of justifying their payments for the next month.

I wanted to cry out 'I don't belong here! I really *want* to work and earn my living!' Bored young clerks looked me up and down with disdain and told me there were no jobs on their books they thought I would fit. I waited the qualifying time and got the inadequate payment, which at least helped stretch my finances and pay the rent.

I began to shop at Top Ryde on Saturday mornings just before midday closing, when the greengrocer and butcher sold off things they didn't want to keep over the weekend. Once I bought a whole box of cauliflower for fifty cents, and I looked up my *Commonsense Cookery Book* (left behind by a domestic science student at the college in Singleton) for all the recipes I could adapt for cauliflower.

I bought rice, pasta and meat on special whenever I had a little money, and some weeks I lived out of the cupboard and freezer, or invited myself to the homes of friends like Elaine and Mick Prest, or Carol and Tom Walsh for a meal.

I was worn down by all of this hardship. If only there was someone I could share the worry of it all with, someone I could talk to, and even share the bills with. But the feeling of aloneness stretched my nerves to breaking point. I cried a lot. Once, when I had a statistics assignment to do for my Macquarie University psychology course, I decided it was all too much. I struggled with the stats at my dining room table, and resented having to submit it on time. Between bouts of tears I thought, next week I'm just going to sit down and cry all week! But by the next week when the assignment was handed in and things seemed not so bad, I could smile at myself.

Rob Hockley, from the chaplains' department at the Royal North Shore Hospital, had been keeping in touch, inviting me to his family's place for lunch or dinner occasionally, and getting me to do odd jobs, like tutoring their daughter, Jayne, for year 12 geography. He spoke to the personnel officer at the Royal North Shore Hospital and she came up with a job for me. I was employed at weekends to mind Vinden House, the nurses' home, from 9 p.m. to 2 a.m. It was only part-time, but it was a real job, and I got paid.

My duties were to do checks with the security men, and to let in the nurses who had been out late. I had a few other tasks, though nothing too onerous, so I could read or study for uni. The pay was good for the hours I worked, and I made enough to cover the rent and the Medicare levy, and had a bit left over for food and petrol. When there was a public holiday on the Monday, or if it was Easter, I got double or triple time for some of the hours, so I ate much better that week. I was able to give up the dole, and felt the return of some self-respect. I was earning my own way.

Then I saw an ad in a local paper for tutors. Ah! I thought. Teaching – I can do that. So I applied, and was able to extend my income by a few dollars each week visiting kids in their homes after school, doing sums, comprehensions and compositions with them. The pay was paltry – ten or twelve dollars an hour for a sixty- or ninety-minute session – and I often had to drive a long way, but I didn't have anything else to do. And even ten dollars could buy a lot of basics like milk, butter and bread, not to mention the occasional chicken for the freezer or rice for the cupboard.

Never at any time through all of this did I think of going back to the convent. I wasn't missing the regimentation at all, and liked being independent and responsible just for myself – and not for others. I knew in my heart the decision was right, and I just had to survive until things improved.

# 22

# The Final Leaving

I am sitting in a large room at Saint Patrick's Theological College, Manly, with a priest who is a canon lawyer, and we are discussing my wish to be dispensed of my religious vows.

'You are nearly fifty years old, and at a time of life when your sisters in the world are well-established.' His gaze is steady, emphasising. 'Most of their homes are paid off, their children are grown up, and they are financially secure. They can look forward to a comfortable life.'

I nod.

'Whereas you have nothing.' There is a wave of his hand. 'You have no security, no home of your own, and probably no means to have these things . . . ever.'

He's looking at me intently. 'Are you sure you wish to leave the congregation which can give you this security into your old age?'

Father Thomas is understanding, but concerned for my welfare. I look up at the vaulted ceiling, then out through the window at the wide sweep of ocean below. How can he even suggest that the need for security, a home and a comfortable life are adequate reasons for going back into the convent? There are times when a life situation becomes unbearable and the point comes when you have to decide to either stay and possibly die inside, or go. This could be in the case of an unhappy marriage, relationship or even a job. In my case it is religious life – membership of the Sisters of Mercy.

When some marriages come to this point, one partner or the other, or both, might decide to stay on for some reason, such as 'for the sake of the children' and they can end up unhappier – even hating each other – and living in a kind of limbo. I have heard women say they would leave if only they had the means to survive. But how could they support themselves and their children?

I have known several unhappy nuns and have wondered if they should have left religious life years before. But in those days it was a disgrace to leave and easier to stay on for the security of having a home and a place to belong to. According to their own lights they were good people, but angry, frustrated, and sometimes bitter. Misfits in their community.

On the other hand, I have known women who have had the courage to leave an intolerable situation – whether it was a marriage or a convent – and have fallen apart because they couldn't cope on their own. They succumbed to the loneliness and insecurity. Some endured breakdowns, alcoholism, drug dependence and personal disintegration.

But right now, Father Thomas is still looking at me in his solicitous way.

'I have to ask you these things to be sure you are aware of

the consequences of your decision. Are you sure you wish to leave the convent?'

'Yes, I'm sure,' is my reply. I *am* sure, and I *am* determined to make a new life for myself.

It had been all such a business. I could have continued being 'on leave' from the convent indefinitely, I suppose, but I wanted the whole thing finished cleanly. A sort of 'honourable discharge'. Two months earlier I applied to my provincial superior to finalise my leaving, but she thought my decision was sudden and made at a time when I was under the effects of a depressive illness (glandular fever). She said she could not support my application.

The alternative was to apply for dispensation from my vows through a canon lawyer. So this was what had brought me to the last of three appointments with Father Thomas. We had discussed the history of my entering religious life, all the years of dedication I had spent in the Order, and my reasons for leaving.

In the end, he said he could see I had thought it all through, and was aware of the consequences of my decision. He agreed to support my application for a dispensation, and to write to my provincial superior to suggest that the humane thing to do would be for her to support my application also. There would be no point in contesting it, he would tell her, as my mind was firmly made up, and the sooner it was finalised the better.

So, under his direction, I wrote the appropriate letter: 'Holy Father, humbly prostrate at your feet, I beg . . .'

I had had a rather uneasy ambivalence for years about the

whole 'mountain-top', 'holier than thou' position the Church had in the world. I felt I had broken free from a lot of the legalism and moral compulsion over the years, and though I still went to Mass on Sundays, I felt no sense of belonging in the alien, impersonal city parishes. Now I found myself in the position of needing to write to a distant Pope for a dispensation from religious life.

I spent my first Christmas after leaving Singleton and coming to Sydney on my own in my little house at Roseville. There was a train strike and services were few to Newcastle where I had family who would have welcomed me warmly. I still had glandular fever and wasn't well enough to take my chances standing up all the way there in a train.

So on Christmas morning I sat alone in my lounge room and watched the midnight Mass from the Vatican. I saw Pope John Paul – a good man, so earnest, convinced, and so full of faith. I felt lonely and cried. I cried for the loss of my youth; for the loss of my dedication; for the loss of my community and friends. Perhaps for the loss of my faith too. Rome – it was all so far away.

Something happened to me that Christmas morning. Or perhaps I merely became aware of what had already happened. Watching the formality of the ceremony from Rome, 'the Church' seemed to me so formal and distant from where most of 'the people' were. Of course, the people *were* the church, but the Ecclesiastical Church – the Pope and his pronouncements, cardinals and bishops – seemed a long way away from life in the suburbs. While I respected the Pope as a very idealistic and holy man, he seemed irrelevant.

Now here I was writing to him. Not that he would read

the letter. Some unknown and detached cleric in the Vatican department dealing with religious orders would consider my application and make decisions about what he thought I should do with the rest of my life. What did this nameless person know of the thirty years of real dedication I had spent? Of the agony I had felt about the decision to leave? Of the pain of establishing a new life for myself? What difference did he think it would make if he decided I should stay in the convent? The days of being able to have me bodily incarcerated in the dungeons of some ancient abbey were well and truly over.

I decided the opinion of the Congregation for Religious was irrelevant to my decision as to the rest of my life.

Nevertheless, I wrote the letter.

Eventually an answer came. I had written the letter in February 1982, and one day in May I met the representative of the Congregation and signed the final papers. I was released from my vows of poverty, chastity and obedience, and ceased to be a member of the Congregation of the Sisters of Mercy.

I agreed to whatever was suggested and signed a statement that I would not, in the future, make any monetary claim on the congregation for the years of service I had given. A once-only payment of $10 000 to help me establish myself in a new life was made to me in consideration of those many years of service.

When I look back it is all a bit vague now. In a way it was an anticlimax. The pain of the leaving and the loneliness and the struggle to survive were all very much present, but the signing of a piece of paper was just that.

In the words of T.S. Eliot, this is the way it ended – 'not with a bang but a whimper'.

When the payment of $10 000 came through, it seemed like a fortune. However, if you divide it by thirty years, it was a pretty small annual rate, but given my financial straits I didn't do the arithmetic but was just grateful and relieved. I bought a better second-hand car, because my old green Toyota bomb was clapped-out. I needed a decent car to get to and from uni and to the Royal North Shore Hospital at night.

Mary Fox, with whom I went to school all those years ago, heard I'd left the convent, tracked me down and invited me to call at her place in Greenwich and have dinner on my way to the hospital every Saturday night. What great meals I had in her little 1800s cottage! Baked dinners with sweets; pasta; grilled steak and vegies; and the warmth of a happy household.

The personnel woman at the hospital found me another job. The Department of Health at Chatswood needed a part-time clerk to help out temporarily, so I turned up there three days a week as the best-qualified records clerk ever. Next, I applied to Granville TAFE as a teacher and was given employment of four hours a week for two terms teaching remedial English and maths at night to a small group of men, mainly migrants. Their zest for life and learning was delightful, and I grew very fond of my 'boys'. Other teachers and the students told me terrible stories of stealing and vandalism in the car park and warned me to lock up well and be careful, but when the end of the year eventually came and I said goodbye to my class, I had had no trouble. My pay came in by cheque once a month and went into the building society against things like car expenses.

By combining all these endeavours, I was now earning enough money to get by in reasonable comfort. I also kept on applying for 'proper' jobs, though – a total of sixty – and heard nothing from most of them. If I rang I always got the same answers: I was overqualified or under-experienced. No one actually said I was also female and creeping towards my fifties.

A cousin who lived in Sydney kept in contact and came to see me a few times. She had been a professional administrator in a large firm but had been retired for a few years, and lamented she was unable to help. Later on she admitted to me she really feared I might never get a full-time job. I, however, still believed that I would, as I had been successful in obtaining bits and pieces along the way.

The Department of Health at Chatswood asked me to work five days a week for a while, and I was very busy with that, teaching at TAFE, the nurses' home and my psychology course at Macquarie. All the while I kept going to uni lectures, submitting assignments and passing exams. I felt more confident in myself, especially since I fitted in so well at the Department of Health, and people there asked me why such a competent person was doing temp work. They said I should apply to join the public service, though it would take me a while to progress up the ranks. I took their advice and applied for the forms for the next year.

I had several interviews for teaching jobs in Catholic schools, was short-listed a few times, and decided that teaching wouldn't be a bad thing to do, now that I had found my feet as a secular person. I was also lonely enough to go on a few blind dates, and began to experiment with reading singles magazines and ads in the local paper. I was earning my own way, finding I could survive life, and began to meet some of the 'available' men out there. It was all a bit scary, but I did meet some nice men, and learnt by my mistakes with others! So, as my first year back in the 'real world' drew to an end, I was more settled. I was still lonely, though, and existence was pretty much hand-to-mouth, but I knew I would survive.

In December I saw a late ad for a senior geography teacher at Saint Scholastica's College for girls in Glebe, and I applied. Terry Quinn (God bless him) had lost a teacher suddenly, so he interviewed me and employed me for the next year, 1983, glad to find so well-qualified and experienced a teacher at that late stage.

I had a proper job at last! But not before the next disaster happened . . .

*It is 6.30 in the morning the day after I told Mum about entering the convent. I am bleary-eyed and getting dressed to go to morning Mass.*

*When I come out to the kitchen, Dad is there having breakfast before he goes to work. He gets up, comes over to me and folds me in his arms.*

*'Mum told me what you've decided.'*

*I'm not sure how to respond to this. Will he be cross too? Will he say I can't go? Then again, this feels all right.*

*So I just say, 'Oh . . .'*

*Then he says, 'I'm very proud of you. I always have been and I always will be. I hope you'll be very happy . . .'*

*It's warm and close, and we both shed a few tears.*

# 23

# Adventures with the Law

On 9 December 1982 I was arrested for shoplifting in Coles at West Ryde, taken to Eastwood Police Station by three policemen in a squad car, fingerprinted, charged and released on bail of $200 to appear at Ryde Court on 20 December 1982.

It was just over a year since I left the convent, and though I was feeling more sure of myself and my new life, the strain of all those months was telling.

I went across to Coles from my unit that day to buy a couple of pots in which to plant some cuttings I had been growing for Christmas presents, and for a packet of razor blades to do some cutting out as part of a calligraphy project I was working on for the same purpose.

When I found I didn't have enough money in my purse, I put the razor blades in my bra and a small pot-plant chain in my bag. I paid for the rest of the things at the checkout, left the store and began to cross the street when I was surrounded by a posse in the middle of the pedestrian crossing. There were two strapping young men and a woman who declared herself to be the store security officer.

She accused me loudly of stealing and demanded I return to the store immediately. I was covered in confusion. People began to stop and stare at the commotion, so I agreed meekly and went back with them.

Then began a nightmare of many weeks that turned into months. I appeared in court and was placed on a good behaviour bond because this was my first offence. I had a good reference from Father Joe, whom I worked with in Goulburn, and I had already taken myself to see Doctor Craig Powell, a psychotherapist, to help me deal with the issues involved. This all helped my case. But I was not prepared to tell anyone – the police sergeant, the court solicitor, the magistrate or the probation people, *anyone* – that I had been a nun. I was too ashamed of the whole affair.

How was it, you may ask, that a law-abiding, middle-aged woman, who had been a nun for thirty years, shoplifted? How indeed? Looking back, I can recognise the stress I'd been under after all those months without proper income, the loss of friends in the convent, and the struggle to keep going. All those months when no one wanted me, when I had so little and felt so powerless . . . And then this big, glittering store had everything laid out to tempt me to take something for myself. They had so much, I had so little, and they'd never miss these little things.

The result of the good behaviour bond was that I had to report weekly to a probation officer at Top Ryde – a 23-year-old girl, just out of training. I could see she was intrigued about me, but I resisted all her efforts to pry into my past. She told me in a patronising way that probation could be a very rewarding time if I decided to use it well. I guess that's what she had been taught to say, but she was trying to teach her grandmother to suck eggs.

The whole experience was heaping humiliation upon humiliation, especially when the probation officer insisted she needed to visit my home to see how I lived. I couldn't refuse, but felt angry and violated under her invasive scrutiny. Eventually our time together ran out when I moved house, and I was able to move on and put one more disastrous episode behind me.

The following is much as I wrote it in my journal on the night I was arrested:

**11pm, 9 December 1982.**

*Today I became a criminal. I was arrested by three policemen in a supermarket and marched off through the crowd of mildly interested spectators, who paused briefly in their shopping routines to watch as I was escorted to a waiting patrol car and we drove off to Eastwood Police Station.*

*I thought how strange it was that three police were needed to arrest and bring in one respectable middle-aged lady – an ex-nun and law-abiding citizen for forty-eight years – over a packet of razor blades (Wilkinson Sword 5s) and a small chain to hang a pot plant in my bathroom. Total value? $2.27!*

*It is nearing midnight now and I think if I write all this down it may be therapeutic and I may be able to*

*sleep. I have been in quite a state since I came home,
and there is no one I feel I can tell.*

As we drove in a perfectly normal way through a normal
world on an ordinary December day, the sergeant turned in
his seat to speak to me.

'How long have you been living in this area?' His voice was
matter-of-fact with perhaps a hint of kindness as it had been
since they had walked into the store office ten minutes ago.

'About. . . .' I blinked back the tears that had been flowing pretty freely, almost unnoticed, and struggled for control
of my voice. 'About . . . six months.' I paused to blow my
nose on the tissues the security lady had thrust into my hand as
we left the office from her own handbag. 'Since . . . Easter,'
I finished.

'And how long have you been out of work?'

There was a much longer pause. The tears flowed so freely
I couldn't get my voice under control at all. The policeman
turned further in his seat to look at me. I avoided his gaze
and looked out the window at the real and ordinary world
passing by, a world I could barely see through the blur of
tears that I couldn't stop, try as I might.

He didn't press me for an answer, but turned back to the
front and all four of us sat in silence till we pulled up inside
the inner yard at the back of the police station. The sergeant
got out and opened my door for me while I gathered my
shoulder bag and the brown paper shopping bag containing
the four items I had bought and paid for. These had been
checked against the docket by the security officer and a
burly young man to see if all the prices complied with the

stock list. Perhaps they thought I might have changed the price tags for cheaper ones, or put one pot inside the other to avoid paying. They were pronounced 'in order' and returned to me when the police escorted me out.

In the office at the supermarket the sergeant had read me my rights: to say nothing if I so wished, or to make a statement in my own handwriting. Again when I got out of the car he reminded me of this and suggested I decide what I wanted to do before I went into the police station. I felt unreal – lost – and not particularly guilty. More humiliated and distressed.

'It's quite clear you've done what they said – shoplifted some articles,' he told me. 'You'll be charged with stealing, because that's what it is.'

I nodded. I had done it all right, no doubt about that. I had been caught and had to live out the rest of the drama. I looked at him for guidance.

'I don't know what to do – what would be best. This is a situation I know very little about.'

He replied, 'I'm afraid I can't advise you on this. I'm not allowed.' His voice was kind as he stood looking at me, and I registered a feeling of appreciation for his treatment of me. There had been hostility and aggression on the part of the security officer and her two stalwart young heavies who accosted me as I left the store.

I followed the sergeant to a fenced-off area – the holding pen, maybe two metres long by one metre deep – with a bench at each end. The gate was bolted behind me on the outside. There were three other police there as well as the three it had taken to bring me in, all going about their business in a matter-of-fact way. For them this was all routine, for me it was unreal and bizarre.

I sat miserably in my pigpen making liberal use of the security lady's tissues and thinking about everything. All the people from the young heavies to the police were only doing their jobs and being fairly impartial about it. No one bullied me or spoke brutally to me, let alone treated me roughly. I was grateful for this. I'd been treated more rudely by the staff behind counters at Social Security, the CES and secretaries at places where I had applied unsuccessfully for jobs.

The sergeant came over several times and asked more questions: 'How long have you been out of work?', 'What was your last job?', 'What school were you last teaching in?', 'Why did you leave your last employment?' I would not give the name of the last school, or say why I had come to Sydney, but admitted it was a private school, a Catholic school. I would not say I had been a nun and left the convent. I was ashamed. He didn't press me. He asked to see inside my money purse.

Another young policeman came over and began to ask me the same questions but the sergeant spoke to him and sent him away. The sergeant came back later to read his version of events to me. He asked me to say 'Yes' or 'No' so that I agreed with what he had written. Next, one of the young policemen took me out of the pigpen and through a door at the back. It was a small concrete corridor, and with a shock I saw bars in the doors opening off it. I had a wild moment of panic. My heart was thudding as I thought, do they lock people up over a packet of razor blades and a pot-plant chain? Then he pointed to a shelf and said, '. . . fingerprints, as you have no previous convictions.' I saw a pad and ink, a large notice requiring all to clean the pad after use, and lots of ink smudges on the notice and the wall. I was mesmerised by the process of inking up the pad and my fingers and printing them one by one (in duplicate) on sheets with red printing on them. We also did my whole four fingers together, and my palms without fingers for each hand. When we were finished, both my hands were covered in thick black sludge which took a great deal of hot water, sandsoap, a little methylated spirits and much rubbing to remove. I thought about Lady Macbeth as I rubbed, and decided that a little water would not cleanse me, either, of this deed.

Back in the pigpen, I was visited by the sergeant before he went out again. He told me – and this time I was sure about the kindness in his voice – that it was nearly all over. I would have to go before a magistrate at Ryde Court.

'There'll be a duty solicitor at the court on the day,' he told me. 'Be sure you get there well before 10 a.m. and ask around till you find him. He'll speak for you and you'll find that a big help.'

'Thank you.'

'You know, the best thing for you would be to plead "Guilty". Do you have any hesitation about that?'

'No.'

'Good. Then you will have it all over and finished in one day. If you contest it, or want to argue about it, the case will be adjourned to another day. And that would only stretch the whole thing out.'

By now tears were flowing again, so I just nodded. Just before he left he leaned over the fence and patted my arm.

'Don't worry,' he said. 'You're not the first to ever do this and, unfortunately, you won't be the last.'

He was gone, and I sat on, numb and miserable.

After a while I was taken to a counter where the sergeant in charge asked me to sign three copies of a bail undertaking, one of which he gave to me with two printed sheets relating to conditions. Then he said I was free to leave, and I walked out the front door of the station. I found myself on the foot-path in an unfamiliar street of a suburb I didn't know. It was about two and a half hours since I had been surrounded and accosted on the pedestrian crossing outside the store, and getting home would be a problem. I crossed the road to where I could see a railway station and sat on a bundle of afternoon *Sun* newspapers outside a deserted news stand to take stock before entering the station.

When the sergeant had asked to look in my purse there were pitifully few coins in it, and I now found they came to just forty-two cents. Not enough for anything. Then I remembered the two twenty-cent coins I kept aside for an emergency phone call. I momentarily wondered who I could ring, and then decided I couldn't ring anybody. I would be too ashamed to tell any of my friends what had happened.

I got up and went into the station to see if I could buy a ticket to West Ryde, only to find the whole place deserted and a sign scrawled on a blackboard that said 'There will be no trains today due to an industrial dispute'.

Back out on the street I asked a passer-by how I could get to West Ryde and she directed me to a bus stop a few blocks away. I was quite exhausted by then and conscious that I must have looked a wreck with my tear-stained face and red eyes, but I couldn't find it in me to care.

When the bus eventually came I asked the driver what the fare was to West Ryde, and found I had just enough for the thirty-minute drive round all the back streets. Once I had reached familiar territory I went to the building society for some more money, and went home to my empty unit and solitary evening, still clutching my somewhat tatty brown-paper bag.

# 24

## Stacey and 'Midnight Matchmaker'

It was a Saturday morning and I had just done my shopping. I pulled into my parking space under the units and, as I got out of the car, a young man working at his car next to mine looked up and said, 'G'day.'

His name was Stacey, and I could see he was only in his twenties, wearing a t-shirt and shorts, feet bare. His friendly smile was wide – white teeth flashing in an open, sun-tanned face.

'Need a hand?' he said, coming over.

'Thanks,' I said. 'But I haven't got much. I'll be right.'

'Interesting car,' he said, standing back to view my little hatchback. 'How many cylinders? What size engine?'

'I really have no idea. Either it goes or it doesn't, as far as I'm concerned.'

'Mind if I have a look?'

'Help yourself,' I said, and that's how it all started.

Forty minutes later I had been upstairs and down again;

Stacey had been under the bonnet, taken my car for a test drive and told me it needed new oil, a filter, spark plugs and water in the battery. He offered to do it for me the next day, Sunday. I was doubtful as I didn't know where to start to get these things, but he offered to buy them for me. He knew somebody somewhere, and they wouldn't be too dear.

Sunday came, and Stacey was into it early. I took him morning tea on a tray and a sandwich for lunch. He was enjoying himself, giving me technical information in a lingo I didn't understand, and getting all black and greasy.

Later, I looked in the freezer, found a chicken and invited Stacey up from his unit downstairs for an evening meal after he'd finished. I checked the pantry and unearthed a tin of pie-apples, so I turned them into an apple pie with custard. I set the dining table with a cloth.

Stacey turned up after six all showered and brushed up, even with shoes. His dark wavy hair was combed to perfection and his wide smile was most attractive. I thought, goodness, he's a handsome boy.

We had a pleasant meal. Stacey told me he came from Western Australia, had finished his term in the army over here and was now a handyman at a private school. He had a good sense of humour and a robust attitude to life. He was also energetic, and offered to take care of any odd jobs I needed doing.

I remember my mother once saying 'If a stray dog follows you home, don't give it any encouragement. And never feed it – or you'll never get rid of it.' She was right. Stacey was lonely – a country boy in the city, in spite of his six years in the army – and he saw me as a substitute for his family who were so far away. I fed him from time to time and he put up towel rails for me, looked after my car and changed light bulbs. He did anything a woman on her own needed a man to do. Well, almost. For me it was quite adequate.

He often dropped in for coffee or asked me down to his unit for a drink. He thoughtfully provided a sweet sherry, which he thought was suitable for a woman of my age and background. I even had dinner there one night and discovered he was quite a creative cook. Sometimes I feared he'd eat me out of house and home, but he and his friendship were worth it.

I'm waiting by the phone, heart pounding, mouth dry, and I'm trembling. I've actually done it! I've phoned 2GB 'Midnight Matchmaker' and now I'm sitting here glued to the earpiece listening to Brian Wiltshire chat away to others, waiting my turn. The clock is getting dangerously close to the witching hour when the program finishes. Milt is forty-two and wants to meet a 35-year-old. He likes sport and owns a boat. Carol is thirty-five, divorced and has two children. She doesn't like garlic or beer bellies, but doesn't mind a beard.

Then the voice cuts in. 'Alice? You're next. Brian will come to you after the break. Are you ready?'

'Yes, thank you.' My voice sounds funny and my heart is beating so loudly I can hear it in my ears. The 'Alice' is strange, but no way am I going to say I'm Cecilia in case someone I know is listening and recognises me. Besides, Alice fits the bill. It was my mother's name, and I certainly feel like Alice in Wonderland.

Suddenly, I'm on! In spite of having a bit of a list written out, I'm tongue-tied. Petrified. Brian is friendly and helpful. Somehow I manage to say, 'I'm forty-seven, never been married – been too busy being a teacher – and I don't mind garlic or beards. I'm not too keen on beer bellies, though. I like live theatre, reading and movies . . . And, no, I don't have any pet hates.'

I'm still shaking. I've hung up the phone. It's over. I've done it. Now, the waiting begins for responses. I can hardly settle down enough to go to bed, but it is about a week before I hear anything. Then a couple of letters arrive, sent on by 2GB.

The first is written on half a sheet of paper, torn out of an old exercise book. It's grubby and the writing and spelling are not too presentable. I don't think you're for me, I say to myself. I write a reply to say, 'Thank you, but I've met somebody.'

The next letter is from Clem, who is from the Central Coast. He's a fifty-year-old widower, owns his own home and is a plumber. I phone him and he sounds nervous, but I'm so nervous as well that it's hard to tell what he's like.

'Yes,' I say. 'Saturday would be fine . . . about five sounds good.' I give him my address. He suggests a drink and a bite to eat at a local club. He'll come on the train and would like to catch a reasonably early one home.

Next thing I know, Saturday arrives and I'm doing a Saturday clean in my unit. It's a left-over ritual from the convent where Saturday charges were a very big deal. As I clean the bath, change the sheets and put on the washing machine I enjoy the mindless therapy of housework. I'm a bit nervous, though. What will he be like? What will we talk about? This is a big gamble. I've *never* really been out on a date as such, but I don't want to spend the rest of my life on my own. I feel I just have to grit my teeth and get into it if I ever want to meet a man.

By 2.30 I have the vacuum cleaner in the middle of the lounge, the bucket and mop in the kitchen, and all the moveable furniture pulled about. Another half-hour or so and I'll be finished, then have a shower and get dressed, in case he's early. Suddenly, above the whir of the vacuum and the sound of the dryer from the little laundry, there's a knock at the door. I push my hair back with a none too clean hand and think, that's Stacey. But instead, I find a slightly stocky middle-aged man standing there, wearing an open necked shirt and with a cardigan over one arm. He looks very clean and neat, in a carefully scrubbed way.

He clears his throat.

'Cecilia?' (I'd confessed to my real name on the phone.)

'Yes?'

'I'm Clem. I'm a bit early. I hope you don't mind.'

My heart sinks as I think of the mess behind me, but I say, 'Hello, Clem. Nice to meet you. Come on in. Don't mind the mess. I was cleaning up.'

He follows me into the shemozzle that is my lounge room, saying, 'I wanted to be early for the train in case I missed it. But I was so early I caught the one before.'

I pull the chairs and table into place and push the vacuum aside.

'That's all right, Clem. Come and sit down.'

He sits, talking a bit too fast. 'I was afraid I wouldn't be able to find the place, but it was easy.'

We have coffee and begin to chat. At first I am very conscious of my old jeans, grubby face and the mop and bucket in the middle of the kitchen. But Clem's so nervous he isn't aware of any of that. He goes quiet and is awkward, but is so obviously an honest, genuine person that I relax.

He tells me how he lost his wife only a few months ago. He's lonely and missing her. I switch easily to a listening mode and encourage him to talk. Somehow, it's already obvious this meeting will not lead to anything long-term for me and I feel almost relieved, in spite of a tinge of disappointment.

After an hour I say, 'Well, Clem, I'd better clean things up a bit. Sorry for the mess.'

He looks about. 'Oh – yes. I see you've been cleaning. I hadn't noticed.' How could he not notice?

'Would you like to watch TV while I get organised?' I ask.

'Ye – es,' he says. 'That'd be nice.'

I leave him watching the football while I put things away and have a shower. He doesn't seem to mind, and looks happy to sit there.

We go to the local Western Suburbs Leagues Club for a drink, talk some more, and have an early meal. He just takes it for granted that he'll pay, and I'm grateful as money is tight. And he's also moved on a bit from the inarticulate awkwardness of the first hour.

'You know,' he says over coffee, 'this is the first time I've been out since my wife died. Except for a drink after work at the pub with the boys – that sort of thing. The first time I've *really* been out.' His hand is shaking as he picks up his cup.

'It's been hard for you, Clem, these last few months.'

'Yes.'

'Do you miss her terribly?'

'Yes, I do. We were together for twenty-seven years. Just the two of us since the girls left home a few years ago.' He pauses, and I sit quietly. 'The house has been empty since she went. It was so sudden. We went to the pictures on Saturday night and she had the heart attack on Sunday.' He clears his throat. 'She died that night. I've been lost ever since. Jen was always there.'

He's a bit choked up, so I say, 'I guess missing her is the price you pay for the closeness you had.'

'That's right,' he says. 'We were close.' He sits quietly for a moment. 'I've been listening to "Midnight Matchmaker" for a while, so I thought I'd try going out and meeting other people, but I think it's a bit soon. I still miss her too much.'

I nod.

'It's been a nice night, though. Thanks. You're a good listener.'

'I've enjoyed it too,' I tell him.

'I don't think I'll do this again for a while. I'm not ready. I need to say my goodbyes.'

We stand up and walk to the door of the club. Outside, he takes my hand.

'You're a nice lady. I hope you find what you're looking for.'

'Thank you, Clem. And you too.'

We part. He goes off to an early train and I head home to a clean unit.

I've survived my first date.

*It's the early 1960s, and I'm visiting Mum and Dad with
another nun as a companion. Maurice has borrowed a big
reel-to-reel tape recorder from somewhere and set it up in
the dining room. We're going to make a spoken 'letter' to
Jim in Wellington. He hasn't been home for a while, and
Maurice thinks this is a good idea as Mum says the doctor
is concerned about Dad's heart.*

*'I've done all this before, you know,' says Dad.*

*We all look at him.*

*'When I was a young fellow in Rutherford fifty-odd years
ago, one of the boys in the hill mob [Dad and his mates]
had one of those early "His Master's Voice" players with
a big trumpet on top.' He waves his hands to make a big
trumpet speaker, and I can see the picture of the dog
looking down the trumpet, listening to his master's voice.*

*He continues, 'Records were on wax cylinders, and if you
got a blank cylinder and fiddled about with the machine,
you could record on it. Not all that clear – your voice
wobbled – but we had great fun. You'd just wipe it and
start again.' He smiles at the memory.*

# 25

## Dracula Romeo and Inner-city Life

When the car turns off the main road into a darker side street, my heart misses a beat. What is he on about? Where is he taking me? Murray is sitting there with a smarmy grin on his overpolished face, saying nothing.

'Where are we going?' I say, feeling the dryness in my mouth and my heart thumping loudly in my throat. We *should* still be on the main road, heading for my unit at West Ryde.

'Now, because you've been a good girl, I'm going to show you Drummoyne Heights.'

Ah – his place. I should have guessed. I've spent the last two hours and ten minutes hearing all about his life and habitat.

Murray is my second flutter into the dating market. Like Clem, he also wrote me a letter after my big appearance on 'Midnight Matchmaker', and this is our first meeting. I made the mistake of giving him my home address and he picked me up to take me to Balmain Leagues Club in his flashy pre-loved Ford.

I look across at him with his dark hair carefully waved and plastered into place with Californian Poppy hair oil. He is still smiling in his unattractive 'Aren't you lucky to be out with the best-looking man in the universe?' way. God, I think, what a jerk! I just can't believe this man can be so self-centred. I think of the two hours at the club – the drinks and Murray's description of his important job in administration at the biscuit factory. How they all depend on him to organise things like transport; how they couldn't do without him. (I think *I* certainly could! I can't wait for this evening to be over.) Then came the bistro meal which we ate to the accompaniment of the pinging and singing and rattling of the poker machines, and we passed on to discussing the details of Murray's private life and loves.

'I'm divorced,' he said. 'Ten years now.' (I understand! She probably couldn't stand another minute.) 'At the moment I'm recovering from a nervous breakdown. I'm getting over a break-up with my last girlfriend. The bitch!' He filled his mouth with a large helping of pie and peas, through which he continued to talk.

'Took me to the cleaners, she did! Drove me mad round the unit, too. Always leaving her underpants and pantyhose hanging in the shower. Nothing worse than always running into women's underwear hanging in your bathroom.' He snorted. 'I told her not to. I told her I didn't like it. And she still kept on doing it!' He banged the table with his knife and fork, and peas scattered about. He took a swig from his beer glass.

'And she didn't look after stuff, either. I'm very careful with my unit. Proud of it. And she left stuff all over the house – papers, books, clothes off the line. Never put things away. Dirty dishes on the sink.' He shook his head and looked at me pitifully. 'No wonder I had a breakdown. I had to ask her to leave and couldn't sleep for days. She took stuff that was mine. Just went. I don't know where. I had to go to the doctor. Missed work. Couldn't concentrate . . .' Then he cheered up. 'But I'm fine, now my nembutal is kicking in.'

And so on it went, and now we were pulling into a dark parking area under a block of units. How can I get out of this? Maybe if I say I want to go straight home . . . Murray leans across to put his arm around me. There is a waft of stale perspiration. I open the door quickly and get out.

We go up the stairs, in the door and through to the lounge.

'This is very nice,' I remark. What else can I say? 'I like the lounge. The curtains tone in so well.'

'I've got a friend who knows a lot about these things, and she chose them. Actually, she lived here for a while.'

Another one! How long did she last? Murray moves around the table towards me with *that* look in his eye.

I say, 'What can you see from the balcony?'

He opens the doors and we step outside. The night air is fresh and I shiver. Maybe I'm just scared. He moves closer again and the arm goes around me. I slip sideways.

'What suburb is that over there?' I point.

'Gladesville.' He moves in on me again, so I turn and go inside.

'I'm tired, Murray – I'd like to go home now, please.'

'Okay, okay,' he says, and I head for the door.

We make it to the car without Murray trying anything else, and when we get to my block of units, he parks underneath.

I thank him, but he's already got his door open. He says, 'I'll see you up the stairs. It's dark around here.'

I'll take my chances, Romeo, I'm thinking.

'It's all right, Murray. Really.' I give in, or maybe I don't have any say because up the three flights of stairs we go. I think of knocking on Stacey's door on the second floor as we pass, reassured by the thought of his 25-year-old, six feet of brawn. But the lights are out. Either he's out or he's gone to bed. I'll just have to get rid of this creep at my door.

My hand is shaking and I can hardly get the key in the lock. My throat is dry and my heart pounding. I open the door, take a step inside and turn to say 'Goodnight!'

But he's not there. He's gone. Somehow, he's slipped or slithered through behind me as I was opening the door. Now he's inside my unit, already sitting on the lounge and grinning his smarmy grin.

'Look, Murray, I'm tired . . .'

'Yeah. But at least you could make me a coffee before I go.'

I sigh and put on the jug. While in the kitchen I wonder how to get him out. I'd like to be able to say 'Just push off, buster!' and make him go, but years of politeness inhibit me. Instead I make two cups of coffee and carry them in with two scotch fingers on a dish. I sit on the opposite end of the lounge with the small table and the tray between us.

Next thing I know, Murray has somehow moved the table and slid up the lounge towards me. I cringe into the corner.

He puts his arm around me and tries to smooch. I smell stale perspiration mixed with aftershave – or is it hair oil?

I wriggle free and stand up. 'Murray, I'd like to go to bed . . .' Oh, my gosh. That's a mistake. That's probably just what he's got in mind himself. I rephrase. 'I'd like you to go home – now. It's late. Goodnight.'

I open the door. I hope he leaves. If it comes to the worst I'll have to rush down and knock on Stacey's door. But what if he's out? Then, unexpectedly, Murray heads out the door as hoped, saying, 'I'll ring you!' and he's gone down the stairs. I lock the door, still shaking. I get changed for bed, but all the time I'm half-expecting a knock on the door. I make sure the bolt is secure.

I sit on the side of my bed for a while. He's unbalanced, I think. What will I do when he rings? I'm sure he will, and I fall into bed. I'm exhausted, so I sleep well.

The next morning is a Saturday, and at 8.00 the phone rings. I answer.

'Hello, lovely lady!' It's him. My heart misses a beat. 'I'm just ringing to say how much I enjoyed the evening. I'm coming over to take you out for the day.'

'No! No, don't do that, Murray. I'm going out. Just getting ready to go away for the weekend.'

'You're trying to put me off, I know! But I'm coming anyway.'

'Well – I'm just going out. Yes, Stacey,' I call out, pretending he's there, 'I'll only be a minute – I'm almost ready! I have to go, Murray. There's no future in this. We don't have anything in common. Please don't call me again. Goodbye.'

As I hang up, I hear him say 'Wait! Cancel whatever it is . . .'

I sit by the phone, shaking. My hands are sweating and my heart is pounding. But I only sit for a moment. I dial Barbara Easterby, a friend in Goulburn, and tell her I'm coming down, and would like to stay the night. I'll explain when I get there. I rush into the bedroom, grab some clothes, run down the stairs to my car and take off within five minutes. I am still half-expecting to see Murray arrive before I can get out of the driveway.

Sunday night I arrive home at 11.30, fearful I will find him waiting outside my door. Instead, there are two big boxes of biscuits and a love letter addressed to 'Lovely Lady'.

Monday, I buy an answering machine and monitor my calls. He keeps ringing but I don't answer him. I follow up a tentative arrangement to move house and set it up for Saturday. After school each day I go out to Macquarie Uni – even on the days I don't have to go. I eat dinner there and each night I stay late at the library. Stacey offers to come up and protect me if he turns up. I ask my brother Tony to come and help me move.

Friday, I have the phone disconnected.

Saturday, I move.

When it came to moving, Stacey was in his element. He knew where to hire a truck, he said he could drive it and he helped me pack up. My brother Tony and his wife Peg came to help, and brought ten-year-old Scott. They all stayed the night. In the morning, Stacey let himself in to finish packing the truck and helped himself to breakfast. Scott found him fascinating. When Stacey had gone downstairs, Scott told us about Stacey's breakfast. His eyes bulged.

'He had eight eggs!' he said. '*Eight eggs!* He kept breaking them into the pan and made an omelette. *And* he had toast!'

I didn't complain. Stacey was such a good friend.

By night-time I was settled in Bourke Street, Woolloomooloo. Stacey had made several trips, carried most of my stuff into the new house, cleaned out the unit at West Ryde and taken the truck back.

My new home in Woolloomooloo was the antithesis of my little unit. It was a big semidetached house with four spacious bedrooms, a lounge room, a dining room, and a partly renovated kitchen. The rent was reasonable because the house was under renovation, and the deal was that the owners could have access to work on it when they needed to. My idea was to advertise for housemates to help with the rent.

The most striking thing about the house was, as real estate people like to say, 'location, location'. From the front verandah you stepped right onto the footpath of busy Bourke Street, and there was always a queue of cars at our front gate waiting for the lights to change at William Street. When you walked up to the corner you met the street girls, often shivering in their skimpy gear, waiting for customers to pick them up. And our tiny backyard was overshadowed by multistoreyed commercial buildings on William Street, with their bright neon signs blinking down over us in the night. It was an interesting place to live for someone who had spent thirty years relatively cloistered in a convent.

Sister Berice from my convent at Singleton was working in Sydney at the time, and was in charge of selling up the Sisters of Mercy novitiate at Waitara when it closed down, so I asked her if I could buy some of the beds and other furniture. Stacey borrowed a truck again from somewhere and we collected beds, chairs, little bedroom units with hanger space on one side and a set of drawers on the other, and study tables from the Waitara novices' bedrooms, and furnished the house with all this ex-convent stuff. We had mats for the floors, crockery for the kitchen and even an old TV which still worked. I found it amusing that my new little 'community' would be living among all these convent hand-me-downs.

The week after I moved in, I advertised in the *Sydney Morning Herald* for housemates, and only interviewed the young people who rang. I figured I would have more control of the place if I had young companions, and that way I could 'make up the game'. I thought that I would organise the household, and the rent they paid me would pretty much cover the rent I had to pay for the house. That way I could save up my salary to buy a house of my own one day.

The people who called ranged from older single men looking for boarding-house-type accommodation to a young man who wanted to know if any sex would be involved in the arrangement. I said 'No', and he replied, 'Not even if I had a nine-inch dick?' I said 'No' again, and wished him luck in finding somewhere to put his nine-inch dick. Not bad, I thought, for an ex-nun!

A lady who rang from the south coast was looking for a place for her two teenage daughters. The elder was to attend teachers' college, and the younger one was already working as an apprentice painter with State Rail. The apprentice currently lived with relatives, but the girls wanted to live together. I had two beds in the large front bedroom upstairs, which also had a closed-in balcony that could be used as a study. This sounded promising to her, so I suggested a meeting. They were coming to Sydney the next day.

When I opened the door to the girls and their mum I got a shock. Not so much because they were Aboriginal, but because I found I had a reaction. I guess I had immediate mental visions of some Aboriginal homes I had seen when passing Eveleigh Street in Redfern, covered in graffiti, with rubbish all over the road, and I didn't want my house to look like that. However, I decided to take these girls as I found them.

Their mum was concerned, as would be all of the mums I knew, about her two daughters being so far from home, in a strange city. She was looking for a safe place for them. I offered them the room, and I needn't have worried. Sharon and Yvette were unsophisticated, friendly and good 'family' to have in the house.

Two young men completed the household. Greg was from New Zealand, John was from Tasmania, and they were both looking for a 'sharing' house. The five of us all got on well, had dinner together at night, talked for ages over the dinner table and laughed a lot. I felt like everyone's favourite aunt. The fact I had been a nun was just 'interesting', and the girls couldn't wait to bring home every nun joke they came across.

I did the shopping, arranged a cooking and cleaning roster and laid down a few ground rules, like use of the phone. Living in a community for so many years was a good preparation for sharing a house. When I came home at night from Macquarie Uni it was wonderful to have someone say to me, 'Come and sit down here and watch TV. I'll get your dinner for you – we kept it warm.' It sure beat the lonely days at

West Ryde when I'd come in at 9.30 p.m. and need to think about getting something to eat for myself before bed.

So we settled into life, just down the road from Kings Cross. We had the occasional male 'customer' ring the door-bell and insist he had been serviced by a young woman here. One came in the wee small hours. He was intoxicated and aggro. Graham – the 'gentle giant' who had taken John's room when he moved out – blocked him from forcing his way down the hall, pushed him out the front door with some gusto and slammed it behind him.

Graham thought he should report it, as he felt the man might have been hurt. He admitted he saw him land hard in the gutter. In the morning when he went up to the police sta-tion, they asked him to go to the hospital and check the identity of a patient admitted after 'a violent struggle'. There was our man – sober, in plaster and sporting a few cuts where he had hit the road. He recognised Graham and shrank into his bedclothes with a quick intake of breath. His story, how-ever, was a bit different from what really happened.

Our neighbours in the shared house next door were friendly and of the 'borrowing a cup of sugar or an egg' vari-ety. Just down the back lane was the entrance to the Matthew Talbot Shelter for Homeless Men run by the St Vincent de Paul Society, and some of the men often spent the day in the sun in the back lane when they left the shelter in the morning. One time a couple of them asked Greg if they could use our hose to put some water in their meths, and settled outside the back gate with their brown-paper bags for a day's drinking and sleeping on an old carpet someone had put out.

That was another thing about the area. People put things

out when they didn't want them any more. There were a lot of people living in illegal squats across the road in houses marked for demolition by the Department of Main Roads, so if a carpet, mattress or old cupboard appeared on the footpath, it didn't stay long.

Sometimes things just disappeared to be used by a new owner, but often they were replaced by something not quite as good. We had an old cupboard in the laundry out the back which had come in from the footpath. It had no doors but Greg scrubbed it out and gave it a coat of green paint. I made a couple of curtains from remnants of material picked up cheaply and it became quite presentable. It eventually migrated inside somewhere.

The renovating owners left another old cupboard on the front verandah. It was full of bits of old carpet and underlay offcuts from the job which might be needed later. We noticed that this cupboard kept slipping out towards the railing near the footpath. I was mystified, because there didn't seem to be that much slope on the floor. I moved it back out of the weather, and it moved to the front again.

Then, one night, one of the boys saw why: an old man slept there on a piece of the carpet with underlay for a blanket. Every morning before we were about he was gone, the carpet and underlay were folded neatly back in the cupboard and there was no sign he'd been there. We used to say there were six of us living there – five inside, and one on the front verandah. That was until someone tripped over him one night just as he was settling down. He didn't come any more after that, and I was sorry. He'd never been any bother, and had found a warm spot for cold nights.

One day I was sick enough with the flu to stay at home from school. I was there when the postman came and I collected the mail from the letterbox, which was on the front fence near the footpath, and just had one of those lift-up lids. In the box that day was a Social Security cheque addressed to someone none of us had ever heard of.

Graham was interested, as he worked for Social Security. He did some research and it turned out this person didn't exist. It was a scam. Someone had invented an ID, given our address and collected his cheque from our letterbox every payment day as soon as the postman came. He must have been very disappointed to see me at home that day. How many other names and addresses did he have?

School at Saint Scholastica's was going well. It had me running to catch up with all the geography I hadn't taught for years, and it was different marching to someone else's drum. I had been the subject coordinator for many years before I stopped teaching. Now somebody else made up the programs I had to teach but the school was a happy one, and it was great to fit back in so easily. What was more, they paid me well. I had no more money worries. My plan to save most of my salary was going well too, and it was very gratifying to see the deposit for my future house growing in the building society.

The whole share-house arrangement was one of my best ideas, and it was a very stimulating environment. The young people were amazed to learn I didn't know *anything* about modern music, or even the Beatles and Abba, let alone INXS (which I had no idea of how to pronounce!). They taught me much by the simple method of changing the kitchen radio from the ABC or 2CH to stations more in tune with their own tastes.

Stacey turned up regularly at Bourke Street to see if I needed jobs done, and to be fed. He became good friends with my young housemates and brought his girlfriend, Christine, to join our circle when she came over to visit from Western Australia. Once, when we were out, he emptied the fridge of all the leftovers – and even the sweets I had made for visitors that evening. He was most apologetic, though. Apple pie was his great delight, and whenever I had made one I learnt to be quite resourceful about where I hid it. Stacey could smell an apple pie even hours after it was out of the oven. It was like a game and no matter where I hid the pie he still found it (though he usually refrained from eating it), and crowed with delight that he had got the better of me in this contest of hide and seek.

Stacey was one of the really good things that happened to me during that terrible year at West Ryde. It was a sad day for all of us when he said goodbye to go home to the west, marry, take up an office job, and raise a family. We've kept in touch, though.

Meantime, my other young friends expanded my horizons in many ways. They thought my emphasis on a tidy house was a bit obsessive and that my taste in TV was quaint. They insisted I learn to watch the soaps on TV channels I hardly knew existed. I found many of the things they told me about life quite eye-opening, like the taking of turns during work hours to have a sleep behind the carriages when they were being repainted at the rail yards, and the things that happened at parties involving alcohol and sex.

They loved it when I bought a kitten, especially the girls, and the cat had a very happy life till it took to sleeping on the second-bottom step of the stairs. It caused World War III in the household when one of the boys accidentally stood on it when bounding down the stairs one day. The girls rushed it to the vet by taxi, and were very distressed when it died. There were tears and violent recriminations, which we only recovered from when I eventually got another kitten from the Cat Protection Society.

Life in the inner city was fascinating, and my social life improved as well.

# 26

## Moving to Chippendale

I was sad when, at the end of the year, we had to move as our landlords decided to begin the renovations full-time. Greg went up the street one Saturday morning and bought the *Sydney Morning Herald*, and we all scanned the 'To Let' columns. He had decided to move somewhere with me, while the girls thought they would try a unit on their own in the eastern suburbs. Graham went off to live with an aunt.

Greg and I set out on our rounds, armed with the paper and a list of the 'open for inspection' times. We headed for Ultimo, Newtown and Chippendale, or anywhere near Sydney Uni, as by now I had finished at Macquarie and was enrolled in a masters degree at Sydney. We saw some run-down, dark, smelly and dirty places, with stained walls and worn-out carpets. Then we came across a terrace house on Abercrombie Street in Chippendale.

The landlord introduced himself as Frank and showed us in. The little house was light and airy, the carpet was clean and the place had been freshly painted. Frank was retired, he told us, and living on the income of several properties, so he attended to things himself. He and Greg got on like a house on fire. In the kitchen, however, I was surprised to see gaping spaces where the doors of the cupboards should be.

'There are no doors on the kitchen cupboards,' I said.

Frank sighed. 'No. That's the short answer. The slightly longer answer is that there used to be, but the last tenants took them off and burnt them in the old fireplace in the dining room.'

A distressed account followed about the previous tenants. How a motorbike was pulled apart and rebuilt on the lounge room carpet, how dirt was ground into upstairs carpets, the filthy bathroom, and how there had been an unbelievable accumulation of rubbish in both the house and the backyard. The whole house, he said, also had a nasty smell. When at last he was able to get the place vacant, he had some retired men he used for maintenance work strip it right out. They threw away all the smelly furniture and carpets, painted everything freshly and laid 'new' second-hand green carpet (which turned out to be older but clean Wilton carpet, much admired later by our visitors who knew about these things). Even the yard was cleaned up. Frank said they had to hire a truck to make several trips to the tip with it all.

Greg and I went into a huddle. After all the places we'd seen, this clean, airy little house with the sun streaming through the back windows looked pretty good, so we said, 'Yes. We'll take it.'

Frank was so obviously relieved to have such respectable and clean-looking tenants that he rang his wife immediately to tell her, and dropped the rent by $5 a week to $95. Even I could tell this was a pretty good deal for a three-bedroom house with separate lounge and dining, even if one of the bedrooms was up a ladder to the attic. I thanked him, and well-spoken Greg made a further good impression by shaking his hand firmly.

Over time, we had a few different tenants for the attic room, until my nephew Sean (my brother Jim's son, from Wellington) asked to move in. He reckoned my housemates were on a pretty good wicket, with such a nice, clean, well-organised house, and me doing the cooking at least every third day.

So there we were. I got yet another kitten, as our Bourke Street kitten had wandered off or been stolen, and we called her Oedipus – Edie, for short, with Puss as her last name – and our happy home was complete. Except for Sheba, who arrived later, by way of adopting me as her new protector and provider. I never knew where she came from – she just appeared. I think she had been letting herself in the back window, eating some of Edie's dinner in the kitchen and sleeping on the lounge for quite some time before I knew about it. When I got home one night I found a tabby cat asleep on the lounge as I came in the front door. I was indignant at its boldness, and thought it was the tabby tomcat from down the street, so I chased it out the window with some energy. But it must have been Sheba, trying us out.

One morning my neighbour Jansis leaned over the fence to talk to me while a dark greeny–grey tabby with lots of black markings sat on the fence between us.

'Cecilia, you're the kind of person who'd take a cat. This one has been hanging around for weeks.'

I looked at the cat sitting there preening itself.

'I've been feeding it,' she said, 'but our lease specifically excludes animals inside, and she wants to come inside all the time. She's such a nice, friendly cat.'

'I don't think so, Jansis,' I said. 'I have one cat already.'

'I wonder where she came from,' said Jansis. 'Someone's loved her – she's so affectionate.'

The cat walked along the top of the fence, leaning towards me as I looked at her. She purred and I put out a finger to scratch her head. 'You're not a bad cat, are you?' I said.

That afternoon when I opened the back door after school the cat was sitting on the doormat. She stood up and stretched as if she had been waiting there for me all day. Then she calmly walked inside, sat on the carpet in the dining room, looked at me, purred, and proceeded to lick herself. She had come home.

Sean was disgusted with me for letting Sheba move in with us.

'You don't know where she's been, Ceal. She's a stray!'

I was hooked on Sheba already, but said I'd make enquiries at school if anyone wanted her. No one did, so she stayed.

Sean was still not happy, and in the end he said, 'Either that cat goes, Ceal, or I do.'

It turned out he wanted to move in with a friend anyway, so I helped him pack. Whenever he visited over the next thirteen years he would look at Sheba asleep on the back deck in the sun or on a lounge chair and say 'Well, Sheba, I guess you won!' But when she eventually died he told me, 'Well – I guess I won in the end!' Poor Sheba had a cancerous growth and had to be put down. She died in my arms.

As for Edie, she wandered off somewhere, but not before the local tom had been busy and both my cats had litters of five kittens each within a few days of each other. Sheba insisted on bedding hers down under my bed in the far corner. I moved them. She put them back. I moved them. She put them back. I gave in and put a box with an old cardigan under the bed. When the kittens were ten weeks old I put an ad in the paper and sold them for a few dollars each. With the proceeds I took both cats around to the veterinary school at Sydney Uni and had them desexed.

By then I was doing a master's degree at Sydney Uni in psychology and had transferred to Saint Augustine's College at Brookvale where I was school counsellor. It was a happy school, and a good job for which they paid me very well to talk to the students.

I set out every morning in my 'new' second-hand hatchback before 7 a.m. to get across the Harbour Bridge before the traffic was too bad, as I needed to be at school about 8. I saw boys in my office before or during school, took some classes and groups, talked with staff and did occasional parent interviews.

It felt as if I had come full circle from the days when, as Sister Mary Scholastica, I was always in trouble for talking to the students about their troubles all those years ago.

Meanwhile, our landlord Frank had become a frequent visitor at the house. He came over each week to collect the rent, often when Greg was there. They became great friends, and had lots of discussions about property ownership and its management problems. One of Frank's cherished projects was a development somewhere up in the Blue Mountains, being held up by the local council. He told Greg that if it came through, he would sell his Sydney houses to fund it.

We realised this meant he would put our little house on the market, and I got the idea to buy it from him. I had already saved some thousands of dollars as a deposit towards this end. Judy, a friend from Newcastle, had lent me $5000 at no interest to be paid back whenever, and Greg Cahill – a nephew and bright young accountancy student from Newcastle – gave me some good advice about how to increase my deposit. I had one credit card which I was very careful to pay off each month, so he said I'd have a good credit record. His suggestion was to apply for several other credit cards on the same day and write on the application forms that I only had one other card. This was true. That way, he said, the banks would each check out the good credit rating on my one existing card, and issue me with a new card. We agreed I'd have to be circumspect as to how much cash I borrowed off these cards, and be able to service the minimum repayment each month until I could pay off the full amount. By doing this I was able to raise a fair deposit, so I started to make enquiries about a loan.

I had spoken to a bank employee about loans some time before but was quite put off by the implication that the bank didn't like to lend to single women, even if they had a good job. They evidently preferred to deal with a man. Someone told me the building societies were more obliging, so I made an appointment in the city with a loans officer. Meantime, I spoke to Frank and we agreed on a purchase price of $52 500. This was a very good deal, given that I sold it a few years later for over $100 000, but at the time it seemed a very big commitment. I asked my nephew Michael (Jim's son from Wellington), who was a mature-age student at one of the Sydney universities, if he would come along for moral support.

The loans officer was a cheery, bright-eyed woman of mature age, who was most encouraging and immediately lowered my age by ten years to make repayment of the loan easier. Allowing for stamp duty and a few other costs, we calculated that I needed to borrow $38 000, which to me seemed an enormous sum. I nervously filled out the forms, provided the necessary documents, and began the exciting process of becoming a home owner.

# 27

# Mary Comes to Town

Butterflies flutter in my tummy as I stop by the mirror for the twentieth time to check my hair, make-up and general appearance. What will they think of me in my new life and about this new start I made at forty-seven? I pat my hair again. What will they think of this little house I'm buying?

It's the May school holidays of 1984, about 10.30 in the morning. Today I have my little Victorian terrace more or less to myself as I wait. My anxious eyes check the place again. Hot scones are cooling on the bench in the tiny kitchen and the kettle is steaming on the old gas stove, ready to make the tea. The table in my dining room is all set with a freshly ironed cloth and my best china, such as it is.

I go out the front door onto the footpath of Abercrombie Street for the fifth time and look up the street. This time I can finally see them coming! They've just turned the corner from the Redfern railway station and are walking up the street. They have the look of a couple who've strayed into the slums of the London docks during the time of Dickens, and expect to meet Fagin or Bill Sykes at the very next turn.

I wave. Mary, my eldest sister, waves back. I can almost sense her relief as she hastens her steps even more and turns to speak to Bill, my brother-in-law. What's she saying? Something like 'Come on, Bill – hurry up. There she is. Let's get inside!'

They step quickly from the footpath into my lounge room, which is what you do in a terrace, and I close the door behind them. Mary sighs audibly.

'Thank goodness we're here. This Redfern is strange. All those Aborigines sitting outside the station, even in the middle of that street. And the mess they've made with all the painting and stuff on the walls of the houses! Don't you feel strange living here? It's not a bit like Newcastle.'

'No,' I say, 'it's not like Newcastle. But I've got used to living here. It's just the inner city, and the Aborigines generally don't bother you. That was Eveleigh Street near the station. Lots of Aborigines live around there.'

'Do you have break-ins and things?' Mary asks.

'Well, I haven't had any. You've got to be careful not to leave anything visible in your car, though, or it might be broken into. But we've got bars on all our windows, deadlocks and security doors back and front as well.'

Mary glances furtively over her shoulder, out through the bars of my open lounge room window, as someone walks by on the footpath right outside.

'Aren't you afraid, living so close to the street? People could look in the window and see you.'

I don't tell her that's exactly what happens. Instead,

I change the subject and say, 'Come and have a cup of tea in the dining room. You must be ready for one after leaving so early.'

'Thanks. That'd be nice.' They follow me to the next room. 'Oh! This is a pleasant room, with that sun coming through the window. And there are your stairs. Do you sleep up there?'

'Yes,' I say.

A terrace house can be a shock for someone from the suburbs – no front fence, no garden, and steep little stairs climbing up the side of your dining room wall. Two up and two down is definitely not what Mary's used to.

'The bathroom–toilet is out here behind the kitchen if you'd like to go.'

'Thanks,' says Mary. 'What a funny little kitchen – but it's got all you need, I suppose. Through this door . . . ?'

I watch as she steps into the bathroom and immediately backs around sideways into the handbasin as she tries to close the door and get to the toilet behind it. What does she think of the tiny space to put her feet, I wonder, while she's on the toilet, perched with her knees almost pushed against the back of the door?

I make the tea and am carrying in scones and biscuits when Mary comes back and very quietly gives Bill his instructions about the bathroom being so small and cramped.

Sheba wanders in from the backyard to check out the visitors.

'Oh, hello puss!' says Mary. 'I didn't know you had a cat. What's its name?'

'Sheba – because she's black but beautiful, like the Queen of Sheba from the Bible.'

'Oh yes,' she says vaguely, not terribly interested in the Queen of Sheba. Then, 'Well, come on puss. Out you go. You shouldn't be inside.'

'I'm afraid I've got news for you. She lives inside.'

'Oh – no! It doesn't, does it? What would your mother say? A cat inside the house!' I note the reproach in the way Mum has become 'your', not 'our'.

Sheba settles herself on the carpet, spread out in a favourite patch of sunlight.

'I like her inside. She's good company.' I smile, and refrain from adding 'and she sleeps on the end of my bed every night'.

I pour the tea and pass around milk and sugar.

'Now,' says Mary, 'who lives here with you? I know you've told me before.'

'Greg, who's from New Zealand and is a sales rep for a big fruit juice company. He's at work today. And Ivan, who's a commercial pilot.'

'A pilot? Really!'

'Yes. Ivan's been flying cargo planes around the Northern Territory and the Kimberley for years, and now he's down here for twelve months to upgrade his licence.' Mary thinks about this, and I can see she's impressed. 'I'm afraid he had a long night at a cousin's party in Chinatown last night, though, and hasn't appeared yet.'

'And do you have to do all the washing and cooking for your boarders?'

'No. They're not boarders. They're called housemates. Everyone looks after themselves and helps around the place. We take turns with the cooking. I usually do the shopping and Greg comes and helps me most of the time.'

There are sounds of movement upstairs as Ivan climbs down the steel ladder from his attic. He knows I'm having visitors and said he'd be going off to his TAFE course. When he appears, Mary's eyes begin to pop. I introduce them and Ivan goes on through to the bathroom.

Mary stutters, 'He's . . . he's Chinese!'

'Mmm,' I say. 'He was born in Australia, though. His grandparents or their parents migrated here long ago.'

'Oh!' she pauses, digesting this, thinking about what to say. I don't offer any help.

'Don't you feel funny,' she says eventually, 'using the same toilet and bathroom? I mean sitting on the same toilet seat after him?'

'Ivan's very clean, Mary. The colour doesn't come off on the seat.'

'No – I suppose not. It's just that . . . I mean, is it really *safe* for you to live with these strangers? You don't know where they go or what they do when they go in and out of here . . . I mean . . .'

'You mean it's not living with family, like you're used to. But it's all right, really. They're both good young people and easy to live with. Especially Greg. He's a real friend. It all works very well.'

'I suppose so.' But she's doubtful. 'It's all so different . . .'

After lunch she pulls out her latest gallery of grandchildren photos and we chat about the family. I tell them about my teaching job and uni studies at night. Then I show Mary around the house while Bill reads the paper.

It's all so different from her suburban house. Mary is not tempted to go up the steel ladder to Ivan's attic and can't quite believe the ladder is the only way to get up there. She's surprised how comfortable my bedroom is, even if a bit small, and intrigued to find the mail has arrived on the lounge room carpet through the slit in the front door.

They're going home to Newcastle early. Mary wants to be safely out of the city and in a train before dark. We stand in my little backyard in the warm sun, relaxed and glad to be here together, sharing our lives briefly. Mary has always been a lovely big sister. She took me to see *Bambi* when I was five, and always had time to listen. When I was a teenager she often had me over for meals or to play with the baby. Despite her undisguised surprise at some parts of my new life, I'm touched that she's made the effort to come so far, in so many ways, to visit me.

I'm able to tell her a bit about things since I've come to Sydney, then she tells me all the news from Newcastle, mainly about my brothers' families. We have some laughs.

'Look,' she says. 'I'm glad we came. I can see you're managing okay, and I won't need to be worrying so much about you.'

She turns and looks back at the house, at the skillion kitchen and laundry tacked on the back below the tiny balcony outside my bedroom, and the dormer window of Ivan's attic poking through the steep slate roof.

'It's certainly different!' she says. 'This place might not be what I'd choose, but if it's what you want, I'd like to help.'

She digs into the pocket of her coat and pulls out a thick roll of grubby banknotes, with a rubber band around them. They are all small currency notes.

'I've been saving up for you. A bit from here, a bit from

there. No one knows about it. Not even Bill. It's just between you and me. I want you to have it.' She pushes the roll into my hand. 'It's not much, but it's to help you buy your house.'

I've got a lump in my throat.

'I hope you'll be very happy here . . .' she says.

Dad is staying at Mary's while Mum is sick in hospital. Mary is careful never to wear her slacks while Dad is in the house. It's many years since the time Dad made her take back the first pair she brought home, and it's only in the last few years that she's decided to wear pants.

She is very proud of her new TV set and says, 'Would you like to watch the news, Dad?'

'No thanks.' He's adamant. 'Don't approve of that new-fangled television stuff.'

He sits at the table with his back to the TV and reads the paper. When the cricket report comes on Mary can see he's listening, then he peeks sideways over his shoulder.

'No,' he tells me when I visit, 'I never watch that TV.'

## 28

## Never So Bad Again

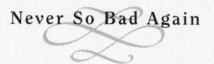

'Things have been really bad . . . but I've survived. They'll never be so bad again. I have a house with a tree in the back-yard, and a cat.'

I am sitting in my chair opposite Doctor Craig Powell in his room at Gladesville, where I've been regularly visiting him after school for nearly twelve months. I met him after my disastrous encounter with the law, when I felt confused and humiliated. I needed to talk through lots of things with someone. Rob Hockley found Doctor Powell for me. He had recently returned to Sydney from overseas and set up a psycho-therapy practice, and he had space for a new client.

So began a painful, but eventually liberating, journey of reflection on my life and all that it had held for me so far. I spent lots of time crying hot tears and pouring out tales of resentment, hurt and pain.

I cried for the loss of my youth; my family life at home; and for the family of my own I had never had. I sobbed for the loss of my friends of thirty years, and the loneliness of my life since I left the convent. I cried bitter tears again over the deaths of my mother and father, the years I had never been able to visit them in our own home, and the things I had never been able to do for them because of the isolation of my life in the convent.

I cried for all the humiliations and seeming cruelties of convent life, and all the little inhumanities and coldness. As I sobbed with the pain of it all, I could tell my understanding doctor that lots of those things which were cold and cruel and seemed inhuman were because 'that's just the way it was'. Not so much 'inhuman', but lacking in warm human values. That was the way religious life had grown to be at that time, and the way people thought it had to be lived.

I told him how the superior opened our letters, and had the right to read or even withhold them from us, both the letters which arrived for us and those we wrote. How we had to ask permission to write a letter. Permission might be refused, and if it was permitted, you were given just one sheet of paper. You then put your unsealed envelope and letter on the superior's desk for posting. This was a humiliating way for grown professional women to live, but again *it was just the way it was*.

The way this custom had originated was lost in the mists of time. It began in the days when not everyone could read and write, and the obligation was put on superiors to open and read the subjects' letters to them and make sure someone wrote a reply for them. It was a small example of a custom that had evolved into an humiliation, but had never begun that way.

Things had changed over the years, though, I told him. By the time I left, many of these distressing customs had been dropped. I needed to talk about them now because I was still hurting from the pain and resentment I had suppressed all those years over the many small inhumane and unjust things I had lived through, and the violence all this had done to a warm, outgoing personality.

I told him of the pain and indecision over leaving the convent, then the insecurity of having no income and applying for the dole. Of the sixty jobs I'd applied for and the hurt I felt that no one wanted me. I had felt a failure, unemployable, and feared what would become of me if I couldn't get a job. I cried at the unfairness of it all.

Through all of these tempests of sorrow, loss and grief, Doctor Powell sat opposite. He let me sob my way through them and very occasionally gave me a brief but warm hug when my fifty minutes was up and he turned me out the door to go to Macquarie Uni, or home, still sobbing and blowing my nose furiously.

He reflected back to me what I was saying, what I was grieving about, and helped me understand my grieving. Though he maintained his impartial distance, I could feel his kindness and sympathy, and was warmed by his understanding and acceptance.

When the tempests of sorrow abated, or passed for the moment, I began to reflect on my life and talk about all those things which come up from the depths when you get talking to a psychotherapist. I talked about religion, home, and all the things in life that had led me to the convent.

It became clear that my dad had been the greatest influence

in my life, whereas previously I'd have said it was Mum. Dad was so upright; such a good man; so sincere in his faith and his commitment to his family. And Dad was so important to us. You loved him, you respected him, and you would never do anything that would have caused him pain.

Dad had been absorbed into my psyche and spoke somehow from deep inside me, influencing my decisions and checking whatever would be offensive to him. It seemed that maybe a lot of my decisions in life had been made to please him, or at least to avoid things that would have distressed him. Would I have left the convent if he had still been alive? Probably not. Was such a strong sense of vocation at sixteen years of age partly fear of what I might do if I embarked on adult life out in the world? Was I afraid of my sexual side and my possible predilection for the hedonistic life if I did go to Sydney Uni?

I didn't know all the answers, so I had to sit with the questions.

But today, as I sit here with Doctor Powell, I've reached a point where I'm at peace with it all, and glad to have come through it. It's a point where I can say, 'I've survived, and it will never be so bad again.' A point where I feel I can let go of the hurts of the past.

I surprise myself with the tree and the cat. The house I understand. I feel secure there. I have a job now and a mortgage, and no one will ever take my home from me. It's mine. Well, mine and the building society's, but I am determined to be independent and safe after all those storms.

But the tree and the cat? Hot tears spring again and I don't know why I'm crying. My doctor is gentle and asks me what is so important about the tree and the cat. I can't answer. It is as if I've been all at sea in a terrible storm, and at last I've found a safe harbour away from the waves which have buffeted and submerged me. At times I've feared I'd drown.

Now, I have anchored my battered barque to this house with a tree. My cat and I are at home, and we face the future together.

# 29

## More Men

The Phoenix Singles Club at the Occidental Hotel, York Street in the city. Saturday night. Thick, choking smoke haze. Brittle laughter above the din of canned music. Couples drifting by, bodies close, swaying erotically in time with the music. People standing alone around the wall, holding a drink in silence. A few groups.

What am I doing here? I shuffle a bit, and think about running home. Then I remember my friend Lenore, who met Ron here, the first night he came, almost as soon as he arrived. I look towards the door, then around the room through the smoke haze. Yuk! I take another sip of my orange juice and lean back against the wall. An attractive thirty-something in a red pants suit says hello to me and smiles as she heads to the bar.

The door opens again, and I look up hopefully. Will it be 'the one'? A scruffy fifty-something fellow shuffles in. No – he won't do. A good-looking man called Matthew appears and asks me to dance and I'm glad to do so, though dancing is hard work for me. I'm not a natural, and out of practice. But standing around with a drink in your hand and feeling like a fool, or worse, like a mutton chop in a butcher's window (not even lamb!), is no fun. You can pick the sleaze element. They stroll around the room smirking, with a calculating look in their eyes, eyeing the merchandise.

Matthew's about forty-five and presentable. His sports coat fits him well, and his shirt is clean and fresh-looking, unlike most of the others. He moves with a quiet confidence that's reassuring and I begin to relax. We sit. He buys me an orange juice, and we talk a bit above the din.

After a while he says, 'This is awful. Can't hear myself think!'

'Me neither!' I shout.

'Let's go and have a coffee somewhere quieter.'

I nod and collect my things. He seems very respectable. He's polite and gentlemanly – opens the door for me, and stands back to let me through.

'My car's around the corner,' he says, as we go down the stairs. 'I don't know why I came here. It's much worse than when I was here before.'

I already know he's a radio operator on a ship, and he's sailing at 3 a.m.

'Never go to bed the night I sail,' he says. 'Always like to go somewhere. A show, or dinner with friends.' He takes my elbow to guide me across the street. 'Nothing that's on appealed to me, and my friends were all busy.'

We turn the corner. 'Where do you teach?' he asks.

'Glebe,' I say. 'Saint Scholastica's College.'

'I know,' he says. 'Down Glebe Point Road. I have some friends who live near there.'

By now we've reached his car. He opens the door and holds it while I get in. We drive down George Street and around a few side streets. It's only about 10.30 p.m., but we can't find anything open. We chat as we drive and I'm feeling more and more comfortable with him. It's as if I've known him for a long time. We drive up to Circular Quay and into The Rocks. There are a few pubs kicking on with loud music blaring.

'I don't think so!' he says.

'Never mind,' I say. 'It was a nice idea. Just drop me at a taxi rank.'

By now we're looking out at Oxford Street, where there are places open, but we feel out of place among the number of men in twos walking arm-in-arm. This is the gay end of town.

'Look,' says Matthew, 'we're pretty close to my place. Why don't we just pop in there for coffee, before you get your taxi?'

'Okay,' I say. It all sounds perfectly reasonable, and it has been so pleasant with Matthew after the Phoenix Club, I'm happy to go on for a bit.

We park under a newish block of units and go up very clean stairs inside the security door. His unit is very modern, with bright-coloured furniture and rugs on the polished floor. It reminds me of an Ikea showroom, but feels lived-in.

'Make yourself at home,' he says, as he puts on a CD of *Peer Gynt*. I've always loved *Peer Gynt*, but I don't say anything. I like this man. I feel at home with him.

I sit on the lounge looking around at the tasteful prints on the wall. I can hear small noises from the kitchen, and begin to smell brewed coffee. Matthew appears with a platter of dried fruit, rice crackers and cheese.

'Won't be long,' he says, and puts it on the table.

I think it's the 'Won't be long' that does it. If coffee won't be long, what happens after that? There's a catch in my tummy, and I look around.

My God! Here I am calmly sitting in some man's lounge room at eleven o'clock at night. What am I thinking of? What happens after coffee? What does he think of all this? What will he expect? Does he think I'm going to go to bed with him? What usually happens in situations like this? I don't know! Panic sets in. The catch in my tummy has become a strangulating knot, and I'm sitting bolt upright on the edge of the chair. How did I get myself into this? I want to go home.

When Matthew appears from the kitchen carrying a tray with milk and sugar, two porcelain china mugs and a pot of steaming coffee, I jump up.

'I'm sorry!' I blurt. 'I have to go home.'

He stands poised with the tray.

'I should never have come.' I struggle to speak through a dry mouth. 'I don't do this. I've been a nun in a convent for thirty years. I only left a bit over a year ago. I'm sorry. I can't stay. I've got to go. I shouldn't be here . . .'

He's looking at me, completely unfazed.

'Okay,' he says. 'But do you have to go right away? Or can we have the coffee first – seeing that it's all made.'

I gulp. 'I don't know. I have to go . . .'

'All right,' he says. 'Just sit down again, we'll have the coffee, and then I'll come down with you and hail a taxi to take you home.'

He certainly doesn't give the impression of a man about to race me off. Suddenly my knees give way, and I sink down on the lounge. Matthew pours the coffee.

'Milk?' he says, in a very matter-of-fact tone that helps rob the scene of its bizarre quality.

I nod a yes.

'And where were you in the convent?' he asks conversationally, as he hands me my mug.

We talk a bit more, and I calm down again. Then, true to his word, he comes downstairs and hails a taxi for me.

'I'll call you next time I'm in port,' he says as he closes the taxi door.

I'm feeling a fool and am glad to escape, but I say, 'Okay.' That'd be nice, I think, but I won't hold my breath.

I knew somehow that he wouldn't ring, so I didn't wait for the phone call that never came.


Charles appears out of the same smoke and deafening sound of a singles-club gathering at the Occidental Hotel in York Street. He is smallish – about my height – and slightly unkempt. His shirt is a little grubby and his wrinkled suit needs a press. He tells me he's a freelance photographer, fifty-eight, and has no ties. Never married.

I listen. I don't have to tell him anything. He doesn't want to know. We dance, we talk and the evening closes about 11.30. When he asks me where my car is and if I'd like him to walk me to it, I'm grateful. It's unpleasant and even dangerous to walk down into The Rocks under the Harbour Bridge where my car is parked.

When we get there I offer to drop him at his car, but he

says he's going home by taxi from the rank at the end of Macquarie Street, which is miles away. I tell him I'll take him there. Off we go. I stop the car near the taxi rank, but Charles doesn't move to get out. Instead, he says, 'Would you like to come to my place for the night?'

'No, thank you.'

'Well, what about your place?'

'No, thank you,' I say again.

'Why not? Don't you like sex?'

I look at him. He's small and grubby, with a slightly musty odour.

'It's not that,' I say. 'I live with a lot of other people.' Though I should have just said 'Look, I just don't want to have sex with you'.

'I'm sure they wouldn't mind,' he says. 'Come on. Or come to my place.'

'No, thank you.' I'm more firm now.

'Well, can I at least kiss you goodnight?'

I relent, and offer him my cheek. Next thing I know, he's fumbling round his waist, I think I hear a zip, and he produces his most treasured possession.

'Look!' he says. I turn and there is his little penis being cradled in two hands like it is the Hope Diamond.

I reach into my mental catalogue of 'Conduct for Social Occasions', and search in vain for a heading about 'What to Do When a Man Pulls Out His Dick in Your Car'. The closest thing I can find are words of wisdom from my mother from the distant past: 'If a boy tries anything, just get out of the car.' But it doesn't fit. This is *my* car.

'Look,' he's saying again. 'Do you like it?'

'Er . . . yes,' I say (just to be polite).

'No, no . . . I mean do you *really* like it?'

'Yes, yes . . .'

'Do you *really*, *really* like it?'

This is getting ridiculous. I have no idea what to do or say next. I have some sort of idea I need to be kind, not just for his sake, but for mine as well. But I'm feeling a bit desperate.

Just at that moment a police car swings around the corner and comes towards us. The 'thing' disappears hastily, the zip flies up and Charles is gone, across the road into a taxi like a rabbit down its burrow.

Thankfully, I never run into him again.

After this experience with Charles, I decide not to brave the singles club again. Where to go, though? How to meet people? I answer some ads in the paper and in a news sheet called *Mr/Ms*. This time I am careful not to give my home address, and arrange to meet for coffee or a meal in a very public place, just in case.

I meet Ned, who lives in Kirribilli just under the Harbour Bridge, and who says he is an anarchist. I've never known one before, but he doesn't seem very anarchic, and leaves a $15 tip after dinner in a restaurant. This is fascinating for someone like me who lives on $15 a week for housekeeping and food. He's generous and good company, but tells me I'm looking for a life companion, and he's not that sort. His young workmates put the ad in for him because they thought he was too nice a man to be on his own, and ought to have a lady friend.

Geoff is an out-of-work labourer who lives with his delight-ful eleven-year-old daughter in a boarding house for single men. He's frightened of losing her, as the Department of Social Services says the boarding house is not a suitable place to care for her. Her mother is gone. The last I hear of him is a phone call to say she's been taken into foster care till he has a job and a better place to live. He's letting go and sinking into despair, and my heart aches for him and for her. I feel burdened that there's nothing I can do to ease their pain.

Paddy is Irish and the only reply to an ad I put in the 'Matrimonial' column in the *Messenger of the Sacred Heart* – a small Catholic monthly magazine put out by the Jesuits. I thought I'd try the *Messenger* almost as a last desperate resort after reading the column for a few months. There were entries like 'country man looking for permanent relationship. Ex-nun welcome' though I did have misgivings about what kind of man would put such an ad in the paper – even if it was a Catholic one.

Paddy suggests the Catholic Club as the place to meet, and I subsequently decide it must be the only Catholic institution he's been in for a long time. He's quite out of touch with changes in the Church, he's small and sleazy, on a disability pension because of operations on his eyes and tells me he wants sex. Can't live without it. He talks about ladies he's had in his housing commission bedsit with the old biddy next door listening at the wall, her ear glued to a glass tumbler. He's definitely not for me.

'I think John would be good for Cecilia, don't you?' says Helen.

The other two women at lunch look at me thoughtfully, weighing up the question.

'Yes,' says Pat. 'He's gentle and intelligent.'

'You really just might enjoy John,' Lenore says. 'It couldn't hurt to meet him.'

I've been invited to this lunch by Pat, one of the teachers I work with, who knows I don't have many friends in Sydney and thought I would enjoy the company. The talk has turned to my search for a man, how it's going, and how hard this sort of thing is.

The conversation goes on, and I'm more or less an interested observer. I'm a bit surprised to pick up that John is Helen's ex-husband. I've gathered Helen is now in a lesbian relationship with a much younger woman. Helen speaks well of John – even fondly – in that patronising, detached way that lesbians sometimes have towards straight men. The other two know him from way back, as they've all been friends over many years. Eventually it's decided that Lenore will invite both John and me to dinner at her place with her husband, Ron.

When the night comes, I find John is slight and dapper. He's intelligent, and good company in a quiet way. Very sincere. But I have the feeling John asks me for my phone number that first time out of some sense that it is expected of him. Even if this is the case, we get on so well that after a couple of dates he relaxes and begins to enjoy things. John makes a point of taking me to interesting places, like to the Pink Pussycat, a mildly sexy show at Kings Cross, as he knows by now my experience is limited. I think he must have a few misgivings, but I'm blithely going along with the idea. It's quite exciting.

We're sitting in a restaurant somewhere in Kings Cross

before the show when John suddenly says, in the middle of a conversation, 'I hope you're not offended by full frontal nudity?'

'I'm not sure,' I say. 'I don't think so. What do you have in mind? Stripping off here and now?'

'No, no, no!' he stammers, in his very proper way. 'I mean the show. There may be nudity in the show.' We both burst out laughing, as he realises I'm teasing him. I laugh a lot with John.

He's a gentleman too. He drives a Mercedes. A very old, well-cared for Mercedes, of which he's very proud. He picks me up to go out, and every time we stop he's out of his seat and around the other side to open my door and hold it for me while I get out. I quite like this attention, and decide I could get used to it.

If we go on a picnic he insists on carrying all the baskets, boxes, esky, cushions and blanket from the car, even if he has to make several trips. He says it's his job as they may be heavy. For someone who spent thirty years lugging around everything to be moved from somewhere to somewhere else in a manless world, this is very pleasant. I feel important and looked after, and I begin to feel very warmly about him. Is John 'the one' I will learn to love, and who will love me?

For the first time I find I feel special, and learn to accept it graciously. I learn how to enjoy dining out and dining in. To enjoy the many things he does to give me pleasure, and the little gifts he finds for me. We talk and talk, and he *is* as gentle as the girls had said.

We have lots of fun together. I find that fun is a commodity he hasn't had a lot of over the years. As I get to know him better, he begins to open up about past hurts. He partly blames himself for the breakdown of his marriage because he thinks he isn't an interesting enough person.

I tell him that *I* find him interesting, and my heart aches for someone who can feel like that about themselves. He says he and Helen had not been close for some time when she fell in love with a young woman. He moved out into a small flat on the side of the house, and left the place to them.

We've now been going out for three or four months and have just been exploring The Rocks after lunch one Sunday afternoon. We went to the theatre the night before, and I'm enjoying the company and cultural life. We come home to my place as usual, and John sits me down on the lounge.

I ask him if he'll stay for dinner.

'No,' he says, 'I'm not staying for tea tonight.' There's something serious in his tone, and I suddenly feel apprehensive.

'Cecilia, you may have noticed I've been working my way through a program I set myself of things I wanted to do with you,' he says.

'No,' I say. 'I haven't noticed.'

'Well,' he says, 'the part of The Rocks I took you to today was the last on my list.'

'Oh.'

'I've known for quite a while,' he says, 'that this relationship had to finish. You're looking for something permanent. I'm not.' He clears his throat. 'So I've been feeling it's unfair of me to lead you on, no matter how much I've enjoyed being with you.'

I'm sitting very still and feel like a block of wood. John takes my hand.

'I'm not a good investment of your time and affections,' he says. 'You're better off without me.'

Inside a voice is screaming 'No!', but I say nothing. I can't think of anything to say.

'So,' he says, 'it's better to make a clean break. I've really enjoyed our friendship and sharing all those things I love about Sydney with you.' He squeezes my cold hand. 'I'm sorry this seems to be such a surprise to you. I thought you would have guessed over the last month.'

'No,' I say. 'I had no idea.' I begin to search for all the hints I haven't picked up, the clues I must have missed.

'Well,' he says again, 'this is how it is. It's better if I just go.' His eyes are misty as I look at him. 'I'm so sorry for hurting you.'

I still can't think of anything to say, so he goes on. 'I think you're such a lovely person and deserve to be happy. I do hope you find the kind of man you're looking for!'

He stands up, kisses me gently on the forehead, and is gone.

I'm left sitting alone on the lounge on a Sunday afternoon.

# 30

## 'Midnight Matchmaker' Again

After John, I nurse my hurt for a couple of months and concentrate on my uni studies and school. This search for a man – a reliable, available, genuine man – is hard work, and fraught with the danger of disappointments. Then I recover a bit, feel a renewal of the urge to find a life companion whom I could love and who would love me.

Where to next? I remember my first foray into dating through 2GB 'Midnight Matchmaker', and decide I'll give it another go. I'm not strictly supposed to call twice, but I've moved and use my Chippendale address. I change my name, make up my spiel and ring Brian Wiltshire again. It's not so bad the second time around, but I'm still nervous. After a week or so, I get a few letters. Some I decline politely, and a couple I answer.

I meet Robert for lunch and have a delightful three hours. He's good company. We have lots to talk about and share a few laughs. The trouble is he's looking for a discreet affair.

Someone to take to the theatre, opera, dinner and maybe occasional sex. His wife spends the evenings, he says, in dressing gown and curlers in front of the TV soaps, and ridicules his choice of the ABC, SBS and live theatre. His business is in both names and it would be financially impossible to separate. I find the idea of being taken to opera, dinner and live theatre very tempting, but we decide it's not what I'm looking for, and wish each other well. Quite some time later he contacts me to tell me he has resolved his situation. He is becoming a minister in his church, and he thanks me again for the few hours of my intelligent company when he felt so trapped.

Eddie lives in Sutherland and is an engineer. He's good company too and helps fix up a few things around my house. He stabilises the little balcony outside my bedroom with an old conveyor belt, and we have a few enjoyable meals both at my home and in restaurants. He's very generous both to me and with his time for the Lions Club, and helps with lots of their functions. The trouble for me is he prefers the stimulation of his charity work and stands me up without notice. Then he rings or arrives the next day full of charm as if nothing has happened. I decide that's not on.

Pedro is Spanish and is a builder from Penrith, specialising in renovations and extensions in the inner city. He also specialises, he says, in playing Casanova to lonely, unappreciated wives whose husbands spend more time at the pub talking about sex than at home doing it. He assures me he knows how to keep a lady happy, and is looking to marry and settle down as he's getting too old for all that. (He's fifty-eight.) I tell him, 'I don't think you can teach an old dog new tricks,' but he says, 'Even an old dog needs a place to lie down in the sun when he is tired.' He is possessive and persistent.

I'm now getting a bit tired of the search again and tell Greg in a moment of disillusion that I'm going to give up and settle for being an old maid with my cats and house. It's all too difficult. He laughs at me and tells me I'm too warm a person to live my life like that. I think what a nice young man he is to say so, but take time off from the search anyway.

After a while, I get one or two letters posted on from a singles magazine in Melbourne. At first I'm confused, as I've never heard of this magazine, but then remember hearing Brian Wiltshire say they have an agreement with a magazine to give a free ad to the people who ring 'Midnight Matchmaker'.

I meet Tony from Kings Cross who designs promotions, and shy Gerard, an airconditioning engineer at the Sydney Entertainment Centre. Tony is keen to invite me up to his nearby unit to see his art collections (just like the fabled stories of 'to see his etchings'). I find it hard to dodge his play for sex. Although Gerard is quiet and shy, he gets amorous too. We don't have enough in common to pursue the relationship. So I go back to my holiday from the Great Search.

Time passes – one month, two months – and I start to get a flood of strange letters, posted on from the singles magazine. They don't sound like responses to anything I might have said: 'Hi! My name's . . . I'm forty-four years young and *I like women* . . . I know how to treat a lady. I believe there must be more to life, as long as nobody gets hurt . . . I am looking for a discreet relationship . . .'

And: 'I found your letter very alluring . . . I am looking for a sensuous woman . . .'

'Alluring' . . . 'sensuous'? What was in that ad?

So it goes on, letter after letter: 'Dear tender sweet lady . . .', 'Dear creature of beauty . . .' There end up being thirty-eight letters like this, some even with photos of very macho-looking guys, all muscles, tight pants and family jewels.

Before I realise what must have happened, I choose a couple of the tamer letters and meet the men. There's Samuel, a charming citizen of the world whose father was a Portuguese diplomat. He's now a businessman from Melbourne, attentive and perfectly charming. We have an enjoyable evening and he says he will ring, but doesn't. I meet two of the other respondents, but both dates feel awkward somehow.

I take the letters down the street to my friend Evelyn, who is also a lady on her own. She's an intelligent professional woman with a grown family and a good sense of humour, and we often share our troubles over coffee. She's mystified too, but then we come up with the idea that the magazine must have made the mistake of putting the reference number they had used for me under someone else's ad.

But what had that ad said? We both search newsagents everywhere we go for a copy of the magazine, but the invariable response is that they always sell out very early in the month, and we are far too late.

Then the bombshell falls. A letter arrives in the form of: 'Once there was a lady who advertised thus . . . and here is a man replying thus . . .' I read what I was supposed to have said: 'Wanted – one damn good male lover by luscious, free-thinking 38-year-old brunette . . .' and so it went on.

I turn hot and cold and rush down the street to Evelyn's. She reads the letter, rocks backwards and forwards and laughs till tears roll down her cheeks. I can't see what's that funny.

'Evelyn,' I say, 'I went out with some of these men!'

She shakes with fresh gales of laughter, and nods as I go on.

'They were expecting a "luscious, free-thinking 38-year-old" who wanted a "damn good male lover". Instead they got a 48-year-old ex-nun, conservative, inexperienced . . . and . . . and not at all luscious!'

'Yes!' she says. 'Yes! Isn't it delightful?'

'No wonder none of them rang me again. They probably went home and said 'Shit! What a night!''

In view of the fact that all these men had paid $20 to have their letters forwarded, Evelyn and I decide to send back to the magazine as many letters as I still have. I'll also tell them it's unprofessional of them to have mixed us up, and ask for a free ad in words of my choice.

I don't receive any acknowledgement or apology from the magazine, but the next month my new ad appears:

Wanted – warm, sincere, well-educated male with a well-developed gunny bone, roughly 47–53 . . . to be friend, confidant and lover to warm, loving and lonely lady, 48. She likes music, theatre and *The Gillies Report* – but what's the fun alone? Widower preferred.

I wait to see what kind of response I'll get this time. I'm a bit perturbed they called my 'funny bone' a 'gunny bone' but, as it turns out, this gave the ad a certain intrigue, as the men tried to work out what a gunny bone was. It didn't really matter, because if they liked *The Gillies Report*, they probably had a good sense of humour anyway.

I thought about the 'widower preferred' part and decided I did prefer a widower. That way there'd be no problem about a Catholic wedding if it ever came to that, and also I'd met such a screwed-up lot of divorced men, that I just thought a widower was likely to be a safer bet.

About 7 p.m. one evening I pick up the phone in my little Chippendale house and ring a North Shore number, mouth dry, heart pounding. I've been through this before but it doesn't get any easier.

'Hello?' The voice sounds very male.

'Hello. I'm Cecilia and I have a letter from you.'

'Oh?'

'Suggesting I ring you.' Who's that I can hear doing the washing-up in the background? He's supposed to be a widower, alone.

'Oh – yes. I'll just take this call in my office.' Deep, firm voice.

Inside, he comes straight to it. 'Well, I suppose we'd better meet. How about dinner? I'm busy for the next few nights and over the weekend.' How many women *did* he write to? Is he taking them all out to dinner? . . . 'How about Monday?'

'Yes, okay – I'm free on Monday.'

'Good. Where do you live? I'll pick you up.'

'I . . . I usually don't tell people where I live straight off . . .' (I've learnt since Murray!) '. . . but you sound all right.'

'Believe me, I *am* all right!'

315

I stammer out my Chippendale address. Maybe I *haven't* learnt so much since Murray.

'I'll see you at seven o'clock then. Oh, and you'd better organise somewhere to go. I don't know your area.'

I don't know my area either. Anyone who lives on $5 a week in their wallet for the small necessities and $15 for housekeeping and food doesn't have a clue where the restaurants *are*, let alone which ones are the good ones! Anyway, I spend the next few days a bit nervous and anxious. Hopeful, too, perhaps.

Come Monday night, I'm still getting my act together at 6.40, after being determined to be ready on time (something I've never been good at). The doorbell rings and my housemate Tony, who has no idea what's going on, answers it. He knows I'm going out for dinner, but not that I've never met this person before. I hear voices floating up the stairs. My God! I think, the man's very early.

As I negotiate the steep little stairs that climb down my dining room wall, I get a glimpse of him. Tall, beanpole, balding head, and well-dressed in a nice navy blazer. He's standing beside the plastered wall in the dining room of my 1880s terrace house, tapping it with a 20 cent piece.

I nod hello, as I wonder what on earth he's doing. It's awkward with Tony standing there. His eyes twinkle cheekily, and he taps the wall again.

'Just testing for rising damp,' he says, then adds, 'it's a bit drummy.'

That's my husband.

We are sitting in a restaurant, upstairs in one of those little two-storey terrace places in Glebe Point Road. It's a small room, with only two or three of the eight tables occupied. We're talking quietly.

Bruce tells me a potted story of his life and career: about his grown-up son and daughter, Greg and Sue. About his wife's death after a long period of ill health; his engineering jobs and now, his work at the Queen Victoria Building renovation site. I manage to find out it was Greg doing the washing-up after dinner when I rang the other night, and that Bruce was busy because he had to work over the weekend. When he finishes he looks at me.

'Well, that about sums me up. How about you? What have you been doing all your life?'

Here is the moment I dread. Do I tell all, or do I tell a bit? Such as, 'I've been a teacher all my life and I've never married'. It has worked before. My tummy is in knots, but I take a big breath and out it comes.

'Well . . . as a matter of fact . . .' he is looking at me so attentively '. . . I . . . I . . . have been a nun – a Catholic sister – in a convent all my life.'

I've found I need to say it several ways. People usually think they must have heard wrongly if I only say it once.

Later, when we laugh about it, Bruce tells me he felt as if his chair went out from under him at this point and he landed on the floor. When he mentally crawled out from under the table, he said he was amazed to see me still sitting there, looking composed and surprisingly normal.

'Well,' he says. There's a pause. 'Have you really? I saw some certificate thing with "Sister Cecilia Cahill" on it in your lounge room. I thought you must be a nurse.'

I tell him about the Sisters of Mercy, teaching and pastoral work; about my present job, my uni study, and buying my little house.

He is still looking at me attentively, but he suddenly says, 'That means you must . . . er, er . . . That is, have you ever . . . ? I mean . . .' He falters to a stop.

'Do you mean am I a virgin?'

'No! No! I don't mean that! I couldn't ask that. It would be too embarrassing!' There's a moment's silence while he deals with this. Then, 'But . . . well, are you?'

It is surprising how this thought affects men differently. At the mention of 'nun' some of them have clammed up and literally run for cover. Others have lit up. You can almost see their fantasies glittering in their eyes. Bruce does neither. I answer his question honestly, but our conversation that night is ours. We talk about it all, he accepts my history calmly, and we spend the evening in pleasant 'getting acquainted' conversation.

At the end of it he kisses me goodnight, with some enthusiasm. When he says he will ring, I find myself believing – and hoping – that he will.

In hot weather Dad likes to sit on a cushion in the doorway of the lounge room. It's a bit cooler there, in the breeze. Mum gives me a cup of tea with a biscuit on the saucer and says, 'Take this in to Dad.'

When I go in, Dad is standing there, looking out the door onto the verandah. Then I see he is really looking out to the street through the verandah louvres. He can see without being seen.

'Just look at that!' he says in disgust.

I look, and there is Noelene, one of the Mahoney girls, coming up the street. Her sleeveless top is a tight fit over her bust, and her breasts are bobbing and bouncing as she walks. Her shorts cling to her bare legs, and her bum is wobbling with every jaunty step.

I feel uncomfortable. Dad's disapproval radiates.

'I can't understand how her parents can let her parade around like that!' he snorts. 'Don't ever think you can dress like her. Just asking for trouble. It's sinful.'

'Er . . .' I say, 'here's your tea, Dad.'

# 31

# Men and Sex

This seems like a good place to think about men and sex in my life.

When I entered the convent and chose to live a celibate existence, it was not a denial of sexuality. A vow of chastity was a choice to live life without sexual intercourse, without giving yourself ultimately to a man, but not to live as a non-sexual being. It was a vow to live as one whose heart is pure.

Nuns are women with all the warmth, femininity, gentleness and understanding common to their sex, but available to many without being locked in a relationship with only one other person, or with a family of offspring to care for. Sex is sublimated, not denied. The choice is to channel sex – female identity – differently.

A religious order of nuns is a female society where women are in charge, do all the day-to-day things and work for others – mostly other women, families or children in the schools. Most are professional women who bring all their womanly attributes to being teachers, social workers or carers for others.

Girls in a male-dominated society who attend a convent school see women in charge, women making decisions and women running the place. These days, this is not so rare. Twenty, thirty or fifty years ago it was unknown to have female prime ministers, consultants or heads of organisations. But religious orders have been the exceptions.

Were there men around in my world as a nun? Not in the day-to-day life of the convent. Parish priests were the nominal heads of the primary schools in their parishes, but few took this to any level of interference. Most nuns as primary principals ran the place. They consulted the parish priest for many things and generally had a harmonious working relationship. Some even formed very good personal friendships.

The priest said Mass for us in the convent chapel, but had no say in the life of the convent. Often he was entertained afterwards as an honoured guest in the parlour by some of the senior sisters in the community. Some priests looked on this as a doubtful privilege and would say disparaging things like 'Bacon and eggs and two nuns for breakfast!' They seemed uncomfortable in a society where women were in charge.

Often older priests ended their days as chaplains in retirement homes run by the sisters, and this was a fairly cushy job, but many didn't look forward to being residents in the homes. They would make such comments as 'O Lord, deliver us from falling into the hands of the nuns in our old age!'

The bishop was in charge of the Religious in the diocese and sometimes made regulations affecting them, such as the running of the schools, but had no say in the life of the congregation. Sometimes they would have liked to. They looked with suspicion on those orders which were run by major superiors in mother houses in other places like Canberra, Ireland or even Rome, and this could cause problems. For example, it caused the split in the Sisters of Saint Joseph founded by Mother Mary MacKillop in Adelaide. Various bishops objected to the authority being placed with the Mother General and wanted to have more control of the sisters in their diocese. This resulted in separate orders – those who stayed with Mother Mary and became the Brown Josephite Sisters, and those who went with Father Tenison Woods and became groups of Black Josephite Sisters.

We mainly saw the bishop for ceremonies of religious reception and profession, and for funerals. He arrived in a cloud of grand expectation and was treated with great respect, amounting almost to adulation. He presided over the funeral or profession ceremony, resplendent in mitre and cope and holding his shepherd's crook, adding a great sense of presence to the occasion, and departed gloriously too, leaving behind a cloud of relief.

Of course our Order was under the control of the Pope and those faceless men who ran the Sacred Congregation for Religious. In 1915 a new code of canon law was introduced telling religious women what they could and could not do, and life was subject to this in the broad outlines. Women were not consulted in the making of laws, but we generally did our own thing within the confines dictated by the Church.

Canon law covered things like owning property, making wills, wearing habits and always going out in twos. You had to apply to the Sacred Congregation for Religious to make some changes, especially if you wanted to leave the Order after you had made final, permanent vows. Sometimes they also stepped in uninvited to discipline orders they thought had gone too far in some way, such as forbidding the Sisters of Charity from running the experimental supervised drug injecting room in Kings Cross in recent years.

However, in day-to-day life at the convent, men were non-existent. I lived with other women in a mostly harmonious society, and sex was a non-issue. Just to clear the air, I never knew two nuns who had a lesbian relationship. People had their close friends, just as in any group, and there were little regulations which encouraged sisters to be 'general' rather than 'particular' in their friendships, and to avoid touching each other. I didn't really understand this emphasis on not having 'particular friendships' for many years, until it dawned on me it was supposed to be a protection against forming lesbian relationships.

When I left the convent I entered a sexual world and decided I would open that door in my life. I didn't want to spend the rest of my life on my own, and I wanted the closeness of a committed relationship with a man. I let myself become aware of the psychological hole at the centre of my being which was meant to be filled by a partner and a family of my own. I was desperately lonely, and certain I had a great deal of love for someone special stored up in me. So that's why I went looking for a man.

I had been fortunate to have warm friendships with some of the men with whom I worked, like Father Joe at North

Goulburn, and Rob Hockley who ran the pastoral care programs. While these friendships were warm, they were not of a
sexual nature. I also knew and liked some of the men I'd
worked with in various other settings.

The problem was, where do I meet the sort of men who
would be suitable and interested in a long-term relationship?
This was not easy for a woman in her late forties in the middle of a big city. And sex? It was an unknown commodity!
I was naïve and inexperienced in this new and frightening
world of sexual encounters. Nevertheless, I gathered my
courage in both hands and set out to 'find a man'. Of course,
as I experimented along the way, I found there were a lot
more toads out there wanting to be kissed than handsome
princes. But I was surprised – even thrilled – to find some
men were attracted to me as a person. Some of these men I
found attractive too, and this triggered off a strong response
in me. I tried letting myself be kissed, and I experimented
with kissing them back. It was very pleasant. However,
when I discovered I had strong sexual feelings in response to
some men, I felt very guilty. Is this right? I would ask myself.
Is it okay?

At this time I was learning hypnosis with Leon Cowan at
his Academy of Applied Hypnosis in George Street, in the
city. One Saturday at an all-day workshop, I was having a
session as the subject, and Leon was demonstrating various
techniques for the benefit of the rest of the group. Somehow
this whole topic of sexuality came up, and Leon very gently
led me through it. I admitted that I was feeling guilty because I
imagined my father judging me and disapproving of me.
I was letting him down. Leon had me imagine my father there

in front of me, talking to me, telling me it was okay to be a sexual woman and that it was a way of loving someone as he had my mother, and as she had loved him. I can't remember the details of the session, but I know it was very healing for me. I was able to look at things differently, while not wanting to be promiscuous with anyone and everyone I met. Leon was there just at the right time for me.

Some of the men I met along the way were walking disasters for a virgin, an inexperienced 'girl' of forty-seven looking for a genuine, committed relationship, but others were kind and gentle. They helped me explore my sexuality, and encouraged me to be warm and responsive. I began with sitting close and holding hands, and progressed to hugging and kissing. I learnt it was okay to be a sexual woman and gradually became comfortable with the role. The move from warm, responsive woman to actual sex was quite natural when it happened. I'd like to say the earth moved, but it didn't. There were no great fireworks. It was painful, messy and only vaguely pleasant. I thought, is this it? After all these years? It was a bit of a fizzer.

The more I thought about it, the more I began to realise that sex was more than just the physical sensation. It was the whole relationship. When I met Bruce I knew it felt right. He was down-to-earth and I liked his sense of humour. He had told me 'What you see is what you get!' and he was pretty right. He was honest and straightforward. Sometimes *very* straightforward. You weren't long in doubt about what he thought of most things.

Bruce was working on the renovation of the Queen Victoria Building in the city when we first met and would often call in after work, especially when they were working late. He'd have to go back to check on things before he went home, so he'd come and have dinner, talk and maybe watch TV with me for a while before he went to the building site about 10 p.m. When he came inside his big work boots would be all white with dust, and his working clothes likewise. It was the same way Dad had looked when he came in from work, and I felt at home with the building-site dust.

Looking back, Bruce definitely reminded me of Dad: upright and honest. I was very comfortable with him. He'd sometimes arrive with a gift for me. Some men might have brought flowers, but Bruce would turn up with a whole rump over his shoulder, or t-bone steaks. After he'd visited a few times he had realised these were not on our menu, as we lived fairly frugally. We ate good food, but bought inexpensive things. The gifts were disconcerting as I was good with casseroles and soups, but had no experience of cooking steak. After I'd spoilt it the first time, I suggested he cook it, which was a much better idea.

Bruce took me out to dinner to local restaurants which I didn't even know existed, and we went to the theatre now and then. I really enjoyed it all. Sometimes on a Sunday afternoon we'd go to The Rocks in the city and sit in one of the Irish pubs with a glass of beer to listen to the music. It was all good fun, and his company was very pleasant.

I eventually met his family and some of his oldest friends. While I had a slight feeling of being 'tried out' in his environment to see how I'd fit, it was surprising how much at home I felt. The friends and relatives were very pleased to meet me. I think they'd been worried that Bruce was lonely, and as he was such a nice fellow, it was a relief for them to see he'd found somebody. As for meeting Bruce's children, Greg and Sue, they made me welcome, though it must have been hard for them to see another woman moving into their mother's place in their family home.

I soon decided Bruce was 'the one'. Sometimes he would stay over at my house in Chippendale and sometimes I visited him in St Ives until we were both satisfied that living together was what we wanted, and I moved into his house for a while after I had a short trip to hospital.

At one stage I thought I should go home to *my* house, where I had a mortgage, a house full of furniture and clothes being looked after by Greg, who was not only busy looking after my two cats, but was also flat-out fielding phone calls for me. He would say I wasn't there at the moment, take their names, then ring me at Bruce's. I'd return the calls from there. I felt guilty and embarrassed to be 'living in sin', and knew it could even cost me my job in the Catholic school if they found out about it and wanted to get officious. So eventually I told Bruce I needed to go home. At this stage in our relationship – six months into it – Bruce decided he would 'make an honest woman of me'. We should just get married, he said. I was more than willing.

So we did.

# 32

## Married at Last

It is the first of March 1986. I am standing nervously outside the chapel of the Royal North Shore Hospital. Peering in, I can see my nephew, Tim, standing up the front in his clerical gear, smiling at me. And there is Gordon, Bruce's only brother, waiting to be best man, and my sister-in-law, Peg, is my matron of honour. The chapel is full and there's a buzz of excitement in the air. Bruce takes my hand in his big warm one, and says, 'Come on, then.'

We walk down the aisle together. I thought I was a bit long in the tooth to have anyone give me away, and anyway, this wedding was *our* choice. As we come through the door, the organ rings out with 'The Wedding March' and everyone stands up and turns around, smiling. It's just a sea of faces, but here and there I see one I recognise. I know them all, but they just merge into one bright collage. Right at the front I see Bruce's 83-year-old mum struggling to stand up, and Bruce leans over and signs her to sit down.

Now we stand side-by-side in front of Tim, and the ceremony begins.

Bruce would have liked to be married in the Ku-Ring-Gai Wildflower Garden at St Ives. I think he was a bit nervous about the big 'church wedding' he thought I might want because of my religious background. A Catholic church was also an alien place for him with its statues, candles and incense. Not that these would all be present at our wedding, but they formed part of his preconceptions.

I had a problem with being married at the Wildflower Garden because Tim, who had been ordained as a priest the year before, would not be able to marry us there. Gardens were not considered suitable places for a Catholic wedding, and I wanted Tim to marry us. I also wanted to be married in a Catholic ceremony because of the number of my relatives and friends who were Catholic and would be distressed if I married 'outside the Church'. For myself, I knew Bruce and I were marrying each other for the same reasons wherever we took our vows. But even though I was disillusioned with the official Church and not fussed about going to Sunday Mass too often any more, there was a part of me still drawn to the Jesus of the Gospel whom I had grown to know within the Church. Once a Catholic, I think you are always a Catholic. Yes, I decided, I would like a Catholic wedding, with Tim. Bruce agreed.

I suggested as an alternative to the big Catholic church wedding that didn't appeal to Bruce that we marry in the chapel at the Royal North Shore Hospital where I had spent so much time involved with pastoral care. The chapel was small and intimate, and I had always liked the filtered light through its lovely stained glass. It had the additional advantage of being an ecumenical chapel, and therefore Catholic, without the unfamiliar statues and whatever other Catholic trappings guests might find uncomfortable. I was very pleased with myself for thinking of this compromise.

Invitations were bought. Who to send them to? How many? And where should we have the reception? Bruce's initial suggestion of having just a few close relatives and friends gave way to my need to share this happy occasion with all those good people who had supported me through the bad times and would be delighted to see this day.

'I don't care if I cook for weeks and have the reception in the backyard!' I said.

'Well, if that's how you feel, that's what we'll do!' said Bruce. 'Only you won't have to cook for weeks. I'm sure we can find someone who'll cater for us at home.'

So that's what we did.

Over a hundred people crammed into the little chapel at the hospital and we celebrated our coming together. Maree, whom I taught in Singleton years before, played the organ. Val, one of the sisters from my community, sang. And there, on the altar rail when we came in, was a lovely flower arrangement from Doctor Craig Powell, saying how delighted he was to see this day. As well as entering the chapel to 'The Wedding March' we came back out to the exultant strains of Jeremiah Clark's 'Trumpet Voluntary'. Though the day is now a blur in memory, the mood of exultation remains clearly with me.

On the way down the aisle when Bruce held my hand very

firmly and squeezed it hard, I thought, he really wants to be here too! It's really not just something I wanted so badly I made it happen! There was elation in my heart at the thought that he wanted to marry me as much as I wanted to marry him.

We had decided we would make up our own order of ceremony, and Tim said all that was essential was that we should declare our wedding vows before the assembled people. We had some interesting moments, though, while we were making up the ceremony.

I'd say, 'I'd like to have this for the reading.'

Bruce would say, 'What have we got to have readings for? Aren't we just getting married?'

And there would follow a warm and frank discussion. In the end we arrived at an order of ceremony I liked, and he was happy to accept. I know the reading we had the above discussion about was eventually considered most fitting. It was from the Song of Solomon and said things like

*Arise, my love, my dove, my beautiful one and come . . .*
*for the winter is past . . .*
*the rains are over and gone . . .*
*and the voice of the turtle is heard in our land . . .*

So many people present in the chapel had been through that winter with me, and had known the cold and emptiness of the land I had travelled! There were a few tears trickling down otherwise tough and unsentimental cheeks that afternoon. Would the kids in Mick Prest's school ever have believed their hard-baked principal would shed a tear at a friend's wedding?

And who'd have thought that Bruce's down-to-earth brother-in-law, Des Barker, the potter, would cry too? Bruce's friends and family all knew the hard road he had also travelled in the last few years, and they were happy that his winter, too, had passed.

Afterwards we all headed off home to the backyard at St Ives where the wine flowed, speeches were made from both sides of the family and everyone continued to celebrate into the night that the new spring had indeed come.

# 33

## On Becoming a Gran

I never thought about becoming a grandmother; grand-children had never entered my scheme of things. But as I sit here looking at a photo of two little boys – my grandsons, D'Arcy and Reuben, smiling back at me from within a little gold frame – my heart warms. They are the light of my life.

You wouldn't think they were brothers. Chalk and cheese. The older with fair, curly hair, soft as clouds on a summer day, eyes sparkling and blue as the sky. The other little one, as dark as his brother is fair, grins cheekily back at me. Already a charmer, he is bright-eyed, bushytailed and able to disarm me totally with his cocky 'Look, it's all right Gran – it didn't break' or 'It doesn't really matter Gran'. Meanwhile, his older brother is alert, interested in life and oh so sensitive.

I was there on the days they were born, almost two years apart. I was there long before they were born, too, watching helplessly as their mum, Sue, struggled off to work day after day with morning sickness which spread through to the evening.

D'Arcy, the eldest, arrived with a characteristic struggle – a trembling shiver at being forced out of the dark, warm place where he wanted to stay and out into a bright, cold world. He screwed up his face, cried and then weed – once, twice, three times – all over the doctor and nurses. There was delighted laughter, and a great cheer went up for the little boy just born. He had to go down to intensive care for observation because of that odd little 'shiver' he gave. It turned out to be nothing to be concerned about – just that our little boy will always need reassurance, because he is apprehensive of change. His mother was anxious as they took the baby away and gave me strict instructions to go with him and keep an eye on him till he was well and truly labelled 'in case I get the wrong one'.

The intensive-care sister attended to him. She wiped and measured, then put that all-important label around his skinny little ankle. She wrapped him in swaddling clothes and I thought she was about to lay him in the clear plastic cot that doubled as the manger. Instead, she turned to me – the fascinated observer – and asked, 'Would you like to nurse him now?'

I froze. My mind boggled. Nurse him – me? This tiny new creature, so fragile *and* yelling lustily, with his little face all red? The sister was standing there, offering me the small white bundle.

'You're the grandmother, aren't you?' she said.

'Er – yes,' I stammered. And for the first time I thought yes, I really am the grandmother! This newest addition to the family I acquired when I married so late in life *was* my grandson – the son of my stepdaughter.

'It's just – no,' I said. 'No – I don't think I'll nurse him right now. I'd better get back to his mother.'

She shrugged and turned back towards the cot with him. I could tell she was puzzled. How could she know how inexperienced I was – that I didn't know anything at all about babies, let alone ones so tiny. I knew I was good with high school students – teenagers. But a new baby? Thirty years of celibate living in a convent hardly prepared you to know what to do with a brand new life.

Then, second thoughts. Something stirred within me. Why shouldn't I hold him? I never thought to have a baby – it was just one of those things about choosing life as a nun. But there was no reason I shouldn't accept this gift now in the late afternoon of my life. Maybe I *could* hold him for a bit.

'Well,' I said awkwardly, 'perhaps I might. Just for a minute.'

I don't know what the nurse made of all this but she smiled encouragement as she came over and said, 'Sit yourself down here and get really comfortable. That's it. Now put your arms like this and I'll give him to you.'

I sat, apprehensive. She put the bundle into my arms. I held him gingerly. It felt strange. I'd never held such a new thing, and he was bellowing loudly. His tiny face was tense and puckered into mounds of red and white crinkles. There were real tears in his little blue eyes, and his body was jerking with the effort of such distress. In desperation, I began to talk to him the way I talked to my cat – quietly, cuddling him, stroking him with my voice. Come to think of it, he *was* like a new kitten.

Then it happened. He liked it! He stopped crying, closed

his little eyes, settled down with a gulp and went to sleep, snuggled on my breast. I don't know how long we stayed there, the childless one and the sleeping babe. I sat gazing at the miracle in my arms and he slept serenely, exhausted by the trauma of his birth. My arms got tired and ached, but I wanted this moment to go on and on. I felt so much at peace, brimming with an emotion I'd never known before.

I was hooked for the term of my natural life.

# 34

## My Sixty-sixth Birthday

It is February 2001. Today is my sixty-sixth birthday and almost twenty years since I left the convent and ceased to be a Sister of Mercy. Now I am wife, stepmother and grandmother. In a few weeks it will be the fifteenth anniversary of our wedding.

Today I wake to the insistent poking of little paws in my back. I turn and look into the liquid brown eyes of my Jack Russell terrier perched on her back legs beside the bed. Bruce is up already and has let her out for the morning, and here she is imploring me to get up and start the day with her. Or at least to put out a hand and pat her tan head, so she can lick me good morning.

I oblige, and stretch luxuriously in the warmth of bed. No leaping out as if the bed was on fire any more. I decide to listen to the ABC 7 a.m. news before I get up, and trail one hand over the edge of the bed to fondle Jackie's responsive ears while I listen.

When I do climb out she is immediately alert and presents me with her rubber squeaky toy, though she has 'killed' its squeak long ago. She wants us to get on with the game of throw and fetch, which is our morning ritual. I throw it, and set out for the bathroom to have my shower.

Dressing is simple these days – bra and undies, T-shirt, pedal-pusher pants and sandals, and I'm done. Back to the bathroom for a quick hairdo and some eye make-up. I can get the hairdresser to put the colour back into my hair, but the eyebrows and eyelashes are dead giveaways of aging. They are colourless and mousy, so I add some eyebrow pencil and eyeliner.

Out in the family room Bruce is sitting in his cane chair in the sun, absorbed in his paper, while eight-year-old Reuben is creeping up on him to say 'Boo!' Today is Friday, so the boys come for an hour before school as their mum goes to work in an early bus. Reuben has let himself in with the emergency key and has his finger on his lips for me to 'Sh . . .' as he tip-toes forward. When Pop is reading his paper, Reuben could almost be an elephant lumbering across the room and he would hardly notice.

'BOO!'

Bruce jumps dutifully and Reuben says, 'Ha! Gotcha, Pop!'

By now ten-year-old D'Arcy has ambled in and says, 'Happy birthday, Gran!' Everyone remembers it's my birthday. We have kisses all round, but no presents yet as we're going to a family dinner tomorrow night, and that's the real 'party'.

Next, I go through the Friday morning ritual of making the boys' breakfast and lunch. Cereal for one, and toast –

'with just butter, please Gran' – for the other, plus a drink of milk. I organise a Nutella sandwich each, and they get their own snacks for morning tea from the supply in the pantry. I make my own cereal and coffee, and start to look at the paper.

By then it's time for the boys to go. Bruce drives them to school while I pack the dishwasher and put the lamb ragout left over from last night's dinner into boxes for the freezer. I saw some lamb neck chops in the supermarket labelled 'Reduced for quick sale' and remembered Mum's stewed chops. I like things 'on sale' – I've never really recovered from the lean years. I cheated, though, and used a packet of lamb ragout seasoning from the supermarket, and added a lot of tiny onions.

When Bruce comes back he insists on getting up into the ceiling to look for a leak in the roof. D'Arcy spied a wet patch on the ceiling of the second bedroom. I'm not keen about Bruce climbing around up there and remind him he's no spring chicken. He tells me not to be stupid, he's perfectly safe and he's been doing this for forty years. He has conveniently forgotten the Saturday morning he decided to climb up and see to the pool heater on the second-storey roof of our old house. While he was standing on the ladder, it slipped and left him hanging on to the sagging guttering, yelling for help.

Today he says in as disparaging a tone as he can muster, 'Look – just come and hold the ladder for me.'

I say 'Men!' as if fifteen years of marriage has made me an expert on them, and I hold the ladder. Up Bruce goes through the manhole in the garage, I pass up his toolbox and soon hear him thumping around up there.

Naturally, that's when the phone rings. It's one of his mates, Kevin Little, looking for a promised phone number about travel insurance. I have a shouted conversation with Bruce through the manhole and eventually I find the number on the desk in the office. I pass it on to Kevin, and then it's time to go back to my ladder-holding duties. Bruce calls for various things – a polystyrene broccoli box I've been saving for something, a piece of wood from the store in the corner of the garage and his bush saw, all of which I pass up. I can't imagine what he's doing with these things.

Bruce re-emerges and declares the leak fixed. Well, he admits, 'it's bodgied up', but he's sure it won't leak again. I'm relieved he's come down safely via the manhole and not through the ceiling somewhere.

He says, 'How about a cup of tea, love? It must be morning tea time.'

I smile at the request. It's a bit of a joke between us. Bruce has 'retired' several times, and I always say the refrains of his various retirements have been 'How about a cup of tea, love?' and 'What's for lunch?'

The first time Bruce retired he was lost. He sat in his chair in the sunroom and read the papers. Then he remembered the local library, and borrowed six books. After that, he sat in the sunroom reading his paper or a book, waiting in vain for someone to need him. All of this interfered with my well-established routines. If I went to the shops he'd ask plaintively 'What time will you be home?' or 'Will you be back for lunch?' This really meant 'Will you be back to get my lunch?' For me, lunch was a non-event. I'd have a sandwich or a piece of fruit when it occurred to me. If I was out, there was no need to rush home. But not any more. Guilt sent me scurrying home to the forlorn man in the corner 'reading his book'.

After a few months of this he went into his 'getting things done' phase. He decided the garden needed to be tidied up, and he dug up and threw out all the daffodils and freesias – bulbs and all – 'because they'd finished'. Plants and weeds alike were pulled up, and he cheerfully admitted he'd never been able to tell the difference. But it was when he set out with his secateurs that disaster really struck. The grapefruit tree became a two-foot high collection of truncated branches (he had to go back for his saw) and the cumquat tree a six-inch high stump. Admittedly it was overgrown and blocked the view, but it didn't deserve to be sacrificed in order to fill the big green bin for several weeks. It became a matter of honour to Bruce to have that bin filled to overflowing every week.

Then, mercifully, he was asked back to work. They had a really big job on, they said, and needed his experience. The young turks lacked the know-how of the wily old veteran. It was balm to his spirit. He pulled out his gear, set the clock for 6 a.m. and was gone for the train by 6.30, happy as a pig in mud. After twelve months of this, however, it wore a bit thin as he remembered golf on Wednesdays and the bowls he had just begun to play when the call came. So he retired again.

This time, we've got it right. The recipe includes lots of bowls, golf, and a new computer. Add to that meetings of his Probus Club and financial discussion group, outings with Probus, and a position as trips and tours organiser for the club. No doubt about it, Probus is a great invention. It's a club for retired professional ('pro') and business ('bus') men who meet once a month and have a business-type meeting to organise activities like tours and interest-group meetings. There's lots of friendship with other men of like mind and background.

But today he's catching up on his office stuff, and retires happily to his desk. As for me, I have a client coming – a remnant from my counselling psychology practice. I left being school counsellor a couple of years after we were married, as I no longer had to pay the mortgage, and went into private practice of various kinds. I had rooms in Gordon for a while, then ran an introduction agency in Chatswood to help other people meet as Bruce and I had done. This was very stressful and only moderately successful, so I returned to private practice with an office at home. I retired from this practice when we moved house in 2000.

My office was on the side of our old house, a nice little room Bruce fixed up for me in what had been the garage and later his business office. It seemed a good time to retire when we moved, and I lost my office. Today, however, Jennifer, one of my past clients, wants to come and talk something over with me, so I see her in the lounge room. This is rare.

When she's gone, I organise left over lamb ragout on toast for lunch. After that I tell Bruce I need a few things from Woolworths and go down to St Ives shopping centre in my little Holden Astra hatchback. Having my own car in which I can come and go as I please is one of the most satisfying luxuries of my life.

I'm back by the time Bruce comes home with the boys after school and I get their afternoon snack of fresh pear and grapes, followed by a chocolate milkshake made with my

Bamix. There's no homework today as it's Friday, and I'm a bit sorry because I really enjoy the homework we do together on Wednesdays. Old teachers never die.

Reuben turns on the cartoon network. D'Arcy and I put plastic covers on several books which missed out last time, and he shows me a library book he's borrowed. It's full of diagrams of various planes over the years, the interior as well as the exterior, and lots of cross-sections. He's been on holidays in planes a few times and is fascinated by their differences. The Boeing 314 – the old flying boat of the 1940s – is particularly interesting to him. In these days of cramped economy-class seats and deep vein thrombosis it looks unbelievably spacious with its lounges and dining room. It even had passenger sleeping alcoves, which D'Arcy can hardly believe. We marvel at how things have changed, specially the price of travel. In those days it was only for the very rich.

We talk about our dinner tomorrow night at Centrepoint Tower. D'Arcy's birthday is a few days after mine, so we have decided to have a combined party. We convinced Pop it really isn't so expensive, as it's two dinner parties in one.

The boys stay with us most Friday nights, as we have declared it a night off for Sue to do anything she wants. Reuben drifts into the office to play the Lego game on Pop's computer, and D'Arcy asks if he can look up his email on my laptop. I get their dinner. They come home from school 'starving' and so they eat early. Bruce and I like to have dinner after the 7 p.m. news on the ABC. I cook them stirfry chicken with sweet and sour sauce, mashed potatoes, carrots, peas and pumpkin, followed by ice-cream and chocolate sauce.

After dinner, the boys go back to the computer or the cartoon network. Bruce asks several times for them to turn it down as he's trying to read the local paper, and then it's news time. While that is on I organise the dog's dinner, make more stirfry chicken and vegies for Bruce and me with a jacket potato, and we eat.

Then it's time for the boys to do PJs, toilet, teeth and bed. There's a racket from the second bedroom until I appear with the *Champion Book* which Bruce got for his ninth birthday in 1938, and we settle down to read a story. I sit on Reuben's bed because he likes to see if there are any pictures, the dog jumps up on D'Arcy's bed, and I read to them all. Bruce washes up the dinner things. Often I hear 'Read another one, Gran!' and, if it's not too late, I do. Then it's 'Lights out!', though D'Arcy reads his *Harry Potter* book with the bed lamp for a while.

The dog and I go back out to the family room and join Bruce to watch TV. About 10.30, when the show finishes, we lock up, put the dog out for a wee before she goes to her bed in the laundry, and head off to bed ourselves. Sometimes we have a cuddle, or just drift off into a satisfied sleep.

# 35

## Reflections on the Journey

It has been a long journey, this search for God, myself, peace and harmony. It is now fifty years since we drove through those imposing gates and up the red gravel drive of Singleton Convent for me to become a Sister of Mercy.

Of all the major players on that day, most have gone ahead into whatever is beyond death. Mum and Dad have both gone, and my brother Jim who drove us all to Singleton died last year. The reverend mothers and novice mistresses I knew have all gone, and even some of the girls I entered the convent with that day have died. The teachers and superiors have gone. Convents are closed, and the secondary school at Hamilton is no more.

And it is over twenty years since the day I drove out those gates for the last time in the convent station wagon.

In a way, religious life was a shock to me. I think I expected it to be a place where people who shared the same hopes and ideals lived together in harmony and sought to bring the same harmony and peace to the people of the world . . . that it would sort of gather them together as a hen gathers her chicks in peace and safety. In a way it was like that, but I didn't see it at the time.

Instead, I found a world that was highly structured and institutionalised. Prayers were in Latin – the Divine Office that we shared with the priests and all the other religious men and women of the world. We sat on opposite sides of the chapel facing each other and took turns to read the psalms, or to say them by heart. Morning, late afternoon and night we met to say Office, as well as the other prayers we prayed in common.

The hardest thing for me were the mornings: rising early in the dark, having been woken by a clanging bell. I have never been a morning person. We dressed by the light of a single candle fluttering in the breeze in the centre of the dormitory, assembled in the cold chapel at some ungodly hour, and were expected to pray. My meditations would become a struggle to stay awake. I'd sit up straight and tall on the little stool in the bottom of my stall and try to concentrate on the points of the meditation for the day. I really didn't care *why* the man went down from Jerusalem to Jericho. If he wanted or needed to go, then okay. The part of the story that appealed to me was when the samaritan man found him, picked him up and looked after him.

I was always tired and terribly hot during summer in all the nuns' gear. And I was often in trouble. In my early days in the Order my high spirits often overflowed in the confinement of the institution. I'd slide down banisters, play practical jokes or tickle someone on the procession to or from chapel at meal times. I walked too fast about the place; I laughed too loud at recreation; I didn't keep my eyes down as I went. I was often late for prayers, or caught talking and laughing during silence time.

The Jesus of the Gospel – the one who wept over Jerusalem; the one who sat tired and dispirited beside the well and asked the Samaritan woman for a drink; the one who went to the wedding parties of his friends – *that* Jesus didn't seem to feature. The things presented as important seemed to be silence, Latin prayers, penance – and conforming. Humiliation was up there too, and I managed to cop more than my share of that from the superiors.

One of the tenets taught was 'The superior is the voice of God'. This was depressing for me, as the superiors didn't seem to think I was good enough. For a long time I hung this on God as well. That wise old priest who told me during my novitiate, 'There was nothing very wrong in the things you did. The worst thing you did was get caught. Just don't get caught!' added some balance for me. Maybe – just *maybe* – it was the system at fault, not me.

So why did I stay? Why did I *want* to stay? There was something deeper in me that believed in the Jesus of the Gospel, and believed this was a way of life to pursue what I believed in. And then, there were the others. The community. My friends. My sisters. I always got on well with them and enjoyed living with them. It seemed very worthwhile to follow my Jesus with these people.

When I was professed and set out as a teacher, a whole new world opened. There were all those children to gather under my wings to teach, to love and to launch on their own lives. I really loved the kids. And I loved the grassroots people and daily life of the community.

I loved the singing and the hymns we learnt. The motets in Latin, the classical Latin Masses we sang in the chapel, the lovely Christmas carols and the exultant Easter hymns. There were special days of exposition where we spent hours just sitting quietly in the chapel with the Blessed Sacrament up on the altar in a monstrance, surrounded with flowers and candles. I loved the concerts for sisters' Feastdays – the dressing-up and acting of comedies, the get-togethers with friends when we'd laugh and talk for hours in the holidays.

For years it seemed very satisfying to follow the Jesus of the Gospel in this community, and 'the Church' – that big institution out there – was just that. Out there. Of course, it impinged on everything we thought and did, but it was possible to lead a very satisfactory life down in the basement, immersed in our own concerns and lives.

In 1977 when I went off to the Assumption Institute in Melbourne for twelve months it was a year of living differently, outside my own community, and in a very relaxed atmosphere. I met interesting people, discovered new ideas and found a lot of others who talked about the Jesus of the Gospels. My greatest discovery was about meditation. It was not wondering about *why* that man went down from Jerusalem to Jericho; it was about opening your heart and mind. It was entering an altered state of consciousness and just being there. It was a revelation that changed my praying and ideas.

I went home a different person and set about spreading the good news with a peace and confidence that had previously eluded me. Then there were weekends for women, prayer days and discussion groups where I shared what I had found. Next, I worked in Canberra running the ashram-cum-conference centre, and later, in the parish in Goulburn. There was also a lot of satisfaction in visiting patients in several hospitals as a chaplain.

When I went back to my convent as superior with the mandate to bring some of my insights to fruition in the community there, it was hard. It seemed they didn't want to know, didn't want to change anything. I felt a frustration and a feeling of being in a dark cellar where people were happy to be in the dark with their candles, not wanting to know about the bright sunlight, flowers and warmth outside.

There was loneliness and there were health problems and, when the doctor suggested I go on leave, anxiety and sadness at the thought of leaving it all behind. But a gradual belief set in that it was the right thing to do. It was time. So I went.

Life was difficult and I struggled to survive physically and financially out in the world. However, there was never any doubt I had done the right thing. Gradually, I also went on leave from formal religion. I had no sense of commitment to a parish in the middle of a big city where I knew nobody. There was no sense of community and belonging.

Eventually, I bought my home at Chippendale. Why was that house with the tree in the backyard and a cat so important to me? For most of my life I had owned nothing. I had to ask permission for everything. I lived comfortably as a nun – more comfortably than I did for that first year outside the convent walls. We had comfortable beds, gracious old buildings in beautiful grounds and we drove new cars every few years – but nothing was *mine*. Everything was 'to my use'. We even used to say things like 'Have you seen the pen to my use? I can't find it'. My shoes, my clothing, my books were all 'to my use'. Our car may have been the latest model, but that was dictated by economics. I had to ask to use it as it was a 'community' car, and not always available when I wanted to go out. Plus I had to have it back on time for someone else to use. And my belongings were necessarily restricted by what I could pack up and move regularly from house to house – and had permission to own.

When I left the convent and set out to find a place to live I was overwhelmed by the fact I had to acquire all I needed. I remember saying to a friend that I had to get a bed, sheets, blankets, towels, a table and chairs – *everything*, even down to salt and pepper shakers. This was quite something for a woman in her forties who had never owned anything.

And, initially, I rented. The landlord decided what I could put on the walls, what kind of curtain rods I could have, where I had power points. I still had to ask to have something mended when it broke or needed replacing. Even so, it was still *my* place. I could go in and close the door. I didn't have to be responsible for anyone, or to anyone, for the way I lived. I could eat what I liked, when I liked, and could come and go as I pleased. There was a great sense of freedom, as well as loneliness.

When I bought my own little house I could do what I liked to it. I bought paintings and put them up where I wanted to. Stacey put curtain rods up for me where I wanted them. I delighted in mixing sand and cement and bits of brick to rebuild the back step, which I built inside a formwork of polystyrene tomato and broccoli boxes, because that's what I had, or what I could get for nothing. Stacey teased me that he was surprised I 'hadn't mixed the cement in the food processor'.

After a few months I had the kitchen redone, and Greg, who was a pretty good handyman, did lots of things about the place to make it more livable. The bathroom was tiny, but we gave it a facelift, a new small bath and tiles for the floor. Is it any wonder I loved that little old house with my own yard and tree, where the cat and I could be 'at home'?

When I moved to St Ives with Bruce I was sad to leave it all behind. Bruce didn't quite understand, as his house was so much bigger, newer and better, plus it wasn't next to Redfern's inner-city problems. So Sheba and I both became North Shore dwellers, and I eventually sold my home to Greg and his future wife, Louise. I think they loved it nearly as much as I did, and they kept restoring its dignity.

There was fulfilment in my work as a school counsellor and in my practice as a psychologist. One of my beliefs has always been a saying attributed to Saint Irenaeus (Bishop of Lyons in the second century): 'The glory of God is Man fully alive.' There was joy for me in helping people stand firmly on their own two feet and be 'fully alive'.

Bruce and I had our sixteenth wedding anniversary the other day, and we are so settled into our life together that we both forgot about it till an anniversary card arrived from Bet. She sent it from Singleton Convent, where she is happily retired and helps out around the nursing home. She goes over there every day to visit the old sisters, writes their letters for them and keeps in contact with their relatives. We are as close as ever, talk on the phone often, and she comes to stay for a week with us a few times a year.

When I met Bruce and married him and his family, I found again that sense of belonging to something warm and close and life-giving. There are people to be loved and gathered under my wings so they may be fully alive, fully themselves and happy. As for Bruce and me – the ongoing romance is our story.

My spiritual journey has come back around to the warmth of a family.

# Epilogue

In the twenty years since I left the convent I have occasionally dreamt I am still there. Or rather, am back there. The pictures often change in a kaleidoscope of memories. Sometimes I am my present age, and at other times I am young again. Sometimes, in the glorious way that dreams have of ignoring boundaries between the now and the then, I am standing on the back cloister of the majestic Singleton Convent with my stepdaughter, Sue, and her two little boys – the only babies I have ever had. Around us the nuns are milling in their long black habits and white starched coifs of yesteryear.

'This is where I used to live when I was young,' I say to them. 'I used to dress like these sisters . . . And look, I always loved those big blue flowers.'

We walk past the masses of agapanthus in bloom and into the chapel while the sounds of the big choir practising carols for the Christmas Mass billow out around us. The organ swells, the harmony crescendos – 'Christmas bells are ringing low, Christmas bells across the snow . . .' – while the old thermometer on the cloister wall climbs towards 100 degrees.

Outside, there is a commotion as a group of laughing young nuns half carry and half drag long seats with the wooden kneelers hooked up behind the seats from the church chancel along the verandah to the chapel.

'These are my friends, and they are moving the seats into the chapel for a ceremony,' I tell the boys.

'Gee, Gran, it looks hard work!'

'Yes, it was hard work, but there was lots of fun too.'

Suddenly a kneeler comes unhooked and swings free, upsetting the balance, and they all stumble, then gasp and collapse with gales of laughter on the seat they have dropped.

Sometimes in my dreams we are all in the big community room together for some gathering. We are laughing and talking. We are all young. In these warm, nostalgic dreams we are always happy, my friends and I. However, when I wake up I never feel I want to go back to the convent. I am sure I am in the right place. And anyway, those times have gone. The long black habits and veils have been changed years ago for simple, secular dresses with a Mercy badge. The community has grown older, and been depleted by death and defection. There have not been any new vocations for years, so there are no young nuns to carry things and breathe life and hope for the future around the place.

There is no choir any more. The nuns with the lovely voices are old or have died. And there are not enough priests to have a Christmas or Easter Mass in the empty chapel. There is only a Mass of Anointing for the old and infirm in the nursing-home chapel every few months.

This is the winter of religious life, and I doubt there will be a new spring . . .

* * *

I have always liked sunsets: the golden glory, the fading rose glow, the quiet peacefulness of completion. When Bruce and I were in Kakadu I witnessed the most perfect sunset I have ever seen from a shallow-hulled tourist boat out on the marshes. The sky blazed with vivid reds and golds, and then the fading glory of the day on high merged with the dead skeletons of trees below, black and stark against the glowing sky. The double splendour of it all was reflected in the open water before me, with the occasional bird winging slowly by.

Sunsets suggest to me the opening stanza of one of the first poems I ever discovered and loved: Gray's 'Elegy Written in a Country Churchyard'.

*The curfew tolls the knell of parting day*
*The lowing herd winds slowly o'er the lea*
*The ploughman homeward plods his weary way*
*And leaves the world to darkness and to me.*

And from a later time in my life these well-loved words of an unknown poet spring:

*I have seen the sky in the evening –*
*It was luminous and serene,*
*And I loved it for its beauty,*
*And I thought of you, my Queen.*

Why have I always loved the end of a day instead of its dawning? Maybe it's because I am not a morning person. The occasional dawns I have witnessed have been wonderful, none more so than the privilege of watching with Bruce as the day slowly banished darkness from the magnificent Grand Canyon. Yet for me, evening, with its sense of completion and fullness and peace, means more.

It means home and the fireplace we had in our family room. It means peace, family togetherness and warmth. It means that the chores of the day are done and the time is now for me – for us – and perhaps for love. The day has been full of busy-ness and demands, but the sunset is full of homing and peace and softness.

Maybe my love of autumn comes from the same sort of place within me. The golden, rich fullness of colour. The sense of the fullness of the year – Keats's 'Season of mists and mellow fruitfulness', especially the 'mellow fruitfulness'. (What a lovely word 'mellow' is. It rolls from the tongue and fills the mouth and the mind with images of sweet, round oranges and mandarins, purple grapes and golden lemons, yellow squash and glorious round pumpkins.) The slowing down of the year as life looks forward to the sleep of winter . . .

D'Arcy said to me one day, 'Look Gran – the trees are dead!'

In his four short years he had not yet become aware of the rhythm of the seasons. The stark deadness of the limbs struck him perhaps with sadness, or perhaps with just shock as he came to a realisation about death.

'No,' I told him. 'They're not dead – they are asleep. They are sleeping through the winter so they can burst out again with new life . . .'

※ ※ ※

Looking back, I am content with the way things have been. If anything had been different, I would not be where I am now. I wouldn't be the person I am now, wouldn't have met Bruce, and wouldn't be part of this family.

Whatever the future holds, I am at peace.

# Acknowledgements

I would like to thank my many friends in the Sisters of Mercy, Singleton, with whom I lived the thirty years of life I have drawn upon for this book. I want to thank them for the companionship and the warm memories I have of those years.

There are many others without whom I would never have put it all down on paper. Special thanks go to the members of my writing group – Robyn Dampney, Liz Hill and Marlene Huggart – for the years of encouragement they gave, and for their skill in pushing me (however unwilling) in the right direction so many times.

Thanks to Patti Miller for the inspiration to begin through her weekend workshop 'Writing Life Stories' and for her help along the way. Thanks also to Bridget Brandon and her program 'LifeStories' for the stimulation to recall and write so many memories, and to her group with whom I shared them.

Thanks to the Varuna Writers' House for including me in their mentorship program, and giving me Meg Simons as my mentor. Without Meg's wisdom and encouragement, I would never have put it all together.

Thanks also to the many friends along the way who encouraged me with their interest, and to the many of my relatives who feature in this story whether they know it or not.

Special thanks go to Selwa Anthony, my agent, for taking me on and pointing me to Catherine Hammond for advice just when I needed it.

Thanks to my publisher, Julie Gibbs at Penguin Australia, and to my editor, Saskia Adams, for her painstaking work.

And thanks to Bruce – to the security of whose love I came late in life, and who has not always understood the need to write, but has been generous with his encouragement and support. And to our family: special thanks to Sue for her friendship and for sharing her boys with me. Thanks to D'Arcy and Reuben for their unconditional love, and to Greg and Robyn for including me in their family.